The Streets of Louth

The Streets of
LOUTH

An A–Z History

Caitlin Green

THE LINDES PRESS

For John, Jeannette, Frances, Evie, Tabitha & Stanley

Published by The Lindes Press
Louth, Lincolnshire

ISBN 978-0-9570336-3-4

Contents

Preface

This is a very different book from my *Origins of Louth*. The aim of that volume was to analyse the origins and development of human settlement and activity in the Louth region, in order to understand how the town of Louth came to be. The present book, in contrast, has a rather different focus. Whilst analytical history is important, there is also a place for simple curiosity about the people and buildings of the place where one lives, works or was brought up. Such very local history can be both fascinating and valuable in its own right—there is a pleasure to be gained from knowing what the street one walks along used to look like, what industries used to take place on it, what used to be there before that building was built or before that area became a car park, and, most interesting of all, who lived on the street in the past, what they did, and what events took place there. *The Streets of Louth* was initially intended to offer brief sketches addressing these questions for each of the key roads in the town. Needless to say, the project has snowballed somewhat since its original conception—the portraits of the key streets are now no longer so brief, and in the end I have attempted to offer at least some information about virtually every road in the town in Louth, along with a few that no longer exist. Moreover, whilst much of the material I have used to write this book relates to the streets of Louth before the First World War (the period for which evidence is most readily available), an attempt has been made to bring the history of most of the roads up to the present day.

In researching this book, I ended up delving far deeper than I originally intended. In doing so, I stumbled across an unexpected corpus of material that appears not to have been utilised before when writing about Louth, but which has many fascinating things to tell us about life on the streets of the nineteenth-century town. The source of this material is the *Hull Packet* newspaper, which was first published in 1787 and issued weekly until 1886, when it was incorporated with the *Hull Daily Mail*. What makes this newspaper of particular interest is that, for much of that time, Louth was considered to be within its district, with J. Jackson of Louth the agent for the newspaper from at least 1800 and detailed reports from the town printed in the news section of the paper. These reports are especially detailed from 1845 through to 1858, when they include a vast wealth of local detail, stories, news and gossip, including regular court reports. The last provide the names and addresses of many of the thieves, drunkards, beggars, brawlers and prostitutes who came up before the courts in Louth during that period, along with details of their crimes, where they occurred, and often what the reporter thought about the participants and the events he related! As such, they are an invaluable resource for the present book, offering a very different perspective on some of the streets of the town. They are consequently used throughout what follows, although some of the events described in these accounts are quite shocking by modern standards, both in terms of the crimes themselves and the punishments (or lack thereof) meted out for them.

With regard to the man who penned these reports, it seems almost certain that he was William Brown, the painter of the famous Louth Panorama (first shown in 1847 and last exhibited in 1856), supplementing his income from writing for the *Stamford Mercury* with regular reports for the *Hull Packet* too. Certainly, the *Hull Packet*'s reporter between 1845 and 1858 was a great fan of the temperance movement (describing the beerhouses of Louth as 'hells of intemperance' in 1858), like Brown, and he was also greatly interested in what was happening in the yard of the 'Warrenite Chapel', which Brown was a supporter and member of. The *Hull Packet*'s correspondent also reported some of the same events as Brown did in the *Stamford Mercury* in a similar way and showing similar interests. For example, Brown's concern in the *Stamford Mercury* in January 1853 over the lack of provision in the new Corn Exchange for 'the wives and daughters' of local farmers who sold 'poultry and butter in the market' was echoed virtually word for word in the Louth report in the *Hull Packet*—given that the *Hull Packet* report was published the same day as the *Stamford Mercury* report (21 January 1853), the only credible explanation is that the same man wrote both articles. Finally, it is worth observing that reports from the *Hull Packet's* Louth correspondent appear to come to an end around the same time that Brown stopped writing for the *Mercury*, shortly before his death in early 1859.

Of course, these newspaper reports were only one of the sources used in preparing the individual street histories below. As the present book is not offered as an academic study, but rather for the enjoyment of the general reader who is interested in the history of Louth and its streets, footnotes and similar bibliographic tools have been avoided here—nonetheless, a brief account of all the major classes of material used in writing *The Streets of Louth*, along with suggested additional reading, is included at the end of this book. With regard to illustrations, in order to keep the length and cost of the volume to a minimum, a decision has been made to restrict illustrations to two maps. These are intended to help readers orientate themselves, the first map being Robert Bayley's plan of the town from 1834 and the second being a modern Ordnance Survey map of Louth. The latter is made freely available under the Open Government Licence v1.0 with the following attribution statement: Contains Ordnance Survey data © Crown copyright and database right 2012. Needless to say, the book could not have been written without the help and kindness of others, and my particular thanks are due here to David Robinson. I also need to thank my partner, children and parents for all their help, support and encouragement whilst this book was being written.

ABBEY PARK

Abbey Park runs south-east from EASTFIELD ROAD and was laid out by 2006, with the houses here being sold as new builds from 2008. The land it is built on was part of Louth Park in the nineteenth and early twentieth centuries, and traces of medieval ridge and furrow have been observed in this area from aerial photographs.

ABBEY ROAD

Abbey Road runs north-east from ST BERNARDS AVENUE before curving round and heading south-east to connect with BROADLEY CRESCENT. It is part of the large, post-World War Two St Bernards Avenue council housing scheme. It appears to have been laid out and partially developed by the time that the 1951 OS map was surveyed, and was fully developed by the time of the 1956 map. The land it stands on was originally part of Louth's old open East Field.

ABBOTTS WAY

Abbotts Way runs south-east from MONKS DYKE ROAD and is part of an early twenty-first-century housing estate developed off an eastern extension of the latter road. The land that it is built on was originally part of Louth's old open East Field, before this was enclosed under the Enclosure Act of 1801, and medieval ridge and furrow has been observed from this area on aerial photographs.

ADA WAY

See ELM DRIVE.

ADRIAN CLOSE

Adrian Close runs west from SEYMOUR AVENUE and is part of the Seymour Avenue housing estate that was constructed off NEWMARKET in the late twentieth century, with Adrian Close begun in the early 1970s. Adrian Close is built on land that was once part of the old open South Field of Louth.

ALBANY ROAD, PLACE & CLOSE

Albany Road is part of a late twentieth-century housing estate that runs west from KENWICK ROAD. Albany Road was being developed at the time that the 1979–84 OS map was drawn up, and it had been completed by the end of the 1980s, as had Albany Place. Albany Close is a more recent development, which was under construction in 2003 and completed by 2006—the houses here were sold as new builds in 2004–07. All three of the roads were built on land that was originally part of Louth's open South Field, and medieval ridge and furrow has been observed in this area from aerial photographs.

ALBION PLACE

Albion Place runs south from the junction of EASTGATE and RAMSGATE, along the side of what is presently a Morrisons supermarket. The street-name Albion Place appears to date from the mid-twentieth century; before this, the road was known as Leake's Court, a name that is now applied to buildings on the south side of JAMES STREET. It is not clear who Leake's Court was named after, although Leakes were certainly present in the town in the eighteenth and nineteenth centuries—for example, William Thorold Leake, whose Louth will is dated 1841, and Richard Leake, whose will is dated 1715.

The earliest witness to the development of this road is Espin's 1808 plan of Louth. On this, a long strip of buildings is shown on the eastern side of the Leake's Court, with two shorter blocks on the opposite side at the southern end. These buildings were still marked here on Bayley's 1834 plan of the town, when the only obvious changes were the establishment of new buildings at the northern end of Leake's Court, facing onto Eastgate, and the culverting of the Aswell spring, which had previously flowed across the front entrance to the court and would have probably had to be forded when entering or leaving it (see further Eastgate and CHURCH STREET on this spring). What the early nineteenth-century buildings on the eastern side of Leake's Court were is uncertain, although they were still there in 1889 and their internal divisions then are suggestive of a largely non-residential usage. In the 1830s and 1840s, Thomas Rose had a brickyard on the east side of Maiden Row (modern CHURCH STREET) and partly under the current

Elizabeth Court, which backs onto the west side of Albion Place, and he may have taken over the business from John Rogerson, who was listed as a brick maker on Maiden Row in Pigot & Co.'s 1828–9 Directory. There was also James Hunter Ryley's brickyard immediately to the east of Leake's Court in the mid-nineteenth century. As such, it is possible that these buildings were somehow associated with the brick-making trade, although some other usage is perfectly possible, with haystacks appearing to be located near to these buildings on Brown's mid-nineteenth-century Panorama.

On the 1839 map of Louth, new buildings are shown on the western side of Leake's Court, and these look like residential houses on the 1889 OS map. Certainly, twenty houses were listed in Leake's Court in 1861, and these were occupied by a variety of working-class people. The heads of the various households in that year included six labourers (for example, Thomas Grantham and William Collins, numbers 2 and 14), a dressmaker (Sarah Elizabeth Thornley, number 3), a groom (Thomas Ryatt, number 4), a carpenter (James Taylor, number 8), two charwomen (Ann Whitelaw and Ann Donner, numbers 9 and 17), a German carpet slipper maker (Elizabeth Younger, number 12), and a blacksmith (John Kirk, number 13). An earlier resident of the street was one Francis Cotchiefer (or Cotcheifer), whose wife, Dinah, was a prostitute—she was charged in 1854 with the beating and robbing of William Horton in a Ramsgate brothel (see further Ramsgate). Another was a woman named Zillah Hutton, who was charged with brawling and creating a disturbance in Leake's Court in 1852. Hutton appeared before the courts again in 1853, when she was charged with stealing a stone of flour from Robert Bee. On that occasion she was discharged, because of a minor fault in the evidence against her—however, she was severely admonished by the court and was then sent to prison the same day for threatening one of the witnesses who had testified against her in the previous case.

In 1889, the brick yard to the east of Leake's Court was marked as disused and the area where Morrisons now stands was home to a coal yard. At the southern end of the court, where Morrisons' car park now is, were two large gasometers used for storing the gas for the town. By 1906, an iron foundry was also marked in the area to the rear of Leake's Court, as it was in the 1930s too. Subsequently, the site where Morrisons now stands was used a garage, and it was redeveloped as a supermarket site in the late twentieth century. On the western side of the street, the housing that was here appears to have persisted into the 1950s, but had largely gone by the 1960s, with Elizabeth Court (facing onto Church Street) built on the land to the west of the road in that period.

ALDER CLOSE

Alder Close runs north from PASTURE DRIVE, and both are part of the HAWKER DRIVE housing estate to the south of STEWTON LANE. This area was fields up until the late twentieth century, when the housing estate here was built—Hawker Drive and HAVELOK CLOSE were built first, with Pasture Drive and Alder Close developed in the 1980s. These fields were already enclosed at the start of the nineteenth century, but they had once been part of the old South Field of the town—medieval ridge and furrow from this has been observed on aerial photographs of this area.

ALEXANDER DRIVE

Alexander Drive is a late twentieth-century residential road that runs north from STEWTON LANE. Up until the Enclosure Award of 1805, the land that Alexander Drive stands on was still part of the town's old open South Field, and medieval ridge and furrow from this has been observed on aerial photographs of this area. In 1876, the railway line from Louth to Bardney was opened and this ran across the land now occupied by Alexander Drive until 1956.

ALEXANDRA ROAD

Alexandra Road was built upon the northern part of the site of the former Louth House of Correction, or prison. This institution was closed and sold for £3,400 in 1872 to John Walmsley (d. 1885), a bone crusher and merchant with premises on both Holmes Lane (HIGH HOLME ROAD) and Walkergate (QUEEN STREET). He demolished the buildings of the House of Correction and used some of the materials—including the old prison clock—to extend and improve his warehouse on the north side of QUEEN STREET. In 1884, the northern part of the prison site was developed for housing, producing Walmsley's Terrace on Alexandra Road. Note, part of Alexandra Road,

4

including the western section of the road itself, originally lay within the 23 foot-high wall that enclosed the House of Correction and on the site of the old prison mill. The rest lay on land beyond the wall, which was home to the prison's cow-house, stable and pigsty in 1872. By 1889, the street was fully developed. In 1891, it was home to a number of people employed by the railway, including a guard, a porter, a fireman, and two engine drivers (George T Wright, number 19, and George Neave, number 15), and this was the case in 1911 too. The road was presumably named after the Princess of Wales, the future Queen Alexandra, who undertook extensive public duties in this period.

ALLISON ROAD

Allison Road runs off BOLLE ROAD, which is the spine of a new housing estate built between NEWBRIDGE HILL and CHARLES STREET from 2006. The estate was built on land occupied by a market garden, Sharpley's Yard and Sharpley's Terrace (on Newbridge Hill), and the Great Northern Oil & Cake Mill (on CHARLES STREET) in the second half of the nineteenth century. Allison Road is built partly on the site of Sharpley's Yard and partly on the site of the Oil & Cake Mill. Inhabitants of Sharpley's Yard in 1861 included two carpet weavers (Matthew and Daniel Buckley), a washerwoman (Ann Brown), a carpenter (Edward Smith) and an agricultural labourer (Robert Codd). The Oil & Cake Mill was run by Richard James Nell, a member of the Nell family of RIVERHEAD, and its site was subsequently used for a wallpaper mill and a canning factory (see Charles Street). In 1951, the houses of Sharpley's Yard and Terrace and the factory facing onto Charles Street were all replaced by a large Lin Pac factory, which manufactured corrugated cardboard for packing. This was in turn demolished in 2003 to make way for the current residential development.

ALMOND CRESCENT

Almond Crescent is a small, late twentieth century housing development that runs north-west from MONKS DYKE ROAD. The houses here were built in the 1970s on land that had been previously the site of a house, associated buildings, greenhouses and an orchard.

ALTHORP GARDENS

Althorp Gardens runs west from ARUNDEL DRIVE and was constructed in the 1990s. The land it is built on was originally part of Louth's old open North Field.

ANDREWS CLOSE

Andrews Close is a late twentieth-century residential street that runs west from BRACKENBOROUGH ROAD. At least some of the properties here were built in 1980 and the land that they stand on was once part of the old open North Field of Louth.

ANTHONY CRESCENT & AMANDA DRIVE

A modern estate, built in the 1970s, which runs east from BRACKENBOROUGH ROAD; Jenkins Close is also a part of this development, running south from Anthony Crescent. The land that these roads and their dwellings now occupy was originally part of the town's old North Field, but in 1805 the Enclosure Commissioners assigned it (along with the land to both the north and the south) to William Stephenson and William Wright. In 1858, the land was offered for sale at auction and was stated then to be arable land occupied by Samuel Plumpton, a local poultry dealer. His business was based in NORTHGATE in 1861, and the fields on Brackenborough Road were presumably being used by him for raising poultry; subsequently, the focus of Samuel Plumpton's business moved from Northgate to MERCER ROW, where the family had a shop for several decades. By 1906, a property named South House—renamed Highfield House Farm in the second half of the twentieth century—had been built on the southern part of the plot of land that Anthony Crescent, Amanda Drive and Jenkins Close occupy. The later houses are arranged around this, with the older house being accessible by a private lane that runs east from Brackenborough Road.

ARUNDEL DRIVE

Arundel Drive runs south from NORTH HOLME ROAD and is one of the main roads of a large housing estate built here in the 1960s and 1970s. The road is absent from the 1968 OS map but it had been laid out and developed on its eastern side by the time of the 1974–6 map. Development on its eastern side occurred a little later, around the time that LONGLEAT DRIVE and BUCKINGHAM ROAD were established. The land that Arundel Drive is built on was originally part of Louth's old open North Field.

ASH CLOSE

See BEECH GROVE.

ASHLEY ROAD

Named after Thomas Ashley, Ashley Road (sometimes Ashley's Road) was built in the late nineteenth century and workers at Ashley's nearby Aswell Iron Works (see CINDER LANE) were amongst those housed there. The houses on the west of the road had been built by the time the 1889 OS map was created, but those on the east had not; they were, however, present on the 1906 OS map. Early inhabitants included George Hodgson, agricultural implement maker, and his sons Richard and Roger (a blacksmith and an apprentice blacksmith), who lived in Pretoria Terrace on the east side of Ashley Road in 1901. Although primarily residential, Joseph Capes is recorded as running his firewood dealership from Ashley Road in 1919. Ashley Road was built on land previously occupied by the same nursery that saw 24 apple and 19 pear trees cleared in 1840–1 to make way for the British School on KIDGATE and which is depicted on Brown's Panorama. The earlier use of this area is recalled in the name Nursery Gardens that has been given to those new properties built at the end of Ashley Road.

ASWELL STREET

Aswell Lane, the original name of the northern half of Aswell Street, almost certainly originated as an early access-way, running from

MERCER ROW and QUEEN STREET to the important Aswell spring and its large pool (see the GATHERUMS & SPRINGSIDE). First mentioned in a Final Concord—a type of document relating to the transfer of land ownership—of 1263 and also in the Louth Manor Court Roll for 1450, Aswell Lane appears to have run between two of the long, thin medieval tenement plots that fronted onto Mercer Row and Walkergate. In perhaps the later medieval and early modern periods, this road to the Aswell spring began to have properties established along it. These new properties cut into the land belonging to the two tenement plots that ran either side of the road, north to south, and were created through the subdivision of these earlier plots. Aswell Lane was, at some point, also extended south of its original terminus, the Aswell spring, in order to become an access road to the Quarry too (see NEWMARKET)—this extension, now the southern half of Aswell Street, was known as Quarry Lane until the nineteenth century. Although it is not clear when this part of the road was constructed, the Quarry itself provided the stone for Louth Park Abbey and so was in existence by the twelfth or thirteenth century. Whatever the case may be as to the origins of Quarry Lane, the southern half of Aswell Street remained almost entirely devoid of buildings well into the nineteenth century, only seeing significant development during the 1840s and 1850s. This can be most readily observed through a comparison of William Brown's preliminary sketches of 1844, which show virtually no buildings here, and his finished Panorama of 1856, which has housing up both sides of the southern half of Aswell Street. The only real gap by the mid-1850s was a lime pit at the top of Aswell Street on the west side, which was used by the lime burner William Hurst in the first half of the nineteenth century (Hurst lived on Aswell Lane in 1841).

In the sixteenth century, we find two interesting references to Aswell Lane. The first relates to the paving of this street, which was apparently undertaken using part of the proceeds from the sale of the bells of St Mary's Church in 1553, following its closure under Edward VI (the sale raised £26 11s 8d, equivalent to around £8,800 today; see BRIDGE STREET on St Mary's Church). In addition, in 1566–7 ten loads of stone from Louth Park Abbey and six from St Mary's were brought to Aswell, and this too has been interpreted as reflecting the provision of paving materials for this street, although it is not actually clear whether these loads of stone were once again used to pave Aswell

Lane or if they were instead used at the Aswell spring site (see the Gatherums for details of the early modern activity at the Aswell spring). The second reference relates to the presence here of an inn in 1536. John Franke, or Frankishe, the Registrar of the Bishop, was apparently staying in the Saracen's Head inn ahead of the Visitation of Louth in October 1536, and it was from there that he was dragged with his books into the MARKET PLACE by Nicholas Melton ('Captain Cobbler') and his company, at the start of the short-lived Lincolnshire Rising. This inn was located on Aswell Lane and is, in fact, first mentioned in John Louth's will of 1459. As such, Aswell Lane not only had a small part to play in the origins of the Lincolnshire Rising, but was also home to Louth's earliest documented inn, which had its origins in the medieval period.

With regard to the location and possible survival of the Saracen's Head into the modern period, it is feasible that there is some sort of intimate relationship between the medieval and early modern inn on Aswell Lane and the modern Turks Head inn, which stands on the north-eastern corner of Aswell Street. The Turks Head appears to be one of the few Louth inns and public houses to have survived since the eighteenth century without a name change, and it was clearly already a significant inn during the mid-eighteenth century, when Christian Frederick Esberger stayed at the 'Turkshead' three times in 1764. In light of this early recording of the Turks Head, the stability of the inn's name, the close resemblance of this name to that of the Saracen's Head, and the location of the inn on the corner of Aswell Lane, it certainly seems possible that the modern Turks Head represents a rebuilding and survival of the earlier inn. Alternatively, it has been suggested that the inn that stood further south on the east side of the Aswell Lane, where Mr Chips' takeaway now is, could have been a survival of the Saracen's Head. Known variously as the Red Lion, the White Hart and the Foresters' Arms in the nineteenth and twentieth centuries, it was apparently known as the Blackmoor's, or Black's, Head before 1789. Of course, it is not impossible that both the Turks Head and the Blackmoor's Head could somehow derive from the medieval and early modern Saracen's Head inn, especially if the buildings and grounds of the Saracen's Head originally encompassed the whole of the medieval tenement that made up the east side of Aswell Lane, running south from Walkergate to the Aswell spring. In this context, it is worth observing that the Blue Stone Inn, another early Louth inn (see UPGATE), is said to have occupied a site running from Mercer Row right the way back to KIDGATE.

Whilst the Turks Head was generally a well-run establishment in the mid-nineteenth century—although the landlady, Jane Morton, was warned in 1858 when her licence came up for renewal, due to a fight on her premises—the same cannot always be said for the Red Lion. In January 1847, the landlord, George Yarnell, found himself in trouble when two police constables went to the Red Lion and found six prostitutes and some men in the bar, drinking and 'making use of conversation of an obscene and disgraceful nature'. He was fined 10 shillings (equivalent to around £40 today) and costs on that occasion, and was 'strongly cautioned as to his future conduct'. Despite this, he was charged once again with harbouring prostitutes in his house in May 1848, with a fine of 20 shillings and 12 shillings costs; he promised on that occasion to be 'more circumspect in the future'! As a result of such 'disorderly conduct' being repeatedly allowed in the Red Lion, Yarnell was briefly denied a renewal of his license that year, although the magistrates later relented and gave him one final chance. He was still the landlord in 1849, but by 1851 he was making his living in Lincoln and the Red Lion had been renamed the White Hart, with Thomas Ryall as the landlord.

The Red Lion inn was not the only area of Aswell Lane where there was an issue with prostitution in the mid-nineteenth century. Indeed, there is evidence for the presence of at least one brothel on Aswell Lane at this time. This was first recorded in 1847, when a complaint was made against Henry Richardson and his wife Susan Richardson, aka Suke Mason, both 'keepers of a most notorious brothel' in 'Aswell-hole'—that is, the area between Aswell Lane and the Aswell spring, accessed by the horse steps. This brothel may have closed in June 1847, as the Richardsons left town before they could be arrested. However, in April 1848 a 'keeper of a brothel in Aswell-lane' named John Marwood was charged with being drunk and disorderly in Walkergate, and the same man is described as 'an old offender of Aswell-hole' in 1850, so it is likely that his brothel was based here too. Whether this brothel was another brothel or simply the earlier Richardson brothel under new management, is unclear, although it certainly seems possible. There are no more incidental references to brothel-owners based in Aswell Hole after this, but this does not mean that the area was now free from prostitution, with several references being made to prostitutes on Aswell Lane itself. In July 1849, a prostitute named Sarah Saunderson and a man named Robert Duckett were both charged with making a disturbance in Aswell Lane, being fined 10 shillings and costs or three months in the prison. Most notable, however, was the apparent attempted murder here of prostitute and brothel-keeper Mary Ann Dauby, of SPOUT YARD, in 1857. Her lover, John Risdale, a painter recently discharged from the 42nd Highlanders, was interrupted by police in Aswell Lane as he threatened to cut her throat with a razor. She had reportedly decided to break it off with him and refused to continue to support him 'with the proceeds of her miserable and degraded calling'. He received a six month prison sentence for his actions, though he could apparently have gone free if he had provided sureties of £50 (equivalent to around £4,000 today).

The Turks Head and the Red Lion/White Hart (renamed the Foresters' Arms from the 1860s through to the 1900s, before reverting back to the White Hart) were not alone as drinking establishments on Aswell Lane. On the opposite side of the street, where a relatively new block of buildings now houses a bookmaker and a Turkish takeaway (2– 6 Aswell Street), there was another drinking spot known as the Black Horse. This was first recorded in 1782 and closed in the early years of the twentieth century. In the mid-nineteenth century, the landlord here was one Thomas Hutchinson, whose methods for dealing with drunks occasionally left something to be desired. Thus, in 1849, Hutchinson was charged with allowing an Irishman named Luke Mooney to become 'helplessly drunk' in the Black Horse and then taking him outside and leaving him in the street, unprotected and at risk of death from passing traffic—for this he was admonished by the Mayor for his cruelty and fined 5 shillings plus costs. There was also a notable business based in Aswell Hole. From 1849, an Irish man ('a son of the Emerald Isle') named Patrick Keys, or Kayes, is said to have kept a 'tramp lodging-house' here. This seems to have been a fairly extensive establishment, as Patrick Kayes is listed as the head of a household containing twenty-three people in the 1851 census, many of whom were agricultural labourers, although one was described as a beggar. By 1855, this lodging house had transformed into a beerhouse under Kayes' management—this was properly called the Nelson but was commonly known as the Rag and Louse, a name which may suggest something of the character of the place. Both Patrick Kayes and this beerhouse are last mentioned in 1861, and the building appears to have subsequently returned to being a lodging house—in 1871 and 1881 it was run by William Kayes, presumably a relative, and in 1891 and 1901 it was run by a George Andrews, William Kayes' son-in-law. In the latter year it housed twelve lodgers, including two Italians who were travelling with a piano organ. In 1911, it was still operating and run by George Andrews' widow, Annie Andrews (née Kayes).

As well as places to buy drink, there was also a site for its manufacture on Aswell Street. This was The Old Maltings, currently an antiques centre and one of the first buildings to be constructed on the southern part of Aswell Street, Quarry Lane, at some point between 1808 and 1834 (when it first appears on a plan of the town). In the later nineteenth century, this building was a brewery and malt kiln belonging to Benjamin Ryley, grocer, brewer and maltster, who died in 1880—he also had a grocery shop at 21 UPGATE. The vats were located at the far west end of the building on the ground floor, whilst the malt and grain were stored upstairs. One of the probable owners of the Old Maltings before Ryley was John Wilson. He was one of two maltsters on Aswell Street in 1835, the only one in 1841, and in 1851 he was still there and his address is confirmed as the Quarry Lane part of the road. By 1856 he had gone, and the firm of Young & Sutton appears to have then taken over the site—certainly, this is the only maltster listed on the road from that year through until at least 1872, and George Sutton, maltster, lived next door to the Old Maltings in 1861, 1871 and 1872. After Ryley, the maltings presumably came under the control of William Hodgson in the 1880s and 1890s—he is listed in directories then as a maltster of Aswell Street, and the 1891 census confirms that he lived next door to the Old Maltings, at no. 40 (he also had the Greyhound Inn on UPGATE). Arthur Soames & Son seemingly had the site in the 1900s and 1910s, as they are listed as a maltster on Aswell Street then; more recently, the front part of the building functioned as a car showroom.

Other places of note on Aswell Street include Thomas Ashley's nineteenth-century Aswell Iron Works, which is said to have employed over 100 men in the 1860s. This is discussed in more detail under CINDER LANE, as only Ashley's showroom was actually located on Aswell Street itself—this was where Otley's shop is now located, on the east side of the southern section of the road, and Ashley is listed as living at 57 Aswell Lane in the 1861 and 1871 censuses. The site of a new building currently occupied by Marmaris Pizzas, at 26 Aswell Street, is also noteworthy. From the 1920s, John Brown (and later his son, Lance) made lightweight 'Le Brun' bicycles here, using metal tubing from Birmingham. The building was subsequently a small, private musical instrument and military items museum for a time, run by Lance Brown in 1970s. One door down, at number 24 (now the southern part of Olivers Wine Bar), there was another interesting business—this was the site of one of the first recorded fried fish shops in Louth, run by Frederick Palmer in 1896. This venture doesn't seem to have been particularly long-lived, as in 1901 James Colbeck's butcher shop was located at 24 Aswell Street. However, by 1909 another fried fish shop had opened on Aswell Street, and this one proved to have rather greater longevity. Run by Robert Hickling, it was based at 19 & 21 Aswell Street, the site of the present-day Mr Chips fish restaurant. He continued to run the business here through until 1919, although it was his son, Fred Hickling, rather than Robert, who was listed as the 'Fish Fryer' in 1911. In 1920, the site was purchased by Daniel Hagan senior and Daniel Hagan junior, and it is still run by the latter's grandson, John. In 1947, fish, chips and peas, along with tea, bread and butter in the restaurant here would have cost 1/7d (equivalent to around 8p, or £2.50 today when adjusted for inflation) according to Mr Chips. Finally, it is worth noting that the entertainments available on Aswell Lane in the first half of the nineteenth century were not limited to drinking and brothels—there was also a dedicated skittle (bowling) alley here in the 1830s, in the grounds of the Red Lion, and another was listed as belonging to the Black Horse on the occasion of its sale in 1906.

AVALON WAY

Avalon Way runs north off BOLLE ROAD, which is the spine of a new housing estate built between NEWBRIDGE HILL and CHARLES STREET from 2006. This road is built on land that was occupied by a market garden in the second half of the nineteenth century, and runs up to two residential properties that stand on the site of the former Holmes Cottage. This was the home of Henry Boothby junior, a boot and shoe seller in the MARKET PLACE, from at least 1856 through to the 1880s, and his son, George Boothby, was listed as a fancy poultry dealer here in 1872.

BADMINTON WAY

Badminton Way runs off LONGLEAT DRIVE. The road is absent from the 1974–6 OS map and it was probably constructed around that time; it had been fully developed by the mid-1980s. The land it is built on was originally part of Louth's old open North Field.

BARTON GATE

Barton Gate crosses ALBANY ROAD is part of a late twentieth-century housing estate that runs west from KENWICK ROAD. Barton Gate was being developed at the time that the 1979–84 OS map was drawn up, and it had been completed by the end of the 1980s. This road was built on land that was originally part of Louth's open South Field, and medieval ridge and furrow has been observed in this area from aerial photographs.

BECK WAY

Beck Way runs north from PASTURE DRIVE, and both are part of the HAWKER DRIVE housing estate to the south of STEWTON LANE. This area was fields up until the late twentieth century, when the housing estate here was built—Hawker Drive and HAVELOK CLOSE were built first, with Pasture Drive and Beck Way developed in the 1980s. These fields were already enclosed at the start of the nineteenth century, but they had once been part of the old South Field of the town—medieval ridge and furrow from this has been observed on aerial photographs of this area.

BEECH GROVE

Beech Grove runs west from LIME GROVE (formerly part of KEDDINGTON CRESCENT). The entrance to Beech Grove is visible on the 1967–8 OS map, but the road is first marked on the 1974 map. At that point, the only development on the road appears to have been a caravan park. Subsequent years saw housing built here, although the northern part of the road wasn't fully developed until after 1990. ASH CLOSE also dates from that time and runs north from Beech Grove; it is mainly built on land formerly given over to a playground.

BEETON CLOSE

Beeton Close is part of the new GRESLEY ROAD residential estate, located north of STEWTON LANE. Up until the Enclosure Award of 1805, the land that Beeton Close and Gresley Road now stand on was still part of the town's old open South Field (medieval ridge and furrow from this has been observed on aerial photographs of this area), and in the mid–late twentieth century there were factories here.

BIRCH ROAD

Birch Road runs off WALLIS ROAD and is part of the large, post-World War Two, St Bernards Avenue council housing scheme, this element of it being laid out after the time that the 1956 OS map was surveyed. Louth & District Indoor Bowls Club and the Mayfair Family Club are both located on this road. The land it stands on was originally part of Louth's old open South Field.

BISHOPS CLOSE

Bishops Close runs south-east from MONKS DYKE ROAD and is part of an early twenty-first-century housing estate developed off an eastern extension of the latter road. The land that it is built on was originally part of Louth's old open East Field, before this was enclosed under the Enclosure Act of 1801, and medieval ridge and furrow has been observed from this area on aerial photographs.

BLANCHARD ROAD

Blanchard Road is part of the 'Weavers Tryst' housing estate that was begun in the late 1990s. It runs south-east from ERESBIE ROAD, the spine of the new development. The estate is built on land that was originally part of Louth's medieval open South Field, although most of

15

the area had been enclosed prior to the 1801 Enclosure Act. The roads within it appear to be named after local worthies of the sixteenth and seventeenth centuries—a Gilbert Blanchard was one of the first Six Assistants of Louth, appointed in 1551, and he was subsequently Warden of Louth several times from 1558 onwards.

BLENHEIM CLOSE

Blenheim Close runs off ARUNDEL DRIVE and is part of a large housing estate built to the south of NORTH HOLME ROAD in the 1960s and 1970s. The road is absent from the 1968 OS map but had been fully developed by the mid-1970s. The land it is built on was originally part of Louth's old open North Field.

BLUE STONE RISE

Blue Stone Rise runs north-west and south-east from MERIDIAN VIEW and is part of a late twentieth-century housing estate running west from UPGATE. The houses here were constructed in the 1990s on arable land that was once part of Louth's old open South Field— medieval ridge and furrow has been identified in this area from aerial photographs. The Blue Stone referred to in the street-name is the Blue Stone, or Louth Stone, that once stood at the junction of Upgate and MERCER ROW (see Upgate). R. S. Bayley, writing in 1834, suggested that this stone could have originally been a 'Druid stone', used 'on Julian Bower for an alter'; JULIAN BOWER lies just to the south of Blue Stone Rise.

BOLLE ROAD

Bolle Road runs west from NEWBRIDGE HILL and is the spine of a new housing estate built here from 2006. The estate was built on land occupied by a market garden, Sharpley's Yard and Sharpley's Terrace (on Newbridge Hill), and the Great Northern Oil & Cake Mill (on CHARLES STREET) in the second half of the nineteenth century. In 1951, the houses of Sharpley's Yard and Terrace and the factory facing onto Charles Street were all replaced by a large Lin Pac factory, which manufactured corrugated cardboard for packing. This was in turn demolished in 2003 to make way for the current residential development. The Bolle family were notable within Louth for several centuries and once lived at Thorpe Hall (see LINCOLN ROAD).

BOWERS AVENUE

Bowers Avenue is a short residential street that runs north from KEDDINGTON ROAD. It was built in the mid-twentieth century opposite the nineteenth-century Grosvenor House, on land that had originally been part of Louth's old open North Field before the Enclosure Act of 1801.

BOWLING GREEN LANE

Bowling Green Lane, or Road, ran south from NEWMARKET—directly opposite the junction between that road and LEE STREET—and through to the Lime Kiln in the Quarry in the late nineteenth century. The lane still runs here, with the Newmarket Car Park on its east, although there is currently no sign to indicate its name. The origins of this street-name lie in the fact that there was a Bowling Green in this area of town from at least the late seventeenth century, this being said to measure 88 yards by 50 yards in the late eighteenth century. The earliest reference dates from 1691, when a certain Thomas North leased the house and the 'Bowling Greene' here for 21 years, at an annual rent of two hens, on condition that he kept the house and green in good order. The Bowling Green appears again in 1717, when it was leased to Robert Pinder for two fat hens at Christmas, or 1 shilling. By the late eighteenth century, however, it appears to have fallen, or to have been falling, out of use; whether this is related to the establishment of a tea garden in this area in the eighteenth century is unclear. So, in 1786 it was known as the 'old Bowling Green' when it was leased to John Brocklesby for 99 years (at a yearly rent of 2s 6d), and when he subsequently assigned it to Cary Parnel Wood in 1799 for the remaining term of the lease, it was simply termed 'a piece of Ground called the Bowling Green situate near the Quarry', a name which would seem to imply that it had ceased to function by this point.

After the eighteenth century, the memory of the former Bowling Green was preserved in the street-name and also in the name of a

17

property that appears to have been located on or close to LONDON ROAD/UPGATE, to the east of Bowling Green Lane—this was Bowling Green House, inhabited by a master lime burner named West Larder from around 1861 to 1885, along with his family and his servant. With regard to Bowling Green Lane itself, there appears to have been little building development in this area until relatively late. There was clearly a house here from the seventeenth century, but on Bayley's map of 1834 there are still only two structures, both on the west side of the Bowling Green Lane, with sheep pens located to the east where there is now a car park. This had changed by 1889, however, when there were buildings along much of the west side of the road. The house that stood on the western corner of Newmarket and Bowling Green Lane was the childhood home of Sir Herbert Broadley around this time (b. 1892, see BROADLEY CRESCENT). His father was Stephenson Samuel Broadley, a wheelwright, joiner, painter and undertaker according to the sign on his house, who was based here from around 1885 and who died in 1922.

BRACKEN WAY

Bracken Way runs south-west from BRACKENBOROUGH ROAD and both the road and the houses here date from the 1990s. The land that they were built on was originally part of the old open North Field of Louth.

BRACKENBOROUGH ROAD

Brackenborough Road (or Lane) is, as the name implies, simply the road from Louth to Brackenborough, though it also functioned as the main routeway northwards from Louth to Covenham and the other Marsh villages beyond. It originally followed a somewhat different line to that which it currently has. The eighteenth-century Brackenborough Road began approximately where NEWBRIDGE HILL now meets HIGH HOLME ROAD and continued the line of Newbridge Hill northwards, rather than beginning around 200 metres to the north-east, off KEDDINGTON ROAD, as it does now. From here it ran north, gradually approaching the present Brackenborough Road from the west before crossing it around two thirds of the way along its main straight. It then carried on diagonally across the land to the east of the current road, cutting the current sharp corner at the end of the road. The course of Brackenborough Road was altered by the Enclosure Commissioners in 1805, who straightened the road, gave it a new starting point off KEDDINGTON ROAD (note, the VICTORIA ROAD southwards extension of the current Brackenborough Road is a later nineteenth-century innovation), and added the sharp dog-leg turn at its northern end.

Brackenborough Road itself was only sparsely developed for much of the nineteenth century, being primarily a road through agricultural land with virtually no buildings along its course, as can be seen on Brown's preliminary panorama sketches of 1844. By the time of the finished Panorama (1856) a few more buildings are visible, including a thin scattering of farm houses and cottages. One of these was inhabited by John Swaby, a farmer of 56 acres, along with his wife and their servants; in 1857, he was one of the inhabitants of the town whom James O'Connor attempted to con into giving him alms, claiming that he was a ship-wrecked sailor. O'Connor was sentenced to two months of hard labour for his troubles. Another notable development on Brackenborough Road since 1844 was Dales' brickyard, opened as an additional brickyard in order to provide bricks—at a contract price of £5,927—for the new Town Hall of 1853–4. The site of this brickyard is now WILLOW DRIVE, and a small windmill can be seen there on the Panorama, most likely used to pump water out of the clay pits.

Thirteen cottages, known as Dales Terrace, are also visible on the 1856 Panorama. They lay alongside Brackenborough Road, immediately to the north of what is now Willow Drive, and were presumably constructed at the same time as the brickyard here, given their name. In 1858, both the cottages and, apparently, the close that contained the brickyard were offered up for sale and advertised in the *Hull Packet*—the close was then described as arable land in the tenure of Thomas Harrison, suggesting that the brickyard had closed soon after it was opened, and the cottages too had tenants (Robert Rook and Ann Gresswell are listed). In 1861, these cottages were all occupied, primarily by agricultural labourers, although a handful of other trades were present too, including a shepherd (William Fletcher, no. 2). The cottages were offered for sale again in 1882, all thirteen fetching a total of £320—equivalent to around £26,000 today, when adjusted for inflation. By the

1950s, the cottages of Dales Terrace appear to have been demolished, in order to make way for new houses here, with Willow Drive being primarily developed over the course of the 1950s and 60s in the close that once lay behind Dales Terrace. With regard to the clay pit here, the main pit appears to have been repurposed as a fish pond by the early twentieth century, and this designation was maintained for much of that century. Since 1990, new housing has been added at the east end of Willow Drive, so that the road now extends to the end of the close and the large pond is surrounded by properties.

Between the 1850s and the 1890s, the character of Brackenborough Road appears to have remained fairly constant, with little new development. By 1906, however, a few new buildings had begun to appear on the south-eastern part of the road, notably a short terrace of seven houses—named Richmond Terrace—and two semi-detached properties named Myrtle House and Lilac House, the latter two bearing the date 1902. In 1911, Richmond Terrace (built by Colonel Richmond) was home to a dairyman, a jobbing gardener, a railway guard, a draper's assistant, and an assistant insurance superintendent. On the west side of Brackenborough Road, Keddington House and a nursery had been constructed at some point between the late 1880s and 1906, and a number of market gardeners are recorded as living on this road in the late nineteenth and early twentieth centuries, including a certain Henry Keal who is listed as a market gardener here in Kelly's Directory for 1905. The process of development along this road accelerated significantly during the 1930s, with the construction of JUBILEE CRESCENT, a small-scale council housing project completed then and named in commemoration of George V's Silver Jubilee of 1935. By the early 1950s, houses had also been built along the south-west part of Brackenborough Road, and from this point onwards the road saw significant further development as a residential area, most notably through the construction of the new, large estate of ANTHONY CRESCENT & AMANDA DRIVE in the 1970s and FULMAR DRIVE in the 1990s. Brackenborough Road saw a degree of commercial development in this period too. By 1964, Dixon's Paper Works, a packaging company, had both been established and closed again on a site opposite Willow Drive. A former employee subsequently took over the site of these Paper Works in that year and converted it into a plastics factory—the resultant firm, C. K. Addison & Co. Ltd., is still based on the same site, currently trading under the name Britton-Merlin Ltd.

BRADLEY CLOSE

Bradley Close is part of the 'Weavers Tryst' housing estate that was begun in the late 1990s. It runs west from ERESBIE ROAD, the spine of the new development. The estate is built on land that was originally part of Louth's medieval open South Field, although most of the area had been enclosed prior to the 1801 Enclosure Act. The roads within it appear to be named after local worthies of the sixteenth and seventeenth centuries—John Bradley was one of the first Six Assistants of Louth, appointed in 1551, and he was subsequently Warden of Louth several times from 1555 onwards.

BRAMLEY CLOSE

Bramley Close runs west from ROBINSON LANE and is part of a late twentieth-century housing estate built to the south of MOUNT PLEASANT. This estate was constructed in the mid-1990s on land that had formerly been used by the Robinson family for its market garden and nursery, and all the roads that run off Robinson Lane are named after varieties of apple.

BREAKNECK LANE

Breakneck Lane is first mentioned in the Manor Court Roll for 1456, when John Cartwryght was fined 4d (equivalent to around £13 today) for not removing refuse placed by him in 'Brekeneslane'. It is mentioned again in 1603, when it was ordered that all those who property adjoined the 'common sewer in Breackneck laine' must cleanse and flush that part of it that ran alongside their property.

Despite these early references, there is little evidence of significant activity on this street before the mid-nineteenth century. Indeed, on the early maps of the town, the street appears almost entirely undeveloped, with no buildings or properties fronting onto it in 1808 or 1834, although some of the buildings belonging to Thornton House on WESTGATE abutted the street. In 1839, what seem to be two properties with associated buildings are shown on the north side of Breakneck Lane where none had been depicted before, but otherwise the street remained largely undeveloped. To the south were gardens belonging to the Sycamores (see CROWTREE LANE), and William Brown's sketches clearly show that the high wall which currently lines the south side of the street was in place by 1844, enclosing these gardens. On the north side, the majority of the street was still taken up with gardens belonging to Westgate House. This was still the case not only when Brown ceased to revise his Panorama in the mid-1850s, but also when the detailed OS maps of the area were drawn up in 1889 and 1906. Only in the post-Second World War period did things begin to change significantly. In the aftermath of the merger of the boys' and girls' grammars in 1965, the gardens of Westgate House were used for temporary buildings for the new King Edward VI Grammar School, and Somersby Court, off GOSPELGATE, was subsequently built on this site in the 1990s. In the same period, the eastern part of the gardens belonging to Sycamores was also built upon, and a new house was constructed on Breakneck Lane where the nineteenth-century buildings mentioned above had been.

In terms of early residents, a single household is listed on Breakneck Lane in the 1861 census—this was that of John Hicks Petty, a horse breaker, who is also listed in this location in the 1861 Post Office Directory. By 1868, Petty no longer appears, but a Richard Bacon is present in the directory of that year as both a horse breaker and a livery stable keeper on Breakneck Lane. By 1872, he too seems to have moved on, and a Richard Medley is listed as a bricklayer and builder on Breakneck Lane—on the Medley family, see EDWARD STREET.

BRIDGE CLOSE

Bridge Close runs east from STATION APPROACH and is part of a late twentieth-century residential housing development built to the north of RAMSGATE. The railway line running south from Louth railway station once ran over this land; it was opened in 1848 and closed in 1970.

BRIDGE STREET

Whether the ancient Barton Street ran down FANTHORPE LANE and GRIMSBY ROAD and forded the Lud at the site of the present bridge or somewhere to the east of this, as has been suggested, the main north–south bridging point across the Lud has clearly been in its present position for several hundred years at the very least. There was already a bridge here in 1808, and in 1824 it was stated to be in need of repair, something which is suggestive of its relative antiquity. Quite how much of this earlier bridge was repaired and how much rebuilt is unclear, but in 1825 it is recorded that the then-substantial sum of £522 17s 2d was paid for 'erecting the New Bridge' here, a description that implies significant works were involved.

With regard to Bridge Street itself, this appears to be a relatively late name for the road here. On Espin's map of 1808, it is named Willow Row, although it is Bridge Street on Bayley's map of 1834 and in Pigot & Co.'s 1828–9 Directory. Even more interesting, however, is the fact that the Corporation Minute Book for 1835 clearly states that Bridge Street was actually once part of CHEQUERGATE, but that this section of the road had been, at some point, renamed. This information is potentially important, as it means that some of the unlocated early buildings and events that are said to have been on Chequergate could actually have been on that part of Chequergate that was eventually renamed Bridge Street. Indeed, it is worth considering in this context whether the medieval/early modern 'Cheker'—an exchequer or accounting house, probably used to collect market tolls and dues—that Chequergate was possibly named from was located on the part of Chequergate that became Bridge Street. Certainly present-day Bridge Street, on the main northern route into town, is a more plausible location for any such Cheker than the medieval back-street that currently bears the name Chequergate (see further CHEQUERGATE).

Perhaps the most interesting building that survives on Bridge Street is Holland's Mill, or St Mary's Mill, on the north side of the bridge. The mill here was run by a Mr Holland in the 1820s and called 'Hollands Mill' then. Nonetheless, the mill was clearly considerably older than this. Not only does the present building bear the date 1755, but in 1824 it was recorded that Mr Holland was liable for the repair of the mill dam of the mill here under the terms of a 200 year lease originally granted to Sir

23

Charles Bolle on 7 April 1653, with Holland being the current assignee of this term. In other words, it is likely that there was a mill at this location from at least the mid-seventeenth century. By 1828–9, John Scott was the miller here, John Holland having gone bankrupt in 1827, and the mill is stated to be a corn mill, although it has been suggested that it was earlier a fulling mill. A corn mill was still marked here in 1906, but by the time of the Louth Flood in 1920 it had become a garage, a role it continued to fill until 1969.

Other buildings of interest on this road include Bridge Street House, built around 1822, and Bridge Street Terrace on the opposite side of the road—the latter, a rather magnificent four-storey terrace of properties, was actually conceived and built as a block of rented houses in 1825, apparently at the same time that the 'New Bridge' was erected here. As interesting as what is still here, however, is what is missing. At one point the graveyard of St James's Church would have been to the south of Bridge Street (it was located both to the north and to the south of the church, see UPGATE), and the Green on Bridge Street has seen finds of skeletons from it. Similarly, at the 'north end of Bridge-street' there was, according to Robert Bayley in 1834, the 'Lodge for the Poore Men' that is referred to in the Churchwardens' Accounts from 1528 to 1569. This was apparently superseded by 'Spittlehouse' on SPITAL HILL, which was being used as the town's poor house in 1572.

Also once present off Bridge Street, but now gone, were a number of buildings to its south, where there are now two green areas. The houses here can be seen on Espin's 1808 plan of the town, with the current path between the greens running on the line of a lane that separated two blocks of buildings. These buildings and the lane can just be observed on William Brown's finished Panorama of 1856 too. Brown was a particular critic of the houses here, which were known as the Feoffee houses. In 1845 he declared them to be 'disgusting', a danger to carriages due to their closeness to the road, and 'a reproach to public decency' due to both their sight and smell! With regard to their origins, the name 'Feoffee houses' and their location on land that was probably part of the original churchyard of St James's Church (see above) suggests that they are somehow related to the 'house in the churchyard', mentioned in 1574, that the twelve feoffees—trustees holding a fee, an estate in land—of Wright's Coal Charity stored coal in, the coal being distributed to the poor of the town in the winter. Wright's Butter

Charity, set up in 1575, similarly had twelve feoffees who stockpiled butter to be distributed to the poor of Louth in winter, the butter being stored in 'a little house in the churchyard'. The Feoffee houses were eventually taken down in 1888, and the area was levelled and grassed to become the Jubilee Ground in honour of Queen Victoria, although the buildings on the western green area remained in place until after the Second World War.

North of the bridge, there was a large pool on the eastern side of the road in 1808, just before CISTERNGATE. This was the pool of 'Small Wells'—a spring ran southwards from this pool to join the Lud, and in 1592 William Blanchard bequeathed £3 for the dressing of Small Wells and the Aswell spring, implying that Small Wells, like the more important Aswell spring, saw a degree of religious veneration in that period (see the GATHERUMS & SPRINGSIDE). By 1834, the pool is depicted as being much smaller in scale, and on the map of 1839 and Brown's sketches and painting of 1844–56 it is not identifiable. On the opposite side of the road, a short lane ran (and still runs) south-west from Bridge Street. Immediately to the north of this lane, and accessed from it, is The Mount, or Mount St Mary. This large house—which dates from the early nineteenth century, or perhaps a little earlier—was owned by two maiden sisters, the Misses Pettener, at time of Brown's Panorama. Two interesting archaeological finds have been made from the grounds of Mount St Mary. The first is a Neolithic flint knife, which could be up to 6,000 years old. The second is a medieval (fourteenth- or fifteenth-century) secular, domestic building, surviving as chalk foundations, floors, surfaces and walls associated with worked stone blocks, medieval tile, glass, pottery and animal remains.

At the end of this little lane is an equally interesting place, the Old Cemetery or St Mary's Burying Ground. This was the site of the medieval St Mary's Church, or Chapel, and the lane leading up to it from Bridge Street was probably called 'Chapple Hill' in the early modern period in reference to this (Chapple Hill is mentioned in 1603, when Thomas Daie was fined for not sweeping this road each week and for allowing refuse to accumulate there, and St Mary's was regularly referred to as 'St Mary Chappell' in contemporary records). Although it has been sometimes suggested that the former St Mary's here had Anglo-Saxon origins and was the original parish church of Louth, this seems unlikely. There is, in fact, no actual evidence to support this hypothesis, and one of its main modern proponents has retracted his support in recent years. He notes that a more careful study of the evidence actually indicates that St Mary's was never more than a medieval chapel of ease, and that many of the supposed references to this church in fact relate to a chapel dedicated to St Mary which lay within the parish church of St Herefrith-St James (see UPGATE on this church and its history).

Whatever its origins and medieval usage, it is clear that the history of St Mary's as a place of religious worship ended in the mid-sixteenth century. It was closed under the Chantries Act of Edward VI, and the windows were walled up and the bells taken down in 1550. The proceeds from the sale of the bells and other items were used in 1553 to pave ASWELL STREET and dyke and hedge Haregarths in the South Field (see LEGBOURNE ROAD). In 1551, the former St Mary's was being used by the Grammar School, although it was soon found to be too cold and inhospitable for teaching and the school was relocated to SCHOOLHOUSE LANE. The Warden and the Six Assistants of Louth were subsequently granted a license by the Bishop of Lincoln for the demolition of St Mary's in 1560, and the steeple blew down soon after this. In the mid-seventeenth century, that portion of St Mary's which survived was apparently serving as a Lodge for Poor Men—Robert Osney's gift of 1636 gave three cottages on NORTHGATE to support six poor children and 'such poore single men as shall inhabit in St Maries Church', and payments were certainly made to poor men living there in 1638 and 1639. The remaining buildings and the churchyard were later let to Sir Charles Bolle in 1655 for 99 years, with the proviso that the town should be able to use the site as a plague house and burial ground if Louth were visited by the plague or any infectious disease. These buildings were finally demolished in 1749, and the exact site of St Mary's within the Old Cemetery is no longer known.

With regard to St Mary's Burying Ground itself, this was not in use before the eighteenth century, with the usual burial place for the town being then St James's Churchyard. From about 1700, St James's Churchyard was supplemented by St Mary's, and the people of Louth were able to choose between St James's and St Mary's up until 1770—after this, however, St James's Churchyard was discontinued as burial ground. Although St Mary's Burying Ground was enlarged in 1827, there were repeated complaints in the nineteenth century about the state of the cemetery here. William Brown, writing in the *Stamford Mercury*, complained in 1845 about the 'unconsciously offending sheep' that grazed here and, more seriously, about the great difficulty in finding space for new graves at this point. So, for example, no fewer than four older coffins were disturbed during the burial of Mrs Good in 1845, including the remains of one spectator's father, dead and buried for 17 years. This was not, apparently, a unique occurrence in this period, and a new burial ground for the town was opened on LONDON ROAD in 1855, although burials continued to be take place at the Old Cemetery for a number of decades. Indeed, the last burial in St Mary's Burying Ground was that of Richard Foster, who died on 8 June, 1890. As might be expected, there are a number of ghost stories attached to this place. One is that the ghost of John Baly, a priest of Trinity Gild who was betrayed by an associate in 1517 after he had broken into the chest at the end of the high alter, haunted St Mary's Churchyard. Another ghost is supposedly that of a grave-digger, who fell backwards into a grave and broke his neck, and there are also tales of a skeleton who glides around the Old Cemetery, wheeling his own head in a wheelbarrow. Both of the latter ghosts are claimed to have been exorcised at the end of the nineteenth century. Although most of the gravestones now cannot be read, because they have been moved from their positions and stacked in ranks to create an open, grassy area, there were clearly some intriguing inscriptions. Indeed, one excited sufficient interest in 1832 to find its way into the regional newspapers. In June of that year, J. Burman, a joiner of Louth, was reported to have erected a gravestone for his wife that displayed the following Old Testament passage: 'And all the people shouted, and said, God save the King' (1 Samuel 10.24). Many people are said to have daily gone and seen this gravestone, the visitors being 'astonished that such a passage should be selected for a wife's epitaph'!

Finally, a few of the earlier inhabitants of Bridge Street ought to be mentioned. One notable resident and local Councillor was Dr Thomas Philbrick, a general practitioner and surgeon who lived at Bridge Street House. He leased a garden extension on the opposite side of the Lud, and in 1838 built a latticed bridge (depicted on Brown's Panorama) to connect Bridge Street House to this. In 1848, two of his female servants were apparently the victims of William Hopper, a bricklayer of Louth, who was charged with 'indecently exposing his person with intent to insult' them—he was sentenced to three months in prison (see also EASTGATE and HORNCASTLE ROAD). Kenrie Hampson, a baker and corn dealer, was also based on Bridge Street in the 1840s. In 1849, 6s and 6d was stolen from Hampson's cash box by 'a boy of very tender age' and was used to buy a pistol from George West, a gunsmith at the Fish Shambles on Eastgate. When Hampson learned of this, he took the pistol back to West's shop and informed him of what happened, but the gunsmith refused to take the pistol back and return the money, an action for which he was condemned by the Mayor, J. B. Sharpley. Hampson also seems to have had some trouble with his servants: in 1847, Mary Copeland was charged with stealing a brooch and several items of 'wearing apparel' from her master, Hampson. In the 1850s, another tradesman on Bridge Street—Thomas Snowden, a butcher—appeared twice before the local magistrates. On one occasion, he was the victim of fraud, with Mary Starkie, of Binbrook, being charged in August 1851 with obtaining meat from Snowden's shop under false pretences, by claiming that she was collecting it for his customers when in reality she kept it herself. On the other, he was the victim of an assault by his wife, Elizabeth, who apparently attacked him, 'demolishing a great portion of his household goods'. The charge was eventually withdrawn on her promising not to offend again, and Thomas and Elizabeth Snowden were still together in 1861, when they were living on EVE STREET.

BROADBANK

Broadbank is usually considered to be, in origin, an eighteenth-century road, and it does not seem to be present on Armstrong's 1778 plan of the town, although it is marked on Espin's plan of 1808. In the first half of the nineteenth century, Broadbank consisted of two distinct parts. The southern part, running north from NORTHGATE, was formerly known first as Lowgate and then as Enginegate. The latter name was adopted after the construction here of the Engine House for the town's fire engine in 1821—this was on the western side of the road on the south bank of the river, and it was demolished and washed away in the Louth Flood of 1920. On a map of the town dated 1839, the name Enginegate is marked between SPAW LANE and Northgate, stretching over both sides of the Lud. As to the northern part of the road, this was known as Broad Bank from at least 1808, when it is marked as such on Espin's plan, although it was apparently also known locally as Byron's Hill in the mid-nineteenth century (after some of the early residents here, see below). By the late nineteenth century, the distinction between the different parts of the road appears to have declined. Although the street-name Broadbank is still mentioned, from the 1861 census onwards Broadbank was included within Enginegate, and the whole road from HIGH HOLME ROAD to Northgate is labelled as Enginegate on the 1889 OS map. This labelling is maintained on subsequent OS maps until the late 1960s, when the whole road appears under the name that it currently possesses, Broadbank.

To judge from Espin's 1808 plan of Louth, there was very little development along this road before the early nineteenth century. In fact, the only buildings that he marked here were the Free School—which, though it was located on Northgate, did stand on the western corner of the junction between Broadbank and that road—and Broad Bank House, apparently the first property to be deliberately built on this road. The latter was depicted in 1808 as a large house with gardens and a lake, situated on the east side of Broad Bank to the north of the Lud. This property appears on William Brown's Panorama and was occupied by the Byron family in the early to mid-nineteenth century, hence the alternative name of Byron's Hill for this part of the road—Christopher Byron, a solicitor on NEW STREET, was living here in the 1820s, and his widow Mary was still at Broad Bank House in 1851. By 1857, the old Broad Bank House, which lay just to the east of the road, had been taken down and a new mansion built on its land, away from the road. This was also called Broad Bank House and was occupied by William Tate—a grocer and soap maker based on UPGATE—from the 1850s through until the 1880s. It was unoccupied at the time of the 1891 census, but in 1901 and 1911 it was the residence of Charles Anderson, a retired butcher. The second Broad Bank House was demolished by the late 1960s and CEDAR CLOSE was built on the land here in the 1970s.

By the 1830s, more buildings were beginning to appear on Broadbank. Bayley's map of 1834 shows houses now present on the western side of the road to the north of CISTERNGATE, and Enginegate south of the Lud also saw development in this period. Of particular note was the building of the Engine House here in 1821 (mentioned above), which in 1872 housed three fire engines, and the construction of a school for girls and infants—the National Girls' and Infants' School, or St James' School—in Enginegate in 1833–4. The latter building was located on the site of the current Broadbank car park until relatively recently and is visible on Brown's Panorama, with a central circle of grass in the school playground and two maypoles. The infants were educated on the ground floor and the girls above, the school having an average attendance of 271 in 1868. In 1841, the Louth Horticultural and Floral Society, founded only four years earlier, held a show on the ground floor of National School here, a meeting that was notable for the apparent bias of the Society against a gifted connoisseur of flowers who happened to be a poor journeyman cabinet maker. Even more significant was the building constructed at the top of Broadbank in 1837. This was the new Union Workhouse, built at a cost of £6,000 to house up to 300 paupers, although there were only 132 inhabitants in 1841 and 179 in 1851. The workhouse closed in 1935 and reopened as the County Infirmary in 1938; its buildings now form part of Louth Hospital.

The period up to the mid-1850s saw further development of this road. In 1839, the land opposite the National School was shown as an empty close, but by 1844, when William Brown made his sketches of the town from the church spire, the properties that currently stand there had been built. Archaeological work undertaken immediately to the east of these properties (where an abattoir was based in the twentieth century) indicates that this area was originally a periodically inundated floodplain of the Lud, which saw deliberate and substantial dumping during the nineteenth century in order to raise the ground level here by a metre or more, thus drying the area out and making it suitable for building. Beginning in 1808, the early nineteenth century plans of the town also show some sort of small channel running from the Lud and encompassing both this area and the current Broadbank car park across the road, something that may be related to the above character of this part of Louth then. North of the Lud, the western side of Broadbank opposite Broad Bank House was developed around the same time, with houses being once again depicted in this area on Brown's sketches but not on earlier maps. In contrast, the eastern side of Broadbank there was still only occupied by Broad Bank House in 1844, with fields and trees to the north of this property. However, this too had begun to change by the time Brown finished work on the Panorama in the mid-1850s—houses facing onto the road to the north of Broad Bank House are shown on his final Panorama, and the buildings of TEMPLE TERRACE (a road leading eastwards from Broadbank) date from 1853.

Moving into the twentieth century, a number of the buildings that were present on the south-eastern part of Broadbank in 1889 (to the junction with Northgate) had been taken down by 1906. Little seems to have been initially developed in their place, although Louth Museum was opened here in 1910 by the Louth Naturalists', Antiquarian and Literary Society—the museum is still on the same site and was renovated and extended considerably in 2003–06. In 1989, this area also saw the construction of a new road entrance into KILN LANE, as part of the development of the Co-operative (Leo's) supermarket in this part of town. The Wilde Memorial Hall was also built on this stretch of Broadbank in 1932, on the opposite side of the road to the museum. This was a single-storey building intended to replace the Parish Rooms, which stood at the western junction of Broadbank and Northgate, where the Free School had been. The Louth Playgoers, founded in 1932, were initially based in the Wilde Memorial Hall through until the start of the Second World War in 1939, when the hall was used as an ARP centre (Air Raid Precautions, responsible for issuing gasmasks, maintaining the blackout and the like). Wilde Hall also accommodated the Guides and Brownies, church bazaars and jumble sales. It was eventually demolished to make way for the modern flats of Northgate Court, and so joined the Engine House, the National School and the second Broad Bank House as a significant building lost from Broadbank during the course of the twentieth century, to be replaced either by new housing or car parking facilities.

In terms of early inhabitants, Broadbank appears to have been a generally respectable neighbourhood. Not only was it the location of Broad Bank House, but by 1861 this road was also home to the rector of Raithby cum Hallington, Henry Disbrowe, and several Methodist ministers and their wives. The general character of the road is perhaps also indicated by the fact that there were a number of people living here whose occupation was described as 'Proprietor of Houses and Lands' or similar in that census, including Ann Sills, John Marshall and Dinah Tomlinson. There were, of course, tradesmen here too, including James Wakelin, the town crier. Wakelin was depicted by Brown on the Panorama, and he was a wood dealer, a coal dealer and a bill poster in addition to his role as the town crier—he lived on Enginegate from at least 1861 through until the 1890s. Broadbank was similarly home to Benjamin Dales in 1861, a master joiner and builder (the father of John

Dales, the man who won the contract for the new Town Hall on EASTGATE in 1853), and Thomas Sutton, a cattle dealer and grazier of 73 acres. Other occupations listed for the inhabitants of this road in 1861 include agricultural labourer, solicitor's clerk, dressmaker, book binder, and omnibus conductor. There were also two boarding houses on Broadbank at that time, kept by Sophia Collis and Hannah Farrow. In 1861, a New York-born book agent named Robert Goodrich was staying in the latter boarding house; he may have been selling copies of Fullarton and Company's *Gazetteer of the World* in the Louth area, as there was certainly a book agent of the same name doing this in the East Midlands region at this time. Nonetheless, despite this general respectability, Broadbank did occasionally find its way into the regional papers. For example, it was reported that Benjamin Minta of Broadbank, 'a labouring man', had committed suicide by swallowing oxalic acid here in December 1848. Rather less serious was a case reported in 1854, when a young man named James Marshall was charged with stealing onions from Jane Goe's garden on Broadbank, for which he was simply reprimanded and made to pay costs. Finally, in March 1846 an assault apparently occurred on this road, with a certain Charles Walker of Keddington attacking an old man named John Child here.

BROADLEY CRESCENT

This road forms part of the extensive St Bernards Avenue council house estate, developed in the 1950s. At the time that the 1951 OS map was drawn up, Broadley Crescent had already been laid out, and the road appears fully developed on the 1956 map of the town. Broadley Crescent was named after Sir Herbert Broadley, a local man who worked for the British government and the United Nations in the mid-twentieth century. Born in 1892, Sir Herbert grew up in a house next to BOWLING GREEN LANE and attended the Wesleyan School in Louth and then the Grammar. In 1912 he joined the British Civil Service, where he worked in the Military Department of the India Office until 1920 and then in the Board of Trade until 1926. From 1926–39 he was managing director of the Berlin branch of an advertising firm, after which he joined the British Ministry of Food and was knighted in 1947. From 1948–58, Sir Herbert Broadley was Deputy Director-General (and, briefly, Acting Director-General) of the Food and Agriculture

Organization of the United Nations, and after his retirement he served as UNICEF's representative in Great Britain until 1968. He was made a Freeman of Louth in 1961 and died aged 90 in 1983.

BUCKINGHAM ROAD

Buckingham Road runs west off ARUNDEL DRIVE. The road is absent from the 1974–6 OS map but had been laid out and developed on its south side by the 1980s. The north side of the road was developed after the surveying of the 1990 OS map, with some of the properties here sold as new builds in the mid-1990s. The land it is built on was originally part of Louth's old open North Field.

BURGHLEY CRESCENT

Burghley Crescent runs off CHATSWORTH DRIVE and is part of a large housing estate built to the south of NORTH HOLME ROAD in the 1960s and 1970s. The road is shown as laid out but without buildings on the 1968 OS map and had been fully developed by the mid-1970s. The land it is built on was originally part of Louth's old open North Field.

BURNT HILL LANE

Burnt Hill Lane—also occasionally called Bunting Lane—runs from EASTGATE to QUEEN STREET and is first depicted on Armstrong's 1778 plan of the town, when it is shown as built up along both sides of the road. The origins of this road are obscure, although both Eastgate and Walkergate (modern Queen Street) are medieval in date, with medieval property boundaries surviving to the west of Burnt Hill Lane on the northern side of Queen Street. It is worth noting that 'Burnt Hill' occurs as a close- or field-name in Lincolnshire and elsewhere; as such, it could be that the street-name derives from an earlier close here or nearby called Burnt Hill.

Burnt Hill Lane was never a significant residential street, despite it being fully developed on the early plans of the town. In 1861, only three houses were listed as being present on the road, along with an additional four that were accessed by passages from Burnt Hill Lane but were

33

actually located in the rear yard of the Warrenite Chapel (now the Masonic Hall) that faced onto Queen Street. Moreover, the road does not seem to have been an especially pleasant neighbourhood in that period. In 1839, William Brown wrote that Burnt Hill Lane was almost impassable in the winter, due to the mud, and claimed that the road stank due to the stagnant water and filth that was allowed to lie there. In addition, some of the people who dwelt either on the road or in the Chapel Yard just off it were of a disreputable character. For example, in June 1847, Mary Bray of Burnt Hill Lane was charged by Sampson Brown with being a common prostitute, frequenting the streets for the purposes of prostitution, and stealing 10s from his person (equivalent to around £35 today). Found guilty, she was committed to the House of Correction for one month as a prostitute. The houses off Burnt Hill Lane in the Warrenite Chapel Yard appear to have been particularly notorious in this regard, being described in 1848 as a 'den of prostitutes', the greater part of which were 'brothels of the very lowest description, and complete sinks of vice and infamy'.

In January 1848, one of these brothels in the Chapel Yard was kept by a prostitute named Fanny Arliss, who was charged with shouting, brawling, and indecent conduct in this yard at night-time, to the annoyance and disturbance of neighbourhood. She was ordered to pay 2s into the poor-box and pay 6s 6d costs. In October, another brothel-keeper here appeared before the courts. This was Eleanor Diana Smith, who was charged with throwing hot ashes over a poor, infirm old woman named Ann Overton, for which she was fined 6d with 12s costs to pay (equivalent to around £50 today). Smith appeared again in late November, when she was described as 'the keeper of a notorious brothel'. She and two of the prostitutes who resided with her, named Ann Taylor and Harriet Wallis, were charged with stealing £40—more than £3,000 today, taking account of inflation—in gold and notes from William Tesch Easten, a cattle jobber of Wooton, who had presumably been robbed during a visit to the brothel.

The actual owner of these houses and brothels was not the chapel in whose yard they were located, but rather one William Brett senior, a hatter and draper based on MERCER ROW. The Louth reporter of the *Hull Packet* argued several times in 1848 that Brett ought to take action to evict his tenants from the Chapel Yard, which they had turned into a 'den of depravity'. There is, however, little evidence that these pleas were acted on with the rapidity that the correspondent desired—there was still at least one brothel there ten months after he first raised the issue. Brett did, however, find himself in front of the local court in October 1849 with regard to these properties, which had been judged so filthy that they posed a danger 'to the health of the inhabitants of the neighbourhood'. He was ordered to pay £2 1s 8d (equivalent to around £170 today) towards the costs incurred by the Sanitary Committee in dealing with the dangers that they saw there.

There were, of course, trades other than the oldest one taking place on Burnt Hill Lane in the nineteenth century. In 1841, both a beer retailer named James Turner and Thomas Darby's veterinary surgeons were listed on this road; James Turner was still listed here in 1849 and 1852, but Thomas Darby was instead listed as Walkergate then, as he had been in 1828–9 and 1835 too—the reason for this variation was that Darby's business was based in the property on the eastern corner of Burnt Hill Lane and Walkergate, now Louth Family Dental Practice. In the 1860s and 1870s, Fanny Horsewood was active as a clothes broker on Burnt Hill Lane, and her husband, James, is listed as trading as a furniture dealer here in the 1880s. In the late 1890s, one of Louth's earliest fried fish shops was based on this road—this belonged to John Morley, who also had a fishmonger's at 19 Queen Street, and it was still in business in 1913. The Wellow Brewery Co. was also listed as being on both Burnt Hill Lane and Queen Street from 1905 until at least 1937, occupying the premises on the south-western corner of Burnt Hill Lane and Queen Street (until recently Thresher's wine shop). The Wellow Brewery was probably continuing a pre-existing brewing business here, as the Nottingham Brewery Co. appears to have been based here in 1900—this company was, significantly, the owner of the Wellow Brewery Co. from 1900, which they ran as a separate business until 1944—and previous to this a Joseph Cornelius Bellamy was listed as a brewer and wine and spirit merchant on Burnt Hill Lane and Queen Street from 1885 to 1896 (in the 1880s, his business was associated with the East & Co. Maiden Row Brewery, on which see CHURCH STREET). In 1905, there was also a grocer's shop on Burnt Hill Lane, run by George Blanchard: by 1909, this had become a confectionery shop and had been joined on Burnt Hill Lane by Wiggen Brothers' printers. Both of these businesses were still here in 1919, but Morley's fried fish shop had closed at some point between 1913 and 1919.

BUTCHER LANE & LITTLE BUTCHER LANE

Butcher Lane and Little Butcher Lane run between two blocks of buildings that separate the CORNMARKET from MERCER ROW. The original medieval market place of Louth extended from the south side of Mercer Row to the north side of the Cornmarket, without any such interruption. It is believed that the western part of this market place was where the butcher stalls, mentioned in the Manor Court Roll of 1450 (see below), were located, with the names Butcher Lane, Little Butcher Lane and Butcher Market (an old name for the Cornmarket) reflecting this original usage of this part of the market place. At some point, the butcher stalls were converted into two permanent blocks of buildings that cut Mercer Row off from the modern Cornmarket, and the small shops on the south of Cornmarket are in fact said to have been used almost exclusively by butchers until the mid-nineteenth century, who slaughtered livestock in front of them. Quite when the butcher stalls here were converted into permanent structures is unclear, although it would seem to have happened by 1603. In that year, John North, draper, and Stephen Bellow were fined 5s each (equivalent to around £50 today) for not repairing 'the pavements between their grounds in a little lane leading from the Beast Market [another early name for the Cornmarket] to the Mercer Row'. This must be a reference to either Butcher Lane or Little Butcher Lane, and if at least one of these lanes was in existence at that time, then the permanent blocks probably must have been too (North and Bellow presumably occupied plots either side of one of these lanes).

In 1671, we find another probable reference to the permanent block of buildings between Cornmarket and Mercer Row. Edward Browne, a mercer (dealer in textiles), leased 'a Bulker & appentice over it in ye beast Market on ye backe side of his house', renting it for 21 years at a rate of 13s 4d '& a barrell of oysters & a pottell [half a gallon] of ffrench wine'! The 'house' of this mercer presumably fronted onto Mercer Row, with Browne then renting structures behind it that fronted onto the Beast Market, or Cornmarket. As to these structures, a bulker is probably a word for a stall and an appentice was an early modern word for 'a lean-to building, a penthouse'. With regard to Edward Browne, mercer, he issued tokens in his name during the seventeenth century and he was also clearly an important figure in the town—he was Warden in 1676–7 and 1683–4, churchwarden in 1666, and one of the Six Assistants of Louth Corporation when he died in 1687.

The area of the medieval market place where Butcher Lane and Little Butcher Lane now exist may have been home to not only the butcher stalls, but also the medieval chapel of St John. In 1450, thirteen butchers were fined for leaving piles of stinking offal both in the common way at the south end of butchers' stalls (probably Mercer Row) and at the east end of the chapel of St John. This account, from the Louth Manor Court Rolls, would seem to indicate that the chapel was not only in close proximity to the butcher stalls, but was also situated to the west of them, given where the offal was placed. As such, a location for the chapel of St John on the west side of the medieval market place—that is, on the west side of either modern Butcher Lane or the Cornmarket—has often seemed the most credible solution to the question of its location. The plot occupied by the chapel was, incidentally, a reasonably sizeable one: in the mid-sixteenth century, it was said to have had an area of one quarter of a rood, which is equal to one sixteenth of an acre, or around 250m². In consequence, the chapel could have occupied a fairly significant proportion of the frontage of the western market place, if it was indeed located there. With regard to the chapel itself, this is first mentioned in 1311, when Roger of Louth, son of William de Lekeburne, granted his brother Master Thomas de Luda some property in the market place that lay next to the chapel of St John. The chapel was demolished under the 1547 Chantries Act of Edward VI, and in 1550 the site was given to Sir Ralph Sadler and Laurence Wynnyngton. It was subsequently sold on twice before the Corporation of Louth finally bought it for 76s 8d in 1567.

In the modern period, Butcher Lane and Little Butcher Lane have been home to a number of businesses. One of these is the current Larders Coffee House, which is based in the premises of Larders delicatessen on Little Butcher Lane—after having been based on Mercer Row from the early nineteenth century, the Larders grocery business moved into its former warehouse here in 1988. Another was the Waterloo Inn in Butcher Lane, which is now Striacroft Jewellers. This was run by William Ackrill in 1828–9 and was subsequently known as Allison's Vaults and run by Allison & Co., wine, spirit, ale and porter merchants of the Cornmarket, who continued to function into the early twentieth century (Allison & Co. had been taken over by Walter Skipworth Foreman by the time of the 1913 directory).

CANNON STREET

It has been suggested that the ancient Barton Street originally ran down BROADBANK and along Cannon Street, before passing through the modern town, rather than running at least partway down the present GRIMSBY ROAD (to the west of Broadbank), as is usually believed. There is, however, no real evidence to support this hypothesis, and what evidence we do have indicates that Cannon Street was an early nineteenth-century road. Certainly, it is not depicted on either Armstrong's 1778 plan of Louth or Espin's more accurate one of 1808, with the site of Cannon Street shown as gardens and allotments on the latter. Indeed, the street appears to have been staked out in 1814, when Eve & Campbell bought a 390 square yard (326m²) plot of land on the new street—a warehouse and showroom, and a joiners' and upholsterers' workshop, were eventually built on this plot, which was located just to north of the Playhouse Cinema. As such, the hypothesis of a prehistoric and Roman origin for Cannon Street must be put to one side. With regard to the name, this is presumably copied from the City of London's Cannon Street, which is located to the east of St Paul's Cathedral; several streets in Louth bear names that appear to have such an origin (see COMMERCIAL ROAD).

Several major buildings are situated on Cannon Street, including Cannon Street House. Built in 1800 as the chapel of the General Baptists on NORTHGATE, this originally had a small burial ground in front of it. After the construction of Cannon Street, the chapel was rebuilt in 1827 (when its capacity was increased to 570) and further altered in 1840. The current facade is said to date from 1851, when the chapel was extended with Sunday School buildings constructed over part of the old graveyard. The chapel stayed in use until 1919, when the Baptists transferred to the Eastgate Baptist Chapel on the corner of EASTGATE and RAMSGATE (Eastgate Union Church) and the Cannon Street chapel was subsequently sold to the Pentecostalists. From 1938, Cannon Street House functioned as the offices of Louth Rural District Council, although it has recently regained a religious role, as the home of the Louth Christian Fellowship.

Another major building on Cannon Street is the Playhouse Cinema. Like Cannon Street House, this was originally a chapel. Built fronting onto the new Cannon Street in 1821 by the Independents (later the Congregationalists), the chapel could seat 500 people. One of its early ministers was local historian R. S. Bayley (1830–6), and Sunday School buildings were added to the chapel in 1871. In 1919, the Congregationalists moved from this chapel to join the Baptists at the Eastgate Baptist Chapel, now Eastgate Union Church. The chapel was subsequently reopened as a theatre in 1922 by F. A. Bradford of Mablethorpe—it was used by Louth Operatic Society for a week each year, and films were shown here. In the 1920s, these were accompanied by the piano and fiddle, with the first 'talkie' being shown in August 1930. In 1935, the building was reconstructed as a small luxury cinema— the current front elevation of the Playhouse Cinema dates from this time, though the original chapel frontage can be still be seen behind it when viewed from across the street or at an angle. In recent years, it has been converted from a single screen to three screens, and in 2012 the interior was refurbished and upgraded.

The final important building here is the Town Hall of 1853–4. Although this primarily faces onto EASTGATE, it also runs along the eastern side of Cannon Street and dominates here, with the road having been widened at this end in order to accommodate it. The Louth Borough Police—first formed in 1823—had their station in the part of the new Town Hall facing onto Cannon Street, with the final 1856 version of Brown's Panorama actually showing the words Police Station painted on the side of the building here (before the building of the new Town Hall, the Mansion House on UPGATE had functioned as the police station). The force in the mid-1850s consisted of a superintendent named John William Tacey, a sergeant and two constables, and it is intriguing to note that Tacey undertook a number of roles from his Town Hall base in addition to his police duties—in 1861, he is listed as not only the chief superintendent of the borough police, but also the sanitary inspector, the inspector of weights and measures, the bailiff to the Corporation, and the 'superintendent of fire police, markets & fairs & for the relief of vagrants'. More recently, the part of the Town Hall facing onto Cannon Street has been used as for the Tourist Information Centre and the Community Access Point. Interestingly, in 1910 David Lloyd George was driven out of the Town Hall and into Cannon Street by suffragettes hiding in a false ceiling, who threw stink bombs at him. He was smuggled out into the road and then taken down a passageway alongside Louth Town and Country Club (formerly the Louth Conservative Club, based on Cannon Street from the late 1880s). This passageway apparently became known as Lloyd George's Passage in honour of this event!

These significant buildings did not stand alone on Cannon Street in the mid-nineteenth century. On the one hand, William Brown's Panorama (last updated in 1856) shows that walled, formal gardens were present here on both sides of the road, to the south of the Baptist Chapel and to the north of the Congregational Chapel. These were presumably the remnants of the gardens that are shown here on the 1808 plan, across which Cannon Street was subsequently laid out. On the other hand, Cannon Street was also the site of some of the most tightly packed working-class housing in nineteenth-century Louth. This housing was located across the road from the Town Hall and the Congregational Chapel (Playhouse Cinema), on the site now occupied by Cannon Street car park. Here, twenty small houses were densely packed into two courts, named Cannon Street Court and Sharpley's Court. The former is shown on Bayley's 1834 plan of the town, and the latter had clearly been added by 1839, as it is present on a map of the town produced in that year. The standard of accommodation here was very poor, with few toilets between the twenty houses. In 1851, the occupants included Samuel Scrimshaw, an engine driver, ten agricultural labourers, and nine laundresses. Something of the cramped nature of life in these one-up, one-down houses can perhaps be had from the description of an accident that occurred here in October 1856. The two year old son of Joseph Smith, a labourer, was left—together with five other children—in the care of an eleven year old girl in one of these houses then. The girl apparently took a pan of boiling water from the fire and placed it on the floor, which the boy, 'running backward in play', fell over into and was 'scalded in a most dreadful manner'. These houses were also home to a number of people of fairly dubious character. For example, in 1855 an Irish labourer of Cannon Street, named Nicholas Corrigan, was charged with 'brutally assaulting', without any provocation, an 'inoffensive agricultural labourer named Ayscough' in WESTGATE; having been convicted several times of similar offences, he was fined 20s and costs, or one month in jail. The houses of Cannon Street Court and Sharpley's Court were finally demolished as slums in 1933.

A number of trades appear to have been undertaken in this street in the nineteenth century. In 1841, for example, a Thomas Vickers is said to have been active in Cannon Street as a smith and bell-hanger, and in 1856, a Thomas Ashley is listed as an iron founder and a whitesmith (one who finishes metal goods) here, having been earlier listed—in 1849—as a blacksmith in the same street. Similarly, in 1868 a James Whisker is listed as a blacksmith on Cannon Street. There were also a number of shopkeepers, grocers and the like whose businesses were located on this road in the nineteenth century, including Harriet Smith (a shopkeeper here in 1856) and Alexander James Furnish (a grocer here in 1868). At the upper end of the social scale, Frederick Sharpley, a solicitor, the deputy coroner, and clerk to the Louth Paving Commissioners, gave his professional address as 1 Cannon Street from 1872 onwards (his business premises were previously listed as being on Eastgate).

CEDAR CLOSE

A 1970s development, built on the site formerly occupied by Broad Bank House and its grounds and fish pond—see further BROADBANK.

CHARLES AVENUE

Charles Avenue is part of a large, mid–late twentieth-century housing estate to the south of KEDDINGTON ROAD. It runs from GROSVENOR ROAD & GROSVENOR CRESCENT through to ADA WAY. Grosvenor Road and Crescent were built first, being present on the 1951 OS map of the town, with Charles Avenue coming later—the easternmost end had been begun by 1959 and the road was nearly fully developed by the late 1960s, although properties were still being built here into the early 1970s. By 1974, the eastern end of Charles Avenue had been joined to Ada Way, part of the ELM DRIVE housing estate. By 1990, CHRISTOPHER CLOSE had been added to the estate, running north from Charles Avenue.

CHARLES STREET

Quite why Charles Street bears this name is unclear; it is possible that it is named after Charles I or Charles II, as has sometimes been suggested, but this is by no means certain. A Roman coin of the emperor Domitian, dated AD 86, has been found on the corner of Charles Street and NEWBRIDGE HILL, but no other indications of Roman or pre-modern activity have been found. The earliest recorded modern activity on Charles Street took the form of an extensive brickworks, the pit of which still survives as a large pond behind Charles Street tennis courts and bowling green. Espin's plan of the town shows that the bridge across the Lud from EVE STREET had been built by 1808, and it is therefore possible that the brickworks on the north side of the Lud here had been opened by this point, as both the 1839 map of the town and William Brown's sketches of 1844 show nothing else present in that area during the first half of the nineteenth century. One of the first owners of the brickyard here was John Dunstan Naull, who had the Charles Street brickworks with John Edwards at the time that Brown was working on the Panorama. He lived in the MARKET PLACE in one of the former 'great houses' of Louth (where the Market Hall now stands), and is listed as a brick and tile maker in the 1828–9 and 1835 directories of Louth. In subsequent years it was run by a number of people, including Charles Titley in 1872 and Frank Darnill in the early twentieth century. In 1913, Darnill's brick and tile works was the only brickyard still functioning in Louth: it finally closed after being damaged in the flood of 1920.

In 1844, Charles Street appears to have been simply the access to the brickyard, which was surrounded by fields, gardens and hedges then. However, by the time Brown had completed his Panorama (first displayed in 1847 and last updated in 1856), things had changed significantly. In particular, the whole of Charles Street had been laid out over the fields through to Newbridge Hill. One of the most striking new buildings depicted here by Brown on the Panorama was the new ironworks of John Sanderson (or Saunderson), with its tall chimney, built on the high bluff where HAWTHORNE AVENUE meets Charles Street. Erected on what had been arable land in the early 1840s, this iron foundry and agricultural implement maker—known as the New Bridge Hill Iron Works—appears to have still been operating in 1891, although John Saunderson is listed as retired, aged 82, in 1901 and the ironworks had been demolished by 1906, to be make way for the southern part of Hawthorne Avenue. Another notable business was Charles Street Mill, a six-sail windmill once located at the north end of MILLERS COURT, which was built on the site of a probably demolished, earlier mill (a mill was present here at the time of the Enclosure Act of 1801 but absent from both Brown's sketch and his final Panorama). John Allison is listed as a miller and baker on Charles Street from 1861 to 1872 and presumably worked out of this mill. From 1885, Hall Brothers are listed as millers here, their windmill surviving the fire that burnt down the adjoining Crown Roller Mills in 1905. Bryan Hall's milling business subsequently moved to the RAMSGATE water mill, and no windmill is marked on 1932 OS map of this area.

In addition to a brickyard, an ironworks and a corn mill, there was also a fellmonger and an oil and cake mill on Charles Street in the nineteenth century. The former, a dealer in hides or skins who might also prepare skins for tanning, is first mentioned in 1856, when Peter Blanchard is listed as a tanner and fellmonger on Charles Street, and he continued to appear in the local directories until 1872. By 1881, his son, Maxey William Blanchard, appears to have taken over the business—he is listed as a fellmonger employing four men in the 1881 census, and in the 1885 and 1889 directories he is listed as a tanner, fellmonger and chemical manure manufacturer on Charles Street. Maxey was probably not the first choice to inherit the business from his father, as his elder brother Peter had also been a tanner. Unfortunately, Peter had been hanged in Lincoln Castle in 1875. On the 17 March 1875, Peter Blanchard junior had met his sweetheart of four years, Louisa Hodgson (of 29 NEWMARKET), after chapel and went back with her to her parents' house. Here they argued about the attention that a young man named Campion had been paying her, a dispute that ended in Blanchard stabbing the young lady in the heart. He confessed his guilt and, although an appeal for leniency was made on the grounds of insanity and his epileptic fits, he was hung by William Marwood in the grounds of Lincoln Castle, using Marwood's famous 'long drop' method. Maxey Blanchard was still in business here in 1891, but in 1896 he is no longer listed as a fellmonger on Charles Street; a Frank Parker is, however, and he may well have taken over the earlier business. By the early twentieth century, Frank Parker's son, Percy, was in charge, and he continued to trade as an artificial manure manufacturer and fellmonger on Charles Street until after World War I.

The oil and cake mill, located on the northern corner between Charles Street and Newbridge Hill, made animal feed—it first appeared as the 'Great Northern Oil & Cake Mill' in the Post Office Directory of 1868, when it was run by Richard James Nell. Nell, a member of the Nell family of RIVERHEAD, died aged 52 in 1868 and the business was taken over by his 19 year-old son, also named Richard James. Richard James Nell junior became a Conservative councillor and, subsequently, Mayor in 1888, and is listed as running the mills here through until 1896. By 1905, however, this factory had been converted into a wallpaper mill for the Free Wall Paper Co. Limited, and it was afterwards the site of United Canners Ltd. This factory canned locally grown fruit and vegetables in the inter-war years, most notably Benedict's Country Garden Peas. In 1951, the canning factory was demolished, to be replaced by a large Lin Pac factory, which manufactured corrugated cardboard for packing. This was in turn demolished in 2003 to make way for a large residential housing development, begun in 2006 (see further BOLLE ROAD). The latter has added a significant number of new houses to the north side of the east end of Charles Street; the south side, in contrast, currently remains undeveloped and occupied by allotments.

Other notable people living and working on Charles Street in the nineteenth century included Charles Dyas, listed as a brewer and builder here from 1856. In 1857, his business had clearly suffered a significant setback, as all his estates and effects were assigned to John Dalton of Hull and Joseph North of Alford (probably his father-in-law), being held in trust by them for the benefit of Charles Dyas' creditors. However, Dyas seems to have survived this setback and continued to trade from Charles Street into the 1870s, although he had retired by the time of the 1881 census. Dyas and his family lived at 1 Charles Street, and Dyas Row (north off Charles Street) is named from him and had been built by 1861. He died aged 70 in 1883, as a result of falling in the Lud between Eve Street and Charles Street while walking home from the Marquis of Granby public house—his friend, Charles Merritt of Keddington Road (a Great Northern Railway foreman platelayer), managed to retrieve him from the river with some help, but Dyas died later that night in his home, after complaining of being cold. Also of note is William Tudor, who is listed as a coach builder based at 3 Charles Street from at least 1881 through until 1896.

CHATSWORTH DRIVE

Chatsworth Drive runs to the south of NORTH HOLME ROAD and is one of the main roads of a large housing estate built here in the 1960s and 1970s. The road is shown partially developed on the 1968 OS map and it was completed by the mid-1970s. The land it is built on was originally part of Louth's old open North Field.

CHEQUERGATE

That Chequergate was at one time rather more extensive than its present-day descendant is demonstrated by the Corporation Minute Book for 1835—this clearly states that BRIDGE STREET was once part of Chequergate, with this section of the road having been renamed at some point. On the one hand, the fact that the street currently known as Chequergate represents only the easternmost part of the original Chequergate is problematical. Whilst we have a number of references to early buildings and events on Chequergate, in most cases we cannot say whether a location on the present Chequergate is meant or one on that part of the street since renamed Bridge Street. On the other hand, the fact that Chequergate once included Bridge Street may help to explain the street-name. The early modern references to Chequergate refer to it as 'the Cheker', and one suggestion has been that the street-name derives from *cheker*, 'ground of chequered appearance'. An alternative proposal, however, is that the name Chequergate may in fact derive from the former presence there of an exchequer or toll house. Certainly, there was a building in Leicester known as 'le cheker' in 1458 and 'the Cheker' in 1525, which was a medieval and early modern exchequer or accounting house, probably used to collect market tolls and dues. Given Louth's status as a significant medieval market town, the idea that Chequergate was the street where such a 'Cheker', or market toll-house, was located would seem to deserve some consideration, and the fact that the original Chequergate included Bridge Street does add considerably to the credibility of this suggestion. After all, present-day Bridge Street, on the main northern route into town, is a far more plausible location for any

45

medieval and early modern Cheker than would be the medieval back-street that currently retains the name Chequergate (the length of road presently known as Chequergate probably had its origins as a medieval back access-way for the properties that fronted onto EASTGATE, see also NORTHGATE).

One of the earliest references to Chequergate occurs in the context of the Petty School (a prep school or elementary school) that was based there. A tenement situated there was given by John Bradley to the Grammar School, and this was converted into the Petty School in 1555–7; the first master was John Laycoke, who died in 1559. The UPGATE (Churchyard) Song School appears to have merged with the Petty School in around 1558, and this school then continued into the second half of the seventeenth century. In 1666, the building seems to have been in poor repair, as part of it fell down in that year, and in 1673 the Petty School was moved to Richard Odling's house, wherever that may have been. The last reference to the school comes in 1681, when John Bucke was paid £4 as his yearly salary (equivalent in economic status to a 2012 salary of around £13,500), and it seems likely that it either merged with, or was superseded by, Mapletoft's Petit Free School on Northgate, established in 1677. Another interesting early reference comes in 1603, when Richard Smithson and Samuell ffisher are charged with fouling the public street by throwing and placing dung 'in the king's highway near the Checker'. In this case, however, the reference could be read as referring to a medieval and early modern toll-house called 'the Checker', of the sort discussed above, with the 'king's highway' presumably being the main northern route into Louth, that is modern Bridge Street, the western part of the original Chequergate.

By 1808, the street-name Chequergate had become restricted to its modern extent. In terms of the character of this section of street, although it had been originally a back access-way for the medieval properties fronting onto Eastgate, by the late eighteenth and early nineteenth centuries there were buildings depicted on both sides of the road here. So, for example, in 1828–9 Mrs Mary Ann Orme, Thomas Hudson and Francis Walesby were listed as 'gentry' living on Chequergate, Richard Paddison was an attorney there, Charles Ryley a mason, and Benjamin Goulson worked as a smith and veterinary surgeon on this road at that time. Moreover, the process of infilling between the river and Chequergate was clearly underway by 1808, and had advanced significantly by the time that William Brown drew his first sketches of the area in 1844. Of particular note were the creation of both LUDGATE & HEALEY'S COURT here, running north from Chequergate. These were the site for not only a large quantity of poor-quality housing, but also significant businesses, such as Esberger's coach building works that were based in Ludgate from 1818. Healey's Court was demolished in the interwar years, as part of the general slum clearances of that period, and the original Ludgate was cleared to make way for the old Telephone Exchange, first constructed in 1965–6 and subsequently extended.

By the mid-nineteenth century, a large number of trades were listed as being present on Chequergate. For example, a baker, flour dealer and miller called John Allison was based here in 1856 (he was subsequently listed on CHARLES STREET, from 1861 to 1872), and a Richard Hubbard is listed as a music professor, engraver and lithographer at 17 Chequergate from 1856 through until 1868 (he had previously been based on NEW STREET, according to the 1849 directory). The latter shop was additionally used by Mr Ross, a dentist from Hull, for the creation of false teeth on the first Wednesday of every month in 1860— Ross manufactured the teeth he fitted and so was able to offer them at half the usual price, according to his advertisements of that year. James Hunter Ryley, stone and marble mason and brick maker, was similarly listed on Chequergate in the 1849, 1856 and 1861 directories (he died in 1867)—he presumably took over the business from the Charles Ryley who was listed as a stone and marble mason on Chequergate in 1828–9. James Hunter Ryley's brickworks were on Eastgate, where ORME LANE is, and he was responsible for building the now-demolished Sessions House on RAMSGATE. Chequergate was also where Frederick Septimus Tate, surgeon, was located from 1861 until 1872, and in 1871 a cottage hospital for the sick poor was established in a house on this road, according to the 1872 White's Directory. This had five beds and was attended to by the local medical practitioners, with Maria Lynn as the nurse. Finally, there was also a short-lived ironworks, known as Chequergate Iron Works, located on the eastern corner of Ludgate and Chequergate—this was shown on the 1889 OS map of the town and was presumably where James Turner, agricultural implement maker, engineer and machine manufacturer of 6 Chequergate was based (he is listed as such in the 1885 directory and in the 1891 census).

In the 1911 census, the inhabitants of the street included a number of people who did not need to work as they lived on 'private means', such as Stephen Weston Marsden of Red House, Chequergate; a dispenser and medical book-keeper, named Charles Pratt; a builder and house joiner called Ellen Hewson, a widow of 70 who appears to have continued her husband's business at 23 Chequergate (Thomas Hewson is first listed as a builder on Chequergate in the 1868 directory); a bootmaker, Francis Clayton; and Paul Strawson, a house painter. Over the course of the twentieth century, a significant number of the buildings on both sides of Chequergate were demolished, first on the south side as a result of the development of the Post Office that fronted onto Eastgate, and later on the north side too, as a consequence of the building and extension of the old Telephone Exchange here.

CHESTNUT DRIVE

Chestnut Drive is a late twentieth-century housing estate, established in the 1970s at the eastern end of EASTFIELD ROAD. The housing estate was built over two of the last remaining fields to the south of Eastfield Road, on land that had originally been part of Louth's open East Field.

CHRISTOPHER CLOSE

Christopher Close is part of a large mid–late twentieth-century housing estate to the south of KEDDINGTON ROAD. It runs north from CHARLES AVENUE and was completed in the 1980s. The land it is constructed on was part of Louth's old open fields until the Enclosure Act of 1801.

CHURCH CLOSE

Church Close runs north off GOSPELGATE and in the nineteenth century its site was occupied by Hyde's Yard. In 1851, a number of households were based in Hyde's Yard—these were headed by a charwoman, a labourer, a chairmaker, a soapmaker's assistant, a pauper, a journeyman cordwainer (cobbler), a master bricklayer, a bricklayer, and a tallow chandler (candlemaker). The charwoman was Mary Waterman— in 1853, she worked as a laundress and used a field off CROWTREE

LANE to dry the items that she washed; a certain James Blizard, of Dublin, was charged in September of that year with stealing four of her shirts from that spot. The soapmaker's assistant and the tallow chandler were David Jackson and John Reed. The presence of these occupations in Hyde's Yard may well reflect the fact that this yard belonged to a soapmaking and tallow chandling business that fronted onto UPGATE in that period. This was listed as Hyde & Sons in 1828–9 and Benjamin Hyde and William Hyde in 1835. By 1841, it had become Hyde & Tate's tallow chandlers and soap boilers, and by 1849 the originally separate Smith firm of tallow chandlers (run by Isaac Smith in 1835 from MERCER ROW) had joined with it to make Hyde, Smith & Tate's grocers, soapmakers and tallow chandlers.

In 1851, the Upgate property of Hyde, Smith & Tate was occupied by William Tate, whilst grocer and soap maker Charles Goodwin Smith lived on CISTERNGATE and a Benjamin Hyde and William Hyde were respectively listed at Southfield House (KENWICK ROAD) and The Sycamores (Crowtree Lane). During the 1850s, Charles Smith appears to have run into problems, as his assets were put into trust for his creditors in 1855. Nonetheless, he clearly survived these problems, as he was still trading in 1861 as part of Smith & Tate grocers, soapmakers and tallow chandlers at the Upgate premises—the business, which the Hydes appear to have retired from by that time, employed nine men and three boys in 1861, down slightly from thirteen men in 1851. By 1872, the firm had become simply C. G. Smith & Sons of 26 Upgate, a name it henceforth retained, though it was also known as Louth Soap Works. Whilst it was listed as on Upgate, and this is where the shop was, the soap and candles were actually produced in Hyde's Yard—on OS maps from 1906, the Soap Works is marked as a large building on the western side of Hyde's Yard, and William Brown marked a warehouse belonging to Hyde & Tate's business on the eastern side of the yard in 1844. The Soap Works in Hyde's Yard were demolished in the mid-twentieth century and C. G. Smith's shop on Upgate was demolished in 1976, with modern properties now occupying the site of Hyde's Yard, which has been renamed Church Close.

CHURCH STREET

Although the name Church Street currently applies to the whole length of road from EASTGATE through to NEWMARKET, this was previously two separate streets. The northern part of the road, to the junction with MONKS DYKE ROAD, was known as Maiden Row (occasionally Maiden Lane) well into the twentieth century, whilst that to the south was originally Long Lane, although it was renamed Church Street in 1864 in reference to the construction of St Michael's Church there in 1862–3.

With regard to Maiden Row, this street was first mentioned in the fifteenth century and linked the eastern ends of two other medieval streets, Eastgate and Walkergate (QUEEN STREET). Maiden Row appears to have been on the periphery of the medieval town and is generally thought to have been largely undeveloped in the fifteenth and sixteenth centuries: certainly, there is no trace of surviving medieval property boundaries on this street and the early references are to pasture here, rather than anything else. So, for example, John Chapman of Thorpe Hall (see LINCOLN ROAD), the patron of John Louth's Chantry, and William Dychaund, the chantry priest, granted a lease of two pastures of chantry land in 'Maydyn Rowe' to Thomas Blaunscherd for 21 years in 1547. The street-name itself probably derives from the medieval Gild of St Mary, which seems to have held land here, given that the manorial court of Louth ordered the Gild of St Mary to repair a defective causeway in 'maydynraw' (Maiden Row) in 1499.

One of the most distinctive features of Maiden Row was the presence here of the Aswell spring. This water course ran all along the back of the properties facing onto Walkergate and was used by the medieval cloth fullers, or walkers, of that road—who stamped on cloth in pure water to felt it and give it a smooth finish—as an essential part of their trade, as well as by other groups including brewers, an industry first mentioned in Louth in 1449 (see further Queen Street and the GATHERUMS & SPRINGSIDE). At some point, the 460 gallons-per-minute or so put out by the Aswell Spring were harnessed to power a watermill, which was located on Maiden Row, with the mill dam just to its east. Quite when this development took place is uncertain. All we can say is that the mill was probably in place by the end of the eighteenth century, as the mill dam is depicted on the 1808 plan of Louth and the mill is referred to in Britton's *Beauties of England and Wales* in 1807. The watermill turned by the Aswell spring is likely to have been originally a fulling mill, representing a mechanisation of the fulling industry that had traditionally taken place in this part of town from at least the thirteenth century: certainly, the mill is described as such in 1807, and this description was repeated in a revised version of that account published in 1819. By the 1820s, however, the watermill on Maiden Row was instead being used to mill corn, having been apparently recently renovated in 1823. In 1828–9, William Farrow was listed as a corn miller on Maiden Row, and he also appears to have been trading as a brewer here then (see below). Other millers listed on Maiden Row include William Raby in 1841, Newby Atkinson from 1849 through to 1856 (he went bankrupt in that year), and James Scarborough in 1861 and 1868: both Atkinson and Scarborough were also listed in the directories as bakers here then. James Scarborough's son, William, was the last miller to work out of Maiden Row—he was listed here in 1872, but had moved to the corn windmill on HORNCASTLE ROAD by the mid-1870s.

After it ceased to be used for a mill, the mill dam was taken over by the brewer William East, who used it for washing barrels (see further below on East). When the brewing industry off Maiden Row and Queen Street came to an end after the First World War, the mill dam was converted into an open air swimming pool. This venture was begun in 1924 by George Bateson, with his son Reginald continuing to run the business until 1955, after which it was leased to Louth Borough Council. The building that they used as an entrance to the swimming pool still stands and the previously indistinct sign on its front has been recently repainted. On the ground floor of this building was the pit that once held that waterwheel of the mill and also a coke-fired boiler that heated the water for the swimming pool showers, whilst the changing rooms for the pool were located up a set of wooden stairs. The pool itself was filled by unheated spring water, fed from the Aswell spring, and in winter it could be covered by ice. It was finally closed in 1970, to be replaced by a covered and heated swimming pool on RIVERHEAD ROAD, with the former mill dam and swimming pool being subsequently filled in.

The watermill and mill dam on Maiden Row were not the only physical impacts of the Aswell spring on Maiden Row. According to the 1808 plan of the town, the tailrace of the mill actually ran down the open street on the western side of Maiden Row, before crossing the road at the north end of Maiden Row (roughly where the zebra crossing is now) and running along the south side of what is now Eastgate, this stretch of road being then known as Watery Lane. Indeed, it is depicted as a sizeable channel on the 1808 plan, and one which took up the entire width of the road just to the south of the junction between Walkergate (Queen Street) and Maiden Row—if the plan is accurate, then one would have had to ford the tailrace here in order to travel south along Maiden Row from this junction. It is unclear both how long the Aswell spring had run down the western side of Maiden Row in this way and whether it had only taken this course after the establishment of the mill dam and water wheel on this road, whenever that may have been. However, it is worth noting that in 1603 Richard Rookesbie and a Mr Oglethorpe were both fined for not making a sufficient fence between their grounds and 'the common sewer [water channel] in Maidenrow', and Rookesbie's property seems to have faced onto both Maiden Row and Walkergate. In light of both these points, it seems credible that the Aswell spring did follow something like its early nineteenth-century course in the early seventeenth century, though whether the mill dam had been constructed by then remains uncertain. As to when this water course was culverted over, this is likely to have taken place at some point in the early nineteenth century, as the tailrace of the mill is not depicted on Bayley's 1834 plan of Louth.

By the nineteenth century, Maiden Row had become relatively built up, especially on the south-western side, where the mill was, and on the eastern side, north of the junction with Queen Street. It was also home to a number of significant businesses in the nineteenth and early twentieth centuries, in addition to the watermill and swimming pool already mentioned. Perhaps the most noteworthy of these was touched on above, namely the brewing trade, an industry that had made use of the waters of the Aswell spring since at least the mid-fifteenth century (see the Gatherums & Springside). In 1828–9, William Farrow of the Maiden Row mill was also listed as a brewer and beer retailer on this road, and his son Thomas was a brewer here in 1835. By 1841, however, the Farrows had departed and William East junior had established himself as a brewer on Maiden Row, perhaps taking over the earlier business (William East senior was presumably the William East who was landlord of the Turks Head inn, a maltster and a hop merchant on ASWELL STREET in the 1820s and 1830s). William East's business was listed as on both Walkergate and Maiden Row in 1849, and by 1856 the company name was East & Co, with the brewery being known as the Maiden Row Brewery from at least 1861 until the 1890s. The malt kilns for this business were located behind Walkergate, off KILN YARD, and the main brewery buildings occupied a site fronting onto Walkergate, which then ran along Maiden Row and behind Walkergate, with the old mill pond being used to wash beer barrels from the mid-1870s. East himself lived at Maiden Row House, to the south of the brewery buildings and next to the mill pond. Recently renovated, this building has William East's initials picked out in black painted bricks on Church Street gable of house. The East & Co. business was acquired by Thomas Montague Winch in 1895–6, and the building alongside Maiden Row still bears the 1897 name of the brewery on its side: T M Winch & Co. By 1898, the brewery was trading under the name Soulby, Sons & Winch (E. H. Soulby & Sons was a brewery in Alford), though by 1909 the buildings here were used only for storage and distribution, brewing apparently having ceased on this site in 1902. From the mid-1920s, the buildings became the print works of W. K. Morton & Sons of Horncastle, and this use continued after the 1959 acquisition of the site by Allinson & Wilcox, printers and bookbinders, through until this company moved out onto the FAIRFIELD INDUSTRIAL ESTATE in 2004.

As well as a brewery, there were also places to buy drink on Maiden Row in the nineteenth century. One was the Globe Inn, located immediately to the north of the old mill house on the western side of Maiden Row. This closed in 1950 and is termed an inn in the 1901 Eastern Counties Directory, though it seems previously to have been counted as simply a beerhouse—so, the 1872 directory lists it as the Globe beerhouse on Maiden Row, its proprietor being Michael Jacob. Jacob is first mentioned as a beer retailer here in 1868 and this Maiden Row beerhouse seems to have remained in his family's hands until at least 1900. Before Michael Jacob, Anthony Reece (sometimes spelled Reace or Reast) ran this establishment in 1851, 1856 and 1861, and he in turn may have taken it over from William Tuxworth. The latter is named as a beer retailer on Maiden Row in the 1841 directory and his property is listed immediately after Raby's milling business in the census of that year—as such, it seems credible that it was the Globe. However, if it was, then Tuxworth must have moved properties between 1841 and

1851, as he was still an innkeeper on Maiden Row in 1851, when Reece was in business, and he was moreover listed as being on the eastern side of the street then, not the west. If the Globe beerhouse did indeed exist in 1841, then it may be worth considering whether this was the premises from which the Maiden Row miller, brewer and beer retailer named William Farrow sold his beer in 1828–9, given its location next-door to the old mill house.

In addition to the Globe, there were two other notable drinking establishments on this street: the Magpies, or Three Magpies, and the Brickyard Arms. The former is first certainly recorded in 1861, when it was located at 15–17 Maiden Row and Edward King was listed as the 'innkeeper' here (he had previously worked as a railway porter in 1851). It is unclear whether the Three Magpies existed before this, although it is not impossible that it was the beerhouse on the eastern side of Maiden Row that William Tuxworth was described as 'innkeeper' of in 1851 and still ran in 1856. The Magpies stayed in Edward King's family into the 1870s, but by the 1880s Richard Burnett was in control. It was the site of a coroner's inquest in 1881, which saw Dr Sharpley investigating the death of a ten week old baby, Charles Wilkinson, on Walkergate—he concluded that the boy had been accidentally smothered whilst sleeping in the same bed as his mother—and in 1901 the Three Magpies was termed an inn, rather than a beerhouse, in the Eastern Counties Directory of that year. It continued to trade through the first half of the twentieth century, and was run by the Soulby, Sons & Winch brewing company in 1951, when this was purchased by J. W. Green Ltd (later Flowers Breweries Ltd)—the buildings that housed it were demolished in the 1960s to make way for Elizabeth Court. The Brickyard Arms, also known as the Paul Pry (a popular comic character from an early nineteenth-century play), was located at 31 Maiden Row, now the site of the Salvation Army's hall. Charles Johnson is listed as the 'publican' here in the 1861 census and he appears as a beer retailer on Maiden Row in various directories from 1842 through to 1868. Certainly, the beerhouse existed in that period, as in April 1849 an Irish bookbinder called Ann Carry was charged with stealing a bonnet and a glass from the Paul Pry beerhouse. This beerhouse looks to have closed by 1871—Charles Johnson is listed simply as a labourer living at this address, rather than a beerhouse keeper or publican, in the census of that year, and in the 1880s this address had become the site of the Holy Trinity Mission

Room. By 1905, the Salvation Army had moved into its barracks here, according to the local directories.

Maiden Row was also home to trades other than milling, brewing and innkeeping. In the 1830s and 1840s, Thomas Rose had a brickyard on the east side of Maiden Row, near to the north end of the road and partly under the current Elizabeth Court. Rose's Yard was marked here on the 1889 OS map of the town, and cottages for his workers were located on the opposite side of the road, where the bus station now is— these were demolished in the late 1950s. In 1841 Rose was also listed as a lime burner and was said to be about to establish a glazed pot factory in Louth, which he did do—when his business was sold by auction in 1850, after his death, it was as Louth Brickyard and Pottery, and Rose himself was described as a 'potter' in a newspaper report of the previous year. How long there had been a brickyard on this road is unclear, but Rose was certainly not the first brick maker to be located here: the 1828–9 directory lists a John Rogerson as a brick maker on Maiden Row, and Rose's brickyard could have been a continuation of this earlier business. The 1828–9 directory also lists a tannery and fellmonger (a dealer in hides or skins who might also prepare skins for tanning) on Maiden Row, run by one Elias Croft. By 1835, this looks to have come under the control of John Gilsthorp or Gelsthorp, who continued the business here into the 1840s. As to its location, the Gelsthorp tannery is listed on Walkergate instead of Maiden Row in 1849 and 1856, on Maiden Row in 1861, and on both in 1868. This would suggest that it was probably based on the northern junction of Maiden Row and Walkergate, opposite the brewery buildings on the southern side—that is to say, on the site of the modern bus station, behind the nineteenth-century housing that fronted onto Maiden Row from at least 1834. Indeed, a tannery is marked in this location in 1889, and the Gelsthorp tannery was still listed on Maiden Row in the county directory for that year (it was last listed there in 1896).

As might be expected from its location within the industrial zone of pre-twentieth-century Louth, Maiden Row wasn't always the most pleasant or orderly street. One of the earliest recorded offenders here was a Nicholas Skifflinge, who was charged in 1603 with fouling the common street in 'Maidenrowe' by throwing and placing dung in it. More serious was the case of James Moffatt, slater, of Maiden Row, who was charged with 'outrageous conduct' here in May 1858. Sergeant

Wilson apparently encountered Mrs Moffatt running around Maiden Row, seeking protection from her husband who had threatened to slit her throat and cut her into two halves. James Moffatt was found lying on his doorstep—roused by the sergeant, he caused a great disturbance, and when the police tried to make him go inside, he brandished a large chopper at them, daring them to interfere with him. He was fined 5s and costs, or 21 days in jail. Another unhappy incident occurred in July 1856, when James Horsewood of Walkergate was charged with being drunk and creating a disturbance in Maiden Row: described as a 'cowardly ruffian', he was apprehended in the act of beating his wife in the public street. Prostitutes and the like were also to be found on this street in the mid-nineteenth century. In May 1851, it is recorded that a 'nymph of the pavé' (prostitute) named Fanny Jepson visited Tuxworth's beer shop in Maiden Row with an agricultural labourer called William Scupham, before taking him to 'two brothels in that neighbourhood' (see further the Gatherums & Springside on Jepson). Similarly, in January 1854, Sarah Atkin—'a notorious drunken and disorderly character'—was charged with grossly indecent conduct in Maiden Row.

Some of the Maiden Row business owners also made appearances in court. William East, for example, appeared as the victim of an assault in August 1849—a certain George Sowerby, 'a well-known disturber of the peace', was charged with kicking his backside in a violent manner several times! In contrast, Anthony Reece of the Globe beerhouse was charged with assaulting a woman named Rebecca Hewitt in August 1852. Her husband was a brewer in the service of William East, and the road to the brewery was said to be through Reece's premises—Hewitt claimed that she was going to see her husband and Reece stopped her, pushing her violently out into the main street. Reece, however, argued that Hewitt was in the habit of going onto his premises and quarrelling with his wife and her sister, 'applying epithets to them which females least like to be designated by and reflecting upon their chastity'. After trying to warn her from doing this again, she attempted to enter his premises once again and so a scuffle ensued, in which Rebecca Hewitt tore the clothes from Anthony Reece's back. The court found in favour of Reece, directing Hewitt to pay costs and stating that it ought to be she, not Reece, in the defendant's box. Finally, William Tuxworth was charged in June 1852 with permitting drunkenness in his beerhouse on a Sunday and selling beer at nine o'clock in the morning on a Sunday—he was discharged of the first and found guilty of the second, being fined 10s and costs (equivalent to around £42 today).

The southern part of Church Street was known as Long Lane before 1864. It was renamed in that year by the local 'Improvement Commissioners', the new name referencing the recently constructed St Michael's Church on this road. St Michael's had been established as a separate parish in 1863, as a response to the mid-nineteenth-century population expansion in the Newmarket area of Louth, which had seen significant numbers of working class homes built there. Designed by James Fowler of Louth and built in 1862–3, the church cost £3,266 to build and equip; the responsibility for the debt was assumed by Canon Wilde, the rector of Louth, and it had been paid off by 1866. In 1864, a bazaar in the Town Hall raised £300 to buy an organ for the new church, which was erected where the Lady Chapel now stands. From the first, it was an Anglo-Catholic church and, as such, was opposed by some in the town—in 1872, for example, a ten-day mission by the 'Arch Ritualist' Rev. Robert J. Ives at St Michael's led to protest meetings in the town. In addition to the High Church St Michael's, there was also a small Methodist mission chapel opened at south end of Church Street in 1868 by the Free Methodists, at a cost of £350. This was closed in the 1970s, due to falling membership and the difficulty in providing ministers, with local Methodists consolidating on the large Eastgate chapel. The chapel was converted into a residential dwelling in recent years.

The Sunday and Day Schools associated with St Michael's Church began in December 1864 and were initially run in an old carpenter's shop on ST MICHAEL'S ROAD (number 4). By 1874, the number of children at the school had become too large for the limited accommodation available there, and so it was decided that a new school had to be built. Designed by James Fowler to cater for 370 children, the foundation stone of St Michael's School was laid on 29 April, 1875, and the school opened in January 1876 on the site now occupied by numbers 37–53 Church Street. Mr and Mrs Adams were the masters and the cost of the school was £689, with £255 towards the cost raised via a bazaar in the Town Hall. From 1882, the master of the school was Mr Gregory, who was famous for his wooden leg and his habit of sleeping in front of the fire—one day, some of the boys actually set his leg alight. He was dismissed in 1887, as he was an uncertified teacher and this was not permitted under the terms of a grant of £145 from the Education

Department that the school managers sought in that year. St Michael's School was made a free school in 1891 (previously, school fees had been collected each Monday) and senior pupils transferred to Monks' Dyke School on MONKS DYKE ROAD in 1939, leaving St Michael's with only the younger pupils. The state finally took control of the school in 1951, and in 1974 the school was moved from Church Street to a new site on Monks' Dyke School playing field. Five years later, the Church Street premises were demolished and the site is now occupied by modern residential properties.

The early plans of Louth only show the northernmost end of Long Lane. In both 1808 and 1834, there were some buildings at this end of the road, but the situation further south is unclear. The 1839 map of the town depicts far more of the road, although it adds but a handful of properties on the eastern side of the road to those shown in 1808 and 1834. In contrast, it would seem that buildings had been constructed all along the eastern side of Long Lane by the middle of the nineteenth century, with some present on the western side too, to judge from William Brown's Panorama (begun in 1844 and last updated in 1856). The 1851 census similarly list 44 properties on Long Lane in that year. These buildings appear to have been primarily residential in character, and in 1856 the only traders listed as based on Long Lane were a baker (Joseph Edman, who had previously been based on GOSPELGATE), a butcher (Charles Hubbard), a cowkeeper (Thomas North), a shopkeeper (John Parker) and a tailor (Charles Crofts). In 1861, only the last three were still listed on this road, although there was a market gardener named Tagg also listed on Long Lane then.

In general, the Long Lane part of modern Church Street appears to have been relatively peaceful, although there were occasional incidents here that made their way into the local press. So, for example, in 1849 a man named John Grantham was charged by a youth called Watkinson, aged about 14, with assaulting him. Watkinson was apparently a common nuisance in Long Lane, where he lived, and had been violent and 'very saucy' to John Grantham, who therefore thrashed him with a stick. The court said that Grantham had been wrong to strike the boy, but due to the clearly mitigating circumstances of the well-known bad character of the boy, a fine of only 1s and costs would be levied!

CINDER LANE

Cinder Lane was laid out in 1855, at the same time as improvements were made to Kidgate school, and it was originally a private, gated road—the gates were usually kept open for traffic, but were shut once a year in order to preserve its private status. The name itself most probably has its origins in the cinders from the iron foundry on Cinder Lane being used to stabilise the road surface there and fill in pot holes and ruts created by carts. This iron foundry belonged to Thomas Ashley's Aswell Iron Works, and is said to have employed over 100 men in the 1860s, some of whom lived on nearby ASHLEY ROAD (only Ashley's showroom was located on ASWELL STREET, despite the name). It was located on the east side of the road, south of the school, in the area where school buildings and the playground are now to be found. The Iron Works made ploughs, fertiliser spreaders, horse shoes, mowers, reapers, and the like, and in July 1857 Thomas Ashley won first prize for an agricultural implement (a plough for light land) at the North Lincolnshire Agricultural Society show, which was held at Louth that year. The foundry finally closed a few years before World War I.

On the west side of Cinder Lane was Joseph Smalley's saw mill. This made chairs, carts and wheels—it was located in the premises with a lantern roof and an impressive tall chimney that still stands there today. This business is first mentioned in the 1856 directory and last appears in the 1913 directory. Like Ashley's Iron Works, Smalley's business was listed as being not on the private Cinder Lane, but rather on Aswell Lane, where Smalley presumably had a showroom—he is certainly listed at 69 Aswell Lane in later local directories and occupied this property in the censuses from 1861 to 1911. Also on Cinder Lane was the Strawsons' sweet factory. The Strawson family started selling sweets from 28 and 30 Aswell Street in the 1900s and 1910s, but scaled up from this as a wholesale trade. Their sweet factory was on the east side of Cinder Lane, where Kidgate School playground now is; the smoke from the boiler apparently used to travel under the road to exit through the tall brick chimney of what was Smalley's saw mill.

CISTERNGATE

Cisterngate has its origins in the medieval period, being first mentioned in 1396. Although the street-name is occasionally spelled Saxongate (as on Espin's 1808 plan of the town, where the street is marked as 'Cistern Gate or Saxon Gate'), and this has been seen as a reference to supposed Anglo-Saxon activity in this part of town, the name Cisterngate is usually believed to derive instead from a personal name Saextan, with the 1396 form of the name being *Saxtanegate* and other early forms including *Saxtengate* and *Sestrangate*. Furthermore, it is worth noting that, whilst the idea that the Anglo-Saxon settlement of Louth was based on the north bank of the river has sometimes proved popular, the evidence we presently have suggests that it was actually located on the south bank, with the north bank only really being developed later in the medieval period.

Although Cisterngate/Saxtanegate was plainly in existence by the late fourteenth century, we currently have no indications as to the nature or density of the activity there then. However, in the 1540s and 1550s the street was apparently considered sufficiently remote from the main town community that a cottage there could be used as a 'plague house' to isolate victims in. A John Bello was in charge of this cottage on Saxtengate—the Churchwardens paid 3s 4d for its use in 1543 and it was still being used to isolate victims ten years later, with Bello also being paid 18d in 1546 to take provisions to Welton le Wold, so that the plague-infected residents of that village wouldn't need to visit town. Other early references to the road include a payment by the Churchwardens of 2s in 1540–1 (equivalent to around £500 in wages today) to a man living on Cisterngate who had caught the plague, so that he could leave town and live in the country instead. In 1549, there is also mention of a tenantless cottage on 'Sestrangate', which John Almonde had granted to the recently dissolved Gild of the Holy Trinity.

In the seventeenth century, there are two notable references to this street. The first is a reference to a building called 'Bradly Hall' on Cisterngate. Formerly owned by an unidentified member of the important Bradley family of Louth, this was leased to Will Patchett in 1676 for 31 years at a rent of 12d per annum. The other comes in the 1660 will of Sir Charles Bolle, who left to his daughter Anne Bolle 'my house in Sesternegate', for which he apparently paid 12s per year to the

Warden of Louth. However, despite these occasional references to properties in this area, Espin's plan of 1808 confirms that there had been relatively little development of the town north of the Lud before the early nineteenth century. With specific regard to Cisterngate, there are some houses and formal gardens shown on the western half of the south side of the road, but nothing on the north side and no development on the eastern half of the south side either. The situation was little different in the 1830s, although what would become GRAY'S ROAD was starting to be laid out on the south side by then. In contrast, William Brown's sketches of the town, made in 1844, show significant activity, with properties now present on both sides and at both ends of the street. The sketches and the subsequent Panorama (last updated in 1856) also offer a better view of the formal gardens and grander houses that were then located to the south and to the north of the street at its western end. Whether some of those on the south side were the houses (or the successors to the houses) that belonged to the Bolles and Bradleys on this road in the second half of the seventeenth century is uncertain, although it seems credible. The garden of what was called 'Cistercian House' in the late nineteenth century is particularly interesting, on account of the large, and sadly unidentified, statue of a man with his arms outstretched that clearly held pride of place in the garden.

Although Cisterngate was always a primarily residential street, there were some businesses here from an early date. In 1849 and 1856, for example, Henry Hopper had a shop on this road, and from at least 1849 through to World War I there was a bakery and shop at 18 Cisterngate, run first by Thomas Broddell and later by William Tuxworth, John Preston and, in the twentieth century, Joseph Bontoft. In terms of criminal behaviour on the road, Thomas Burke, a labourer, was charged with fighting and creating a disturbance at night on Cisterngate around Christmas, 1850. More seriously, Thomas Williams of Cisterngate, an agricultural labourer from North Wales, was charged (along with two other men) with possession of four or five stone of wool that couldn't be accounted for. However, other than these two incidents, the street and its inhabitants appear to have been relatively peaceful in the mid-nineteenth century.

COMMERCIAL ROAD

The name Commercial Road was said by William Brown, writing in 1852, to have been coined in imitation of the London road of that name (see also CANNON STREET and LUDGATE). The road itself had been already laid out by the time that the 1824 OS map was surveyed (c. 1818–20), although it had few buildings present on it at that time, and the situation appears to have been little different in the mid-1840s, to judge from William Brown's sketch of 1844. By the time of the Brown's final Panorama (1847–56), however, the street had clearly developed significantly, and in the 1851 census Commercial Road was something of an enclave for mariners, with eleven of the inhabitants of twenty-two houses there being connected to the canal. So, for example, one household was headed by Elizabeth Smart, described as a sloop owner, who lived with her nephew, Horby Smith, who was a mariner. Another was occupied at the time of the census by Jane Hardcastle, a mariner's wife, and her three children. This maritime character soon declined, along with the canal itself. By 1871 the total number of mariners had dropped to six, and in 1891 there were but two mariners living on the road compared to six railway workers, something illustrative of not only the changing nature of this area of town, but also one of the reasons for this change. The railway workers in 1891 consisted of a fireman, a railway servant, an engine driver, a guard, a clerk and a ticket collector.

During the twentieth century, Commerical Road saw a number of new developments, including the construction of a Methodist mission chapel here in 1925. There hadn't been a chapel in the RIVERHEAD area since 1854 and the new chapel remained active until the 1970s, when it was finally closed down due to falling membership and the difficulty in providing ministers (the local Methodists consolidated on the EASTGATE chapel). Other, more recent changes to the road include the erection of a large store at the northern end of the street in the mid-twentieth century and the construction of a handful of new residential properties on the western side of the street. The one time that Commercial Road appeared in the mid-nineteenth-century police reports in the *Hull Packet* was in 1848, when William Beattie, a shoemaker from Long Sutton, was brought up before the court on a charge of begging on this road (he was discharged). The only other relevant report relates to the death in 1850 of Richard Hardcastle, aged four, the son of a mariner and presumably that Jane Hardcastle who is mentioned above. The boy had been left alone in the house by his mother, who went to fetch a pail of water, when his clothes caught fire—he was so badly burnt that he died within three hours of the incident.

CORNISH WAY

Cornish Way runs between the two ends of BOLLE ROAD, the latter being the spine of a new housing estate that was constructed from 2006 between NEWBRIDGE HILL and CHARLES STREET. The estate was built on land that was formerly occupied by a market garden, Sharpley's Yard and Sharpley's Terrace (on Newbridge Hill), and the Great Northern Oil & Cake Mill (on Charles Street) in the second half of the nineteenth century. In 1951, the houses of Sharpley's Yard and Terrace and the factory facing onto Charles Street were all replaced by a large Lin Pac factory, which manufactured corrugated cardboard for packing. This was in turn demolished in 2003 to make way for the current residential development.

CORNMARKET

See MARKET PLACE & CORNMARKET.

COXEY HILLS ROAD

Coxey Hills Road, on the southern part of London Road, was one of roads planned out by 1805 Enclosure Award. Judging from aerial photographs and a comparison with the enclosure map, it still exists today as track running south-west from London Road. The road ran in the direction of Coxey Hills, now on the southern side of the LOUTH A16 BYPASS.

CRESCENT, THE

In the aftermath of the Louth Flood of 1920, the refugees from the flooding were housed in temporary accommodation erected in a field on HIGH HOLME ROAD that lay to the east of MILL LANE, known locally as 'Canvas Town' and later as 'Hut Town', after the construction of more robust temporary accommodation for the people here. An aerial photograph of 1926 indicates that Hut Town consisted of around twenty-five long huts arranged in fives lines on this field. In 1930, The Crescent was built to replace Hut Town as a small-scale council housing project; the houses constructed here had hot water, bathrooms and electricity.

CROWTREE LANE

The origins of Crowtree Lane appear to lie in an early track or footway from Hallington to Louth. In 1602, Thomas Bradeley was accused of having walled up and obstructed 'a foot-way at Claye pittes in the South Field at the west end of Gospell leading through his close to Hallington... to the great inconvenience as well as of inhabitants as of strangers coming to market', and he was fined 20s in 1603 due to his continuing failure to remove the obstruction. Given the description of this 'foot-way' as running from the 'west end of Gospell' (GOSPELGATE) to Hallington, and the fact that a close named Clay Pits Wong or Clay Pitts Close existed into the modern period at the east end of Crowtree Lane (see below), this footway is likely to have followed, at least in part, what is now Crowtree Lane. The footway presumably ran along the present line of the road, before following a route across to join HALFPENNY LANE. Certainly, a road following such a route is shown on Armstrong's 1778 map of the Louth area. Under the Enclosure Award of 1805, modern Crowtree Lane was laid out as a road running along the boundary between four old closes (now Westgate Fields) and the open South Field, probably on the line of the existing track.

Crowtree Lane, as it currently exists, extends down to the Hubbard's Hill Mill in the valley. This watermill is believed to have been built around 1788 by Charles Chaplin for spinning wool, and it remained in the Chaplin family until 1905, working as a corn-grinding mill. An early tenant of the mill from the 1820s to the 1840s was the baker and flour dealer Edward Hackford, whose main premises were listed on EASTGATE and MERCER ROW; in 1841, the day-to-day running of 'Hackfords Mill' seems to have been in the hands of a journeyman miller named Barzillai Elsey. The mill finally ceased to function in 1920, when it was damaged in the flood of that year. In 1872–3, the Louth Water Works Company (formed 1871) bought an acre of land at the valley bottom near to the mill, and bored down until it found water. The waterworks consequently built there were designed by James Fowler and were originally twice as large as the surviving buildings. They used steam to pump the water up to a reservoir on HORNCASTLE ROAD, from where the town was supplied by gravity. This development altered the water flow to the watermill and led to construction of a reservoir (now the pool in Hubbard's Hills) and the straightening of river course to the mill in 1877. The roadway alongside the new river course was probably constructed then too, giving access to Dog Kennel Farm across the bridge dam (this farm was previously accessed via a track from the LINCOLN ROAD through the Thorpe Hall estate). This length of road now allows vehicular access to Hubbard's Hills, which was given to the town of Louth as a memorial for the wife of Auguste Alphonse Pahud, Annie, in 1907 (see WESTGATE). Westgate Fields, the other major green area off Crowtree Lane, was not transferred to the town until 1936, although there had long been a pathway through its closes that the residents of town had used, with people depicted promenading along it on William Brown's mid-nineteenth-century Panorama.

Before the early nineteenth century, Crowtree Lane served only a handful of properties, the most notable of which was perhaps The Lodge. This was built on Clay Pitts Close (or Clay Pits Wong) at the eastern end of Crowtree Lane in 1797 by the Corporation for the Head of the Grammar School, at a cost of £940 (around £85,000 today). The Lodge overlooked the Goose Pool and functioned as both a new boarding-block and a house for the headmaster: one of the first boarders to live there was the future Sir John Franklin, the Arctic explorer. With regard to the Goose Pool, the name of the close it was located in—Clay Pitts—suggests that it may have been at least partly artificial in origin. This pool is usually thought to be the pool after which Gospelgate is named (it stood close to the western end of this road), although it appears to have been one of a number of medieval pools located on or near Gospelgate. Certainly, traces of another probably medieval pool have recently been found to the south of the western end of Gospelgate, and yet another was discovered through excavations behind the Greyhound Inn at the eastern end of that road, although the Clay Pitts Close pool appears to have been the most notable and long-lived of these pools. It was this pool that Alfred Lord Tennyson recalled from his boyhood—in around 1818, a boy named Hyde gave him a strong cigar while at the Grammar School, and Tennyson smoked all of it and then threw the end in the old Goose Pool. The pool is clearly shown and extensive on the 1834 plan of the town, but it is not marked on later maps.

The other major property on Crowtree Lane in the first half of the nineteenth century was The Sycamores. This appears on Thomas Espin's 1808 plan of the town, and it was done up for the Hobart family in the 'artisan mannerist style' by Louth architect C J Carter in around 1837. It can clearly be seen on both Brown's sketches and the final Panorama, with a tall wall enclosing its gardens and running down the south side of BREAKNECK LANE. The Sycamores was the site of Miss Elizabeth Leak's Ladies' Academy in the 1840s, which 'Claribel' attended, and was owned by William Hyde in 1851. A local ghost story is attached to this house—supposedly, a small man in a kilt regularly used to emerge from the garden door of The Sycamores and run across the road to the large tree that used to stand opposite in the Grammar School grounds. The Sycamores was purchased by the Grammar School in 1973 and used as a boys' boarding house until 1989.

By the end of the nineteenth century, Crowtree Lane had only seen a little additional development. Perhaps the most important of these was the construction of the new Louth & District Hospital and Dispensary here. This was designed by James Fowler and was originally opened in 1873, at a cost of £2000; in 1913 there were beds there for 19 patients. It finally closed in the 1980s and was reopened in 1989 as the new boarding house and sixth form centre for King Edward VI Grammar School, being renamed Foundation House. There were also two large houses marked on the south side of Crowtree Lane on the 1889 OS map of this area, called The Elms and The Hill. The former was the home of Alixa Smith in 1891—a widow living on her own with three servants—and Christopher Ingoldby, attorney, in 1861; it was renamed Elmhurst in the twentieth century. The latter was the home of Thomas Falkner Allison, solicitor with the firm of Allisons & Allisons of MERCER ROW, in 1891, who had lived there since at least 1861, and before that The Hill would appear to have been inhabited by Miss Frances Emeris in 1841 and 1851, a woman of independent means who had previously lived on Gospelgate in 1835 and who died in 1853. Indeed, The Hill, unlike the Elms, is shown on the 1839 map of the town, and as such it is one of the oldest properties on Crowtree Lane. In addition, to these large houses, there were also residences of a more modest status on Crowtree Lane in the nineteenth century. The terrace of houses next to Little Crowtree Lane that is present on the 1889 map also appears on Brown's finished Panorama of 1847–56, but these houses are not shown on his preliminary sketches of 1844 nor are they apparent in the 1841 census. In 1861, they were inhabited by a range of working-class people, including Sarah Upton, a dressmaker; Eliza Taylor, a seamstress; John Tuxworth, a blacksmith; and Charles Robinson, an agricultural labourer.

The twentieth century saw increased activity along Crowtree Lane. Some of this was associated with the expansion of the Grammar School, which led to a new science block and sports block being built close to the road (at the beginning and near to the end of the century, respectively) and the conversion of the old Louth & District Hospital into a sixth form centre. There was also an expansion of housing in various places along the road, the most obvious examples of this being the late twentieth century houses built on the south side of Crowtree Lane overlooking Westgate Fields. Finally, the second half of the twentieth century saw the erection of Crowtree House residential care home between The Elms (known as Elmhurst since the early twentieth century) and the Louth & District Hospital, as well as the creation of the golf course off Crowtree Lane and the conversion of The Hill into the clubhouse of Louth Golf Club, founded 1965.

CUPPLEDITCH WAY

Cuppleditch Way is a modern road running west from BRACKENBOROUGH ROAD; the properties here were still being constructed in 2006. The land it stands on was once part of Louth's old open North Field.

DALTON'S LANE

When the Market Hall was built in 1866–7, it removed a narrow passage between EASTGATE and the MARKET PLACE called Dalton's Lane. This was presumably the same passageway as the Daulton's Lane and Dalton's Yard that are mentioned in 1681.

DAVEY CLOSE

Davey Close runs west from BRACKENBOROUGH ROAD and its eastern end is depicted on the OS maps of the town from 1889 onwards. The road appears to have been extended westwards in the mid-twentieth century, with a handful of structures built along it. In 2003, the land off the road was still largely undeveloped, but by 2006 houses had been built on both the south side of the road and at its western end, with some further residential development taking place there by 2008.

DAVID AVENUE

See ELM DRIVE.

DOVE CLOSE

See SWALLOW DRIVE.

EASTFIELD RISE

Eastfield Rise runs south from EASTFIELD ROAD and follows the line of the nineteenth- and earlier twentieth-century boundary between Louth and Louth Park. The road and houses here were constructed in the 1990s, with at least one of the properties built in 1994.

EASTFIELD ROAD

Eastfield Road runs through the old East Field of Louth, one of the medieval open fields belonging to the town, which was hedged in 1547. Although the present road was laid out by the Enclosure Commissioners in 1805, 'Eastfeilde laine' is actually mentioned in 1603. In that year, Thomas Bradeley, Richard Shalder, and Thomas Massingbearde were ordered to make a 'sufficient causeway and market-way in Eastfeilde laine, over against their properties' (probably enclosures rather than habitations). These gentlemen had apparently allowed the lane to remain defective for a long time, to the great inconvenience of the inhabitants of Louth and strangers coming to market, and so were fined 10s, 40s, and 26s 8d, respectively. A road following this route and heading past Louth

Park Abbey towards the Marsh villages is also depicted on Armstrong's 1778 map of the Louth area.

The early nineteenth-century Enclosure Act allowed the open field land between Eastfield Road and the Canal (see RIVERHEAD ROAD) to be used for housing. One notable property subsequently built on this road was the large house facing onto Eastfield Road that is now occupied by Douglas Electronic Industries. This was constructed for Robert Norfolk, a mid-nineteenth-century oil miller, seed crusher, and merchant, who lived there with his family and servants. The little lane 50 metres east of Norfolk's House led to Norfolk Place, where a row of cottages were built for Norfolk's workers. A second major property was Eastfield House, which was built for the family of William Nell in around 1879. They moved to this large, grand house from their previous home in Trinity Terrace, EASTGATE, and the new house both reflected the gentry aspirations of this family and was close to Nell's business concerns at the Riverhead. The family suffered a major financial collapse in 1881–2 and were forced to move out of Eastfield House and into Sydenham Terrace, on NEWMARKET. Eastfield House now houses Lincolnshire County Council's Adult Social Care and Children's Services area offices.

Another important building on Eastfield Road was the Holy Trinity Parochial School, constructed on the corner of Riverhead Road and Eastfield Road in 1865. Costing £800, it was enlarged five years later to accommodate 380 children. James Christian was the first headmaster and in 1875 Malachi Bice began nearly 40 years as headmaster. It came under the control of Lindsey County Council, as Louth Trinity Council School, by 1920, and by 1922 the name had been changed to Louth Eastfield Road Council School. The older pupils were lost to the new Monks' Dyke School in 1929, but the younger ones continued to be taught there for a period. In the 1960s, the Juniors were transferred to the new Lacey Gardens Junior School, off LACEY GARDENS, which had opened to cater for the population of the new ST BERNARDS AVENUE estate. The Infants came later, in 1979, when they moved to new buildings adjacent to Lacey Gardens, now known as Eastfield Infants' School. The old Holy Trinity Parochial School was used by Lincoln Technology College from the 1980s and was finally demolished in 2007 to make way for flats.

Eastfield Road saw few non-residential uses in the nineteenth century, with the only business listed here in 1868 being Samuel Sharp's bakery and Mary Buttery's shop, a situation which had changed little by the mid-1880s. However, there was some industrial activity on the little lane off Eastfield Road that lies east of Robert Norfolk's house (see above) through until 1857—a five-storey windmill was located here, which belonged to the Griffin family and ground bark for the Riverhead tannery, until it burnt down due to overheating. With regard to the early inhabitants of Eastfield Road, they were, unsurprisingly, often associated with either the canal or the industries of the Riverhead. So, in 1861 Benjamin Beaumont and Charles Ladlow of numbers 9 and 14 Eastfield Road were shipwrights; William Wray of 13 Eastfield Road was a ship carpenter; William Jackson and George Armitage of 2 and 3 Eastfield Road were merchants; William Brant, John Brant, Moses Chatterton, George Gray, and John Forman of 31, 32, 33, and 35 Eastfield Road worked in the steam flour mill; Thomas Procter, John Skins, William Leedham and John Mitchell of 18, 19, 22 and 24 Eastfield Road worked at the oilcake mill; Mary Chapman of 4 Eastfield Road was a sailor's wife; and Thomas Cole of 21 Eastfield Road was a farmer and the collector of the Navigation tolls. In addition, there were a number of people who were of independent means or described as gentlewomen, including Ann and Elizabeth Barr, of 28 Eastfield Road, and Emily Howard, of number 15. In 1891, the situation was broadly similar, with the inhabitants of the street consisting of a mixture of merchants and business owners, people of independent means, shipwrights, and workers in the Riverhead industries, although fewer of the last class were recorded then than was the case earlier in the century.

The twentieth century saw significant further development along Eastfield Road, most especially on its southern side, which had seen little activity in the nineteenth century beyond the building of Eastfield House. By the mid-1950s, not only had St Bernards Avenue and PARK AVENUE been constructed running south from Eastfield Road, but the line of houses to the east of the entrance to Park Avenue had also been erected. The mid-twentieth century also saw significant infilling of the nineteenth-century development on the northern side of Eastfield Road, creating an almost continuous line of houses here, as well as the use of Robert Norfolk's old house as a factory and the establishment of the fire and ambulance station on the southern side of the road. In the 1970s, the eastern end of Eastfield Road was developed still further with the establishment of the CHESTNUT DRIVE estate, running south from Eastfield Road over what had been two fields.

EASTGATE

The first mention of Eastgate comes in a charter of Thomas de Luda, chapter clerk of Lincoln Cathedral, which was drawn up in 1317. He provided an endowment to pay for a daily mass to be said for the salvation of his own soul, and for the souls of his father, William, and his mother, Margaret, his brother, his benefactors, and all the faithful dead. The endowment included six messuages (usually defined as a dwelling house with outbuildings and the site on which it stood), three of which were on Eastgate. Although this is the first documentary reference to this road, it would seem that Eastgate already then extended down to its junction with NORTHGATE, as one of the messuages was said to be near Padehole (an old name for Northgate). The archaeological evidence confirms this impression of Eastgate having been an early and important street in medieval Louth. So, for example, sherds of Anglo-Scandinavian pottery have been discovered on Eastgate from the site where Meridian House now stands, and the block of preserved medieval property boundaries to the east of the Fish Shambles is complemented by a substantial quantity of twelfth-century and later pottery from 47–51 Eastgate (currently Peacocks, just to the north-east of the Fish Shambles), chalk wall foundations of probably medieval date, two pits and a possible gravel surface. Further evidence for medieval activity in this part of Louth comes from 76a Eastgate, where medieval pottery sherds were found along with a red-brown baked clay layer that may reflect a medieval hearth or oven. Finally, medieval deposits were also found a little further to the west, during trial trenching at the Eastgate end of the Market Hall in 1989.

Aside from Thomas de Luda's messuages, early documentary references to Eastgate include a record of a number of men being fined for placing refuse in Eastgate near to St James's church in 1453, and another record of a Roger Stutt and five other men being fined for not making sufficient footway against their houses in Eastgate in 1603. In 1575, at least two tenements on Eastgate were owned by a Richard Wright, with a yearly value of 32s—he granted these to pay for hardened

71

cloth and butter to be purchased and distributed to the poor of Louth each winter after his death. The charity he set up continued to function into the nineteenth century, when part of its income was used, from 1878, to endow scholarships at the Grammar School. Quite where these tenements and houses were on Eastgate is uncertain, however, as is the location of the 'Barne in Eastgate & a Cottage' that Thomasin Cooke paid one fat turkey in rent for in 1717.

With regard to the development and extent of pre-modern Eastgate, it is often thought that the town had come to encompass the whole of Eastgate down to its junction with CHURCH STREET by the end of the medieval period. Of course, if this was the case, it does not mean that all parts of the road were equally well developed in the medieval period or after. Certainly, Eastgate to the east of the Northgate junction appears noticeably less built up than Eastgate between UPGATE and Northgate on Espin's detailed 1808 plan of the town, and it may well be that this was true earlier too, with this part of Eastgate—along with the equivalent section of QUEEN STREET—probably being peripheral to the main core of the medieval town. Likewise, the 1778 Armstrong plan of Louth shows buildings all along most of Eastgate up to the Northgate junction, aside from an almost complete absence of structures along one part of the south side of the street, between Upgate and the Fish Shambles. Whether this area of Eastgate was really so undeveloped in the late eighteenth century is more questionable, however. No such absence of structures is apparent on Espin's only slightly later plan of 1808, and Armstrong's plan is not only far less carefully drawn than Espin's, but also appears to be somewhat inaccurate in places. Furthermore, even if there were no structures there then, it need not mean that this section of the south side of Eastgate was always without buildings before the later eighteenth century—indeed, the narrow property units at the western end of Eastgate have been considered to be, in origin, probably medieval burgage plots, and medieval deposits were found close to the surface at the Eastgate end of the Market Hall in 1989, as was noted above.

Turning to look at that section of Eastgate beyond the junction with Church Street, it is worth noting that this section of road appears not to have been classed as part of Eastgate through until the mid-nineteenth century, instead being marked as a separate road known as Watery Lane on the 1808, 1834 and 1839 plans and maps of the town. This name derived from the fact that the tail race of the Aswell spring flowing down the south side of this road after it exited Maiden Row (see Church Street and the GATHERUMS & SPRINGSIDE). The spring must have crossed over to the north side of Watery Lane/Eastgate at some point— perhaps near Byford House?—and it eventually flowed south from the road, across marshy ground, to join the Lud near to Bryan Hall's RAMSGATE water mill. One of the earliest buildings to be built on this section of what is now Eastgate was the House of Correction, or prison, which stood on the corner of Eastgate and Ramsgate. This institution was first mentioned in 1661, when Thomas Grantham—a leading Baptist Dissenter—was imprisoned there for six months, and in 1671 Charles Kilburne, the keeper of House of Correction, set up 'school' for poor boys and girls in the prison. This was the so-called 'Jersey School', which saw the town's orphans and poor young people moved into the prison and set to work preparing hemp for sale to local ropemakers. This institution lasted a long time, for 60 years later, in 1732, the Jersey School Master (the keeper of the House of Correction) was fined £5 for allowing pauper named Jonathan Parrott to escape his school. The House of Correction remained a mud and stud building until 1754, when the keeper's house fell down and the Corporation was forced to rebuild it. It was enclosed by a twenty-three feet high wall, had a treadmill added in 1820 (in south-west corner, where the War Memorial now is), and housed 119 inmates in 1851. The prison was finally closed in 1872, due to new requirements regarding the required quality of prisoner accommodation, and it was subsequently demolished by its new owner, John Walmsley, who had bought it for £3,400. He used some of the materials from it—including the old prison clock—to extend and improve his warehouse on the north side of QUEEN STREET.

The site of the old House of Correction was eventually split into a new road (ALEXANDRA ROAD) and the Orme almshouses, which were built in 1885 and designed by James Fowler. These provided independent, one-bedroom accommodation for ten elderly single gentlemen, who were required to be over 55 years of age, Church of England lay members, and bachelors or widowers. The trust was set up by the Rev. Frederick Orme with an endowment of £7,200, to be invested in the maintenance of the houses and in providing each pensioner 5s a week and a new long coat every four years. To the east of these remained the purpose-built County Police Station of 1866 and the

Sessions House, built in 1874 to replace that which had stood in the prison grounds. The former has been replaced by a new police station on EASTFIELD ROAD, whilst the latter functioned as the local Magistrates Court through until 2008, when this function was removed to Skegness—from May 2011, the Sessions House has had a new lease of life as the home for Louth Town Council. Further to the east still is The Priory. This was built by Thomas Espin in 1818, on land called Brick's Close that he had bought in 1805. Espin moved the Northgate 'Free School', of which he had been the master since 1790, to The Priory, along with its boarders. The Priory was subsequently used as classical commercial boarding school from the early 1840s, under Alexander Tallents Rogers, and more recently as a retirement home and (from 1977) a hotel.

On the opposite side of Watery Lane/Eastgate to the House of Correction and The Priory were a number of industrial concerns, located to the west of where the railway line once ran (the southern part of the bridge over Eastgate is still visible, with a mark indicating the level reached by the 1920 Louth Flood). In the mid-nineteenth century, the area to the south of Eastgate and between the railway line and PRIORY ROAD (then called Union Court) was the brickworks of Nicholas Pearson Bellamy. This is visible on William Brown's Panorama (first shown in 1847 and last updated in 1856), and Bellamy & Co. is listed as a brick maker on Eastgate in the 1841 Pigot's directory and the 1849 White's directory—whether it was a successor to the brickworks of Edward Arliss, which were listed on Union Court in 1828–9 and 1835, is unclear, but it seems credible (Arliss is listed at the RIVERHEAD in 1841). By 1889, terraced housing had been established along much of Eastgate between Priory Road and the railway line, a process largely complete by the early twentieth century. The area behind this is shown as containing a large pit in 1889, and by 1906 an iron foundry had been established here. The iron foundry was still marked here on the 1956 OS map, but the area was a Builders Merchant's Yard and Public Works Contractor's Depot in the 1960s; more recently, the houses of PRIORY CLOSE were constructed on this land. To the west of Bellamy's brickworks was Elisha Ryall's ropery and then James Hunter Ryley's brickworks in the ORME LANE area (see CHEQUERGATE for Ryley's stone mason business). In 1889 the brick yard here was marked as disused, with the Eastgate frontage—now Morrisons supermarket and terraced housing—taken up by two coal yards and a timber yard. By 1906, terraced housing had been constructed here and an iron foundry is marked in the area to the rear, as it was in the 1930s too. Subsequently, the area where Morrisons now stands was used a garage, with a bus depot founded to the rear, off Orme Lane.

Continuing east along Eastgate, we pass the former railway bridge and eventually reach Holy Trinity Church. Holy Trinity was first built 1834 as a chapel of ease to serve the Riverhead community, standing on high ground overlooking it. It was rebuilt from 1864 onwards at a cost of £3,515, and the new church was consecrated in 1866, with its own parish formed in January 1867. With some rearrangement of the seating in 1877, the capacity of the second Holy Trinity Church was increased to 800, a significant improvement over the first church, which could seat only 450. The second church burnt down overnight on 1 June 1991, with only the tower surviving, and a new church and community centre was eventually completed here in 1997. In the meantime, services were held in Lacey Gardens School and then, from 1992, at the Scout headquarters on THAMES STREET. Opposite and close to the church are a notable group of large houses, which are visible on Brown's sketches of 1844— these housed nineteenth-century merchants after it had become unacceptable for them to live close to their work in the Riverhead district, as earlier generations had. So, for example, William Nell's family was still based at the Riverhead in 1851, but by 1861 he and his family had relocated into the fashionable Regency-style row of houses on this part of Eastgate. The final building to be noted on this part of Eastgate is The Lincolnshire Poacher Hotel. This was a private house, Park House, until 1954, when it became a public house. In the Second World War, Park House was the Headquarters for the Coldstreams, the Grenadiers and the Hampshires, and Winston Churchill visited it in early days of war and stayed there overnight.

Turning from the former Watery Lane back to Eastgate proper, one of the first buildings met travelling westwards is the Manor House. Although the present building dates from the eighteenth century, it is worth noting that it stands above cellars belonging to an earlier structure, perhaps also a manor house. In the nineteenth century, this was home to Mary Chaworth, one of Lord Byron's early loves. Several supposedly ghostly happenings are recorded for the Manor House, in particular the sight of a man standing in one of the windows of the coachman's cottage at the rear of the property, who is never there when the matter is investigated, although the door to this room always mysteriously opens itself—this was supposedly witnessed by two independent people in 1974. On the same side of the road, just to the east, is another key building, the Eastgate Union Church. After 1919, the Congregationalists, the Baptists and the General Baptists all worshipped in the 1864 Eastgate Baptist Chapel, located on corner of Eastgate and Ramsgate (this was one of the last nonconformist chapels built in Louth). This was one of several chapels and churches at one time or another present on Eastgate. On the opposite side of the road, a little further to the west, was the Louth Free Methodist Church, which was a 1,200 seat 'pillared chapel' built in 1854. Championed by Joseph Larder and John Booth Sharpley, it lay opposite Sharpley's home, Eastgate House (now a dental practice), and was demolished in 1957–8: the site is presently a car park. At the opposite end of Eastgate is the current Louth Methodist Church, which is the only Methodist establishment still in use in town. The first Methodist meeting house in Louth was established in the 1760s, in Rose's Passage off Eastgate (behind the Lloyds TSB bank), and John Wesley preached here on his last visit to the town in 1788, when he was aged 85. In 1805, the current Eastgate site was secured. At its maximum extent, after 1835, the Methodist church here could seat 1,600 worshippers, although the number of pews was reduced in favour of greater comfort in 1854. The church was refashioned in the late 1970s— at a cost of £110,000—removing the Victorian box pews and galleries and adding a new entrance onto NICHOL HILL. Finally, there was also, in 1792 at least, a Catholic church on Eastgate, though its exact location has never been ascertained, and the Congregationalists or Independents met in a loft near the northern, Eastgate entrance to the yard of the Bricklayer's Arms (now the Masons Arms) in around 1800.

Eastgate has also been home to a large number of inns and public houses. The earliest recorded of these is the White Swan. This was first mentioned in an archdeacon's visitation of 1612 as 'The Sign of the Swan' and the present building is believed to date from the seventeenth century; in 1834 it had stabling for 15 horses. Another early inn was The Pack Horse. This was certainly in existence by 1782. Until 1821, this inn had a Swiss landlord named Jean Mari de la Pierre (d. 1822). He disapproved of drunkenness and would only serve a modicum of drink, saying to his customers that when they had had enough, they ought to go home, as their wives and children needed the money. He made a point of closing his house early, but one night some customers tried to thwart him by staying late—his hints to leave were ignored, so he withdrew and then reappeared claiming that there was a fire in BURNT HILL LANE. The men left quickly to see the fire, but soon discovered that there was none, at which point they rushed back to the Pack Horse—they were, however, too late, for the door was locked. Other early-recorded drinking establishments included the Marquis of Granby, first mentioned in 1782 and closed in 1961 (Meridian House is built on the former site of this inn); the Ship & Horns, again first mentioned in the late eighteenth century, then under the name the Royal Sovereign (now the Red Cross charity shop in the Fish Shambles; the present building was constructed in 1888); and the Jolly Sailor, first mentioned in 1782 and closed in 1970 (on the corner of Eastgate and Burnt Hill Lane; now the Sue Ryder charity shop).

Later-recorded inns on Eastgate include the Temperance Hotel, run by Reuben Spivey in 1848. In October of that year, a meeting of the teetotal movement took place in this establishment, and William Brown was elected to preside over the teetotal committee and address the meeting. These premises were demolished in 1965 to make way for a supermarket, and the site is now occupied by Wilkinson's. Another later-recorded establishment was the Woodman, which was located next to the Free Methodist Church. First mentioned in 1841, when Joseph Leaf was the landlord, it finally closed in 2012. In 1847, 'a prostitute of rather ancient appearance', named Ann McDonald (alias Ann Smith) was charged with stealing a pocket watch from a John Smith in the yard of the Woodman—she supposedly sold it 'to a Jew', who then took it to a local pawnshop—and in 1848 Mary Leaf, the hostess of the Woodman, was charged by William Scholfield, a labourer, with striking him on the head with a red-hot poker, leaving visible marks on his face. Her excuse for this violent outburst was that Scholfield had called her by 'a name most irritating to a woman': she was fined 10s plus 12s costs.

Such events were not, of course, restricted to the Woodman's yard in the mid-nineteenth century. So, for example, in 1847 a prostitute from Hull, named Mary Ann Walker, was charged with having behaved in an indecent manner on Eastgate, and in 1849 William Hopper, a bricklayer, was charged with 'exposing his person' on two different days, with the intent 'to insult several females' on Eastgate. Hopper was apparently 'an incorrigible rogue', who had been charged with the same offence in 1848—certainly, at the time of the 1851 census he was incarcerated in the Louth House of Correction (see also BRIDGE STREET and HORNCASTLE ROAD). Other criminal events reported in the Eastgate area in the mid-nineteenth-century regional press included the 1855 case of John Overton, alias George Overton, a journeyman tailor of Eastgate. He was charged by a servant named Maria Hornsey, aged 14, with committing an indecent assault on her: whilst she was drawing water from a pump for her master, Overton grabbed her and kissed her and then pulled her into his house and assaulted her. For this he was fined 40s and costs. Less serious were the numerous cases of drunkenness and disorderly conduct on the street, which were perhaps to be expected given the number of inns here and its prominence as a town thoroughfare. For instance, in 1845 John Rock—'a Hibernian [Irishman] of herculean proportions'—was charged with being drunk and incapable of looking after himself on Eastgate, and in 1849 Michael Pendegrast and John Fearey were charged with being drunk and creating a great annoyance at the time that the local people were 'on their way to divine service'.

Perhaps the most impressive building on Eastgate is the Town Hall. The building is somewhat curiously located at one of the narrowest sections of Eastgate, but has a magnificent decorated Italianate frontage with columns of Caen stone. The original, sixteenth-century Town Hall had been demolished in the early nineteenth century and the Town Council had since made use of the Guildhall in the Cornmarket (see MARKET PLACE) and the Mansion House on Upgate. In the early 1850s, however, it was decided that these accommodations were inadequate and that a new Town Hall ought to be built at the corner of CANNON STREET and Eastgate, on a Corporation property known as the Stall Yard. The foundation stone for the new building was laid by the Earl of Yarborough in 1853, with the Town Hall completed by local builder John Dales in 1854, who had to open a new brickpit on BRACKENBOROUGH ROAD due to the quantity of materials required. The new Town Hall was paid for by the sale of the Guildhall in Market Place and the Mansion House (to Louth Mechanics' Institute) on Upgate, along with a number of other pieces of land—the final cost was £5,927. With the local government reorganization of the early 1970s, the Town Council lost control of Louth's Town Hall, which was passed instead to East Lindsey District Council. Despite this, the Town Council continued to be based in the Town Hall until 2011, when they moved to the old Sessions House, further down Eastgate.

Other notable buildings on Eastgate include the former Electric Picture Palace, built by the Ingleton family on the corner of VICKERS LANE and Eastgate. Opened in July 1914, this once had a magnificent frontage, now sadly replaced by a standard shop front. There were basket chairs in front of the circle and the theatre here put on variety shows and revues as well as films; its name reflects the fact that the Electric Picture Palace was the first building in town to have electricity, which it generated itself. The theatre and cinema here closed in the late 1950s, and in recent years the building has been a Fine Fare supermarket, a Wilkinson's, and now a Heron supermarket. The same site also once housed Louth's first Post Office, established by 1822, with Sarah Allison as Post Mistress. The Post Office moved to the Market Place in 1880s, with sub-offices established on Eastgate (opposite Trinity Church) and Newmarket. The Main Post Office relocated to its present site at the western end of Eastgate in 1928–9, a move which saw the demolition of a number of properties there, both fronting onto Eastgate and behind it. Number 61 Eastgate, a little further to the east, also had—and, indeed, still has—an interesting frontage. Now home to Argos, the magnificently detailed frontage of the upper storeys of this shop dates from 1851. In that year, Batterham's linen and woolen drapers were transformed into Anselm Odling's drapery depot, at a cost of several thousand pounds. Interestingly, at the time of this transformation, there were still apparently a few thatched premises on Eastgate, according to William Brown, though which these were is uncertain. By 1856, 61 Eastgate had been taken over by J. W. Dennis & Son, a manufacturing and dispensing chemist. This important and long-lived local business made 'Lincolnshire Pig Powders' and exported as far afield as China and Japan.

With regard to the shops and businesses of Eastgate, a wide variety of trades are currently represented in buildings that generally date from the eighteenth and nineteenth centuries, including an unusual number of independent butchers and other food shops. For example, Lakings of Louth's butcher shop at 33 Eastgate (along with 1 Nichol Hill behind it) has been thought to date from the late eighteenth century. 33 Eastgate was originally the third Lakings in town, the business having begun on BROADBANK in 1908 and then expanded to two Eastgate sites, first number 71 and later, in 1935, number 33, on which the business finally consolidated under John Laking. Before becoming a butcher's shop, number 33 had functioned as Timothy Wold Topham's bakery, probably from the late 1840s through to the 1870s, and it appears to have continued as a bakery through until at least World War One (Topham died in 1876 and the business was taken over by his son, Titus). Timothy Topham's shop was previously based on JAMES STREET in the 1830s and early 1840s, and the Topham family's mill was listed on Broadbank in 1841 (presumably the mill near the top of Broadbank that is visible on Brown's 1844 sketch, see HIGH HOLME ROAD), on WESTGATE in 1856 (Thorpe Hall Mill, also known as The Old Paper Mill), and then on MILL LANE, off Holmes Lane (High Holme Road) from at least 1872—the latter was a six-sail windmill that was eventually demolished in 1910. Number 8 Eastgate may be even older than number 33: it has been suggested that the building could belong to the early eighteenth century, with a shop window that dates from the early nineteenth century. Used for lodging homeless men in early twentieth century, this shop has also been used as a wardrobe dealership (in the later nineteenth century) and as a newsagent. Further down the road, the present-day independent newsagent and bookseller named Wrights of Louth occupies a building that may date from around 1780. This was used as Platt's grocer shop from 1909 through until 1985, when it became first Parkers' and then Wrights' newsagent and bookshop (Platt's was founded in the 1880s and was, until 1909, located on the western corner of Burnt Hill Lane and Eastgate). Continuing eastwards, number 85 Eastgate has been considered to date from sometime around 1700, whilst 130 Eastgate—until recently Forbes and now Clarks shoe shop—is a pre-1850 building that was once occupied by a cowkeeper, who sold milk from here. His cows were apparently grazed in a field at the back of what is now Harvey's furniture store (where the Northgate car park is currently located).

Finally, attention ought to be drawn to the Fish Shambles on Eastgate, which represents the site of the fish stalls of the medieval and early modern Louth market. Located on the downwind edge of the market, probably because of the smell, the Fish Shambles is first mentioned in 1559. In that year 4d was paid 'to wynter for mending the fyshe shameles' by Louth Corporation, and there was a further payment for wood and work on the 'shammells' in 1564. In 1617, 15s was paid for the making of the well at the 'ffishe shambles', and in 1822, William Coulam was paid £9 12s for erecting the 'New Fish Shambles'. William Brown, writing in the *Stamford Mercury*, complained about the Fish Shambles on several occasions—it was supposedly in a poor condition, without accommodation for those who deal in fish there in 1839; it was dilapidated and fishmongers were offering their wares outside of the bounds of the shambles in 1846; and benches and slabbing for the fish trade had been provided, but offal was nonetheless being slovenly cast upon the cobbles, where it lay and infected the air with its stench in 1856. In 1849, William Armitage's shop in the Fish Shambles burnt down. Armitage was a chemist and inventor—he was drying his detonating fog signals for use by the railways in his oven here when they exploded, causing the building to burn down and Armitage and four others to lose their lives. Interestingly, this accident doesn't appear to have scared off other chemists in the Louth area from making these dangerous items, with several explosions being caused by them over the next two years (see MONKS DYKE ROAD).

EDWARD STREET

The name Edward Street was presumably coined from the presence of buildings to the west of this street that belonged to Louth's Grammar School, refounded by Edward VI in 1551. The earliest of these was The Lodge, which was built as both a house for the Headmaster and a boarding-block in 1797 (see further CROWTREE LANE), and the name Edward Street was certainly current in the first half of the nineteenth century. In the twentieth century the school buildings to the west of Edward Street were added to, first with a purpose-built gymnasium for the Boys' Grammar School on Edward Street, opened in 1906 by Robert Baden-Powell, and then with a new school quadrangle and hall, constructed in 1931–3. The latter buildings allowed the school roll to rise to a historic high of 250 before the outbreak of World War Two and the school itself was moved to the new Edward Street site from its previous home on SCHOOLHOUSE LANE. What the street was called before the construction of The Lodge at the end of the eighteenth century is uncertain, but it clearly existed then, as it is marked on Armstrong's 1778 plan of the town. One possibility is that it was called 'Gospollane'. This street is mentioned in 1317 as being near 'Gospolgat'

(GOSPELGATE), and its name implies that it was a distinct road from the latter that was not only located near to Gospelgate, but also near to the Goose Pool after which Gospelgate is named. In this context, it is worth pointing out that the Goose Pool that Gospelgate is named from is usually believed to be that which stood just to the west of Edward Street, in Clay Pitts Close (see Crowtree Lane), and recent excavations have turned up another probably medieval pool on the eastern side of Edward Street too, at number 9, which may have been filled in as late as the eighteenth century.

In the early nineteenth century, Edward Street was almost entirely undeveloped—the only buildings shown there on Espin's 1808 plan of Louth were The Lodge, off Crowtree Lane but located to the west of Edward Street, and a long, thin building that is somewhat curiously shown as sited within the street, partially blocking it. This building was still there in 1834, when some additional buildings had been constructed opposite the junction of Edward Street and Crowtree Lane. However, it is not shown on the 1839 map of the town, nor on the 1844 sketch of the area made by William Brown. In addition to the apparent loss of this building, the period between 1834 and 1839 also saw the development of the northern part of Edward Street, with a new yard and buildings constructed on the eastern side of the street, to the south of the junction with Crowtree Lane, and buildings also extending halfway down the eastern side of the street by 1839. The yard was known as the 'Brick Yard' in the nineteenth century and was the location of Medley's brickpits, which were said to have been worked until 'quite recently' in 1916 (on the 1889 OS map, the cottages in the Brick Yard were marked as 'Medley's Row'). The Medley family who owned this brickyard were presumably the father and son—Michael and Richard—who lived on Gospelgate and GEORGE STREET from 1841 to 1889 and who were described as bricklayers and builders in the censuses and directories. Michael Medley, d. 1865, was based on Walkergate (QUEEN STREET) in the 1828–9 and 1835 directories, but had moved to Gospelgate by 1841, a move that would seem to coincide nicely with the apparent development of the Brick Yard on Edward Street in the mid-late 1830s.

By the end of the nineteenth century, the gaps that were present in the housing on the northern half of the eastern side of the street had been filled in, though a few structures further south on the road look to have been demolished by the time of the 1889 OS map. With regard to the people who lived on Edward Street in that period, the 1861 census lists several laundresses, dressmakers, shoemakers and bricklayers living on this road, along with a porter spirit merchant (Samuel Bontoft, number 12), a gentleman's butler (Joseph Duckering, number 7), a gentleman's gardener and groom (Thomas and John Metcalf, number 3), a lodging house keeper (Mary Ann Grownsell, number 6), a cowkeeper with six acres (William Fowler, number 4), and the local Registrar of Births & Deaths (William Parkin, number 13). At the end of the nineteenth century, there was a similar mix of people, ranging from labourers and dressmakers through to people living on their own means (Mary Elvin, number 10), a police constable (John Cook, number 9), two grooms (Joseph and George Wilkinson, number 11), and a printer and bookbinder (Charles Mason, number 12). In general, the street appears to have been respectable, with few entries concerning it present in the surviving court reports of the mid-nineteenth century, aside from two prosecutions for begging on this road. However, the Medleys do appear occasionally, usually as the complainant—for example, in 1849 Richard Medley charged one of their bricklayers, William Hopper (a noted flasher in the town, see EASTGATE, BRIDGE STREET and HORNCASTLE ROAD), with stealing four of his trowels and a hammer, a crime of which Hopper was eventually acquitted. In the twentieth century, the major changes to the street occurred as a result of the move of the Grammar School to its new Edward Street site, but there were other changes too, not least the demolition of Medley's Row in the old Brick Yard and the construction of a handful of new properties to the south of the nineteenth-century housing on the eastern side of the street.

ELM DRIVE

Elm Drive and its associated roads—DAVID DRIVE, ADA WAY and STAINESWAY—are located to the south of KEDDINGTON ROAD. Together they form a mid-twentieth-century housing estate that was nearly fully developed by the late 1960s, aside from at the eastern end of Stainesway, which was completed in the early 1970s. The land that this estate was built on had been part of the old open fields of Louth up until the Enclosure Act of 1801, and an area of medieval ridge and furrow field system was found during excavations in this part of town in the late 1990s. Subsequently, this land belonged to The Elms, a large nineteenth-century house located near to the RIVERHEAD. The Elms is currently a care home located at the south end of Elm Drive, but through until the mid-twentieth century the whole area that the housing estate was built upon formed a park attached to this house. In the censuses, The Elms is grouped with the houses of Keddington Road and the 1889 and later OS maps show that The Elms did indeed have some sort of accessway that opened onto that road—this was located just to the west of the entrance to Elm Drive and is currently a footpath down the rear of the houses facing onto Elm Drive, becoming Ticklepenny Walk around halfway down its length. In the nineteenth century, inhabitants of The Elms included Edward H. Cartwright, farmer, in 1891 and Richard J. Nell, seed crusher, in 1861.

ERESBIE ROAD

Eresbie Road is part of the 'Weavers Tryst' housing estate that was begun in the late 1990s. It forms the spine of this new development, running north from LEGBOURNE ROAD and then turning west to match the alignment of STEWTON LANE, which runs just to the north of it. It is built on land that was originally part of Louth's medieval open South Field, although most of the area had been enclosed prior to the 1801 Enclosure Act. The roads within it appear to be named after local worthies of the sixteenth and seventeenth centuries—Lawrence Eresbie was the first Warden of Louth, from 1551–4.

EVE STREET

Eve Street links both JAMES STREET and CHARLES STREET to the medieval NORTHGATE. James Dunn, a local bricklayer, was leased land in Northgate in 1793 by the Louth Corporation in return for an agreement to spend £1,000 in building 'the new intended road from Padehole [Northgate] to the Navigation'. Although James Street was the main result of this agreement, Eve Street is believed to have been also constructed then, as the final section linking the new James Street to Northgate. Certainly, no street is marked in this position on Armstrong's 1778 plan of Louth, whilst Eve Street is very clearly depicted on Espin's 1808 plan of the town. The road had buildings on both side through to the James Street junction by 1808, but beyond this it appears to have been an undeveloped track leading to a bridge over the Lud (probably providing access to the Charles Street brickworks), with what looks like an orchard to its west, where the loading area for the Co-op supermarket is now located. The name 'Eve Street' is presumably a reference to Adam Eve, who had land in this area of town and who had taken over the carpet factory in 1790 (see James Street).

In the mid-nineteenth century, the proximity of Eve Street to the carpet factory on James Street is reflected in the fact that six of the inhabitants were listed as carpet weavers in 1861. Other occupations represented on the street then included a lawyer (Elmil Dawson), a muffin maker (Hannah Lawson), a stonemason (William King, whose place of business was on James Street), a shoemaker (Jacob Dales), a cattle dealer (John Hackforth) and a dye house labourer (Thomas Cook). The street also had a beer retailer somewhere on it at the time of the 1861 census, run by John Badley. In succeeding years, a beerhouse was based at 2–4 Eve Street (1871, George Clark) and 6 Eve Street (1891–1905, Job Robinson), and in 1872 William Barton's brewery was located on Eve Street. The Eve Street Brewery was also recorded in 1885 and 1889, when it was run by Wright Simons and linked to the Shades Tavern at 66 EASTGATE.

A number of other interesting businesses and groups were present on Eve Street around the end of the nineteenth century. For example, the western side of the street near to the river, where once there was an orchard, is marked as the Waterloo Dye Works on the 1889 OS map, with an associated terrace of houses—this was called Waterloo Terrace in 1889, but appears to have been listed as Pulley's Yard in 1881. The Dye Works was presumably owned by Louth dyer Joseph Edward Pulley, who had a shop on Eastgate from at least 1872 and who was listed as a dyer on Eve Street in the 1896 directory. The Louth Laundry Co., which was listed on Eve Street in 1905 and apparently still there in 1909, may have taken over this site, especially as this business is linked to a dyer in its adverts. Subsequently, the site of the Dye Works was occupied by a dog biscuit manufacturer, Ludameaties. Founded in 1938, its factory on Eve Street was gutted by a major fire in 1952 and the factory subsequently moved to THAMES STREET. Since 1989, this site has been used by the Co-operative supermarket, with its loading area facing onto Eve Street. On the opposite side of the street, also next to the river, was Eve Street Iron Works—marked on the 1889 OS map, it is unclear how long this works had been on the street, but it was certainly still in business in the inter-war years, when it was run by Arthur Dunkin, an agricultural implement maker and repairer. The site of the Eve Street Iron Works now lies in the yard of Leake's Masons, off James Street. Finally, the Artillery Drill Hall lay at the northern end of Eve Street, on the north side of the Lud. This belonged to the Lincolnshire Volunteer Artillery Brigade (and later the Lincolnshire Yeomanry Territorial Force and the Royal Field Artillery) from at least 1885, when it was under the control of Captain Robert Ranshaw, and it continued to function as a Drill Hall, depot and headquarters well into the twentieth century (in 1896, the sergeant-major of the Lincolnshire Volunteer Artillery, Robert Holsworth, lived at 3 Eve Street).

FAIRFIELD INDUSTRIAL ESTATE

Fairfield Industrial Estate was developed in the old North Field of the town from the 1960s. One of first factories to set up on the estate was that of the knitwear manufacturer Davenport Stannard Ltd in 1969. Another notable local firm on the estate was Lin Pac—founded in 1959, it was formerly based on CHARLES STREET and originally known as the Lincolnshire Packaging Company; the Louth business was eventually sold to D. S. Smith Packaging in 2003 for £170 million. By 1980 there were 20 firms on the Fairfield Industrial Estate, and a major expansion of the estate came in the 1990s, when East Lindsey District Council purchased an additional 100 acre site in 1995 and undertook a major road building and infrastructure development over the next four years, at a cost of over £6 million. The new extension was opened by the Countryside Minister, Elliot Morley MP, and by the end of the 1990s there were more than 80 firms based on the estate. In the early twenty-first century, Louth's industrial estate has continued to expand northwards, with businesses now established along most of the roads within the estate, including the Louth Indoor Tennis & Sports Centre on Scarborough Road.

The roads within Fairfield Industrial Estate are generally named after local or national places, for example Tattershall Way, Warwick Road, Bolingbroke Road. In terms of underlying archaeology of the land now used by the estate, there have been few finds of note, the chief exception being a large, unabraded sherd of Iron Age pottery that was found on

86

the site of the new Recycling Centre in 2006. Otherwise, the local Historic Environment Record only records the presence of medieval ridge and furrow field systems belonging to the old North Field in this area, notably to the south of Fanthorpe Farm (in the area where D S Smith Packaging is now based, on the west side of the A16 GRIMSBY ROAD); in the area to the east of Belvoir Way; and in the area of Bolingbroke Road, near to the new Recycling Centre. There is also surviving medieval ridge and furrow to the north of the present industrial estate, along with a ditch and slight bank that appears to mark the boundary between Louth and Keddington parishes.

FANTHORPE LANE

Fanthorpe Lane represents part of the ancient Barton Street (also known as Louth Street), a prehistoric and later routeway running from Barton on Humber southwards along the eastern edge of the Wolds. In the modern period, the Scartho and Louth Turnpike—the A16 GRIMSBY ROAD—replaced this road as the main routeway leading north from Louth. The part of Barton Street still functioning as a lane leading north from Louth was termed Fanthorpe Lane locally; it was subsequently cut in two by the construction of the LOUTH A16 BYPASS, which opened in 1991.

A pre-Roman cropmark enclosure has been identified from aerial photography near to Fanthorpe Lane and a Royal Observer Corps look-out post was apparently established on the lane during World War Two. Otherwise, there is little evidence for development or activity along most of the lane, which appears to have been primarily agricultural in nature until very recently. So, the only properties present on Fanthorpe Lane at the end of the nineteenth century were Glebe Farm (now Northfield Farm) and New Farm (now demolished), and its rural character is very apparent from William Brown's depiction of the road on his mid-nineteenth-century Panorama. Moreover, it is interesting to note that the strips of agricultural land at 'Ellerybdale' mentioned in a 1317 charter (of Thomas de Luda, chapter clerk of Lincoln Cathedral) appear to have been situated on Fanthorpe Lane, given that an Egrydale Close was recorded here in 1918. This agricultural character only really began to change in the mid-twentieth century, when a number of houses were built at the southern end of the lane.

87

FERN CLOSE

Fern Close runs south-west from BRACKENBOROUGH ROAD. The house on the south side of the road is marked on the 1889 OS map of this area, with the area immediately to the north of this appearing to be an orchard of some sort in the late nineteenth and early twentieth centuries. In the mid-twentieth century, the road that is now Fern Close had been laid out, leading from Brackenborough Road through to Keddington House and a nursery (off KEDDINGTON ROAD), and a number of new residential properties were built on this road in the early twenty-first century.

FLORENCE WRIGHT AVENUE

Florence Wright Avenue runs east from KENWICK ROAD and had been largely developed by the early 1950s, although the properties at the eastern end of the street date from the late twentieth century. The land that Florence Wright Avenue stands on was part of the town's old open South Field, and medieval ridge and furrow has been observed on aerial photographs of this area.

FREER GARDENS

Freer Gardens runs south-east from MONKS DYKE ROAD and is part of the large, post-World War Two, ST BERNARDS AVENUE council housing scheme. It doesn't appear to have been laid out by the time that the 1951 OS map was surveyed, but it was laid out and developed by the time of the 1956 map. The land it stands on was originally part of Louth's old open South Field.

FULMAR DRIVE

Fulmar Drive runs eastwards from Brackenborough Road. Built in 1990s, the houses here were being sold as new builds in 1995–7. The houses on Shearwater Close, which runs north off Fulmar Drive, were sold as new builds in 1998. As of 2012, developers are reported to be considering building a new estate of 140 homes off Fulmar Drive.

GATHERUMS & SPRINGSIDE

The Gatherums (from Scandinavian *gatu-rum*) was originally a rough track or droveway which ran alongside the two major springs and their pools that were located in this area of town, namely the Aswell spring and St Helen's spring. Both of these springs were first recorded in the mid-thirteenth century, although they are likely to have been significant foci for the town in earlier periods too. For example, holy wells and springs dedicated to St Helen are now thought to have their origins in an early Christianization of cult-sites dedicated to a Romano-British pagan water-goddess known as Alauna, whose name could easily deform to 'Helen'. Likewise, the Aswell spring is 'the spring by the ash tree' and a possible location for 'the ash tree at Louth' where the pre-Norman wapentake of Louthesk met to discuss and arrange the business and legal affairs of the surrounding district.

In the medieval and early modern periods, there are a significant number of references to these springs. By the middle of the thirteenth century, the courses of both St Helen's spring and the Aswell spring had been diverted in order to supply Louth Park Abbey via the Monks' Dyke (see MONKS DYKE ROAD). According to a charter of 1315, the monks had originally paid a rent of 4d a year for the right to channel water from the two springs through to the abbey, until John Siadeway discharged them from this obligation, and both the springs and the monks' right of way here are first mentioned in a document of 1235–53. The Aswell spring, which flowed at around 460 gallons-per-minute, was also a key source of fresh water for the town, something reflected in the fact that fines were fairly frequently handed out for its defilement in medieval period. So, in 1431, Robert ffynche was reported to the Manor Court for washing newly dyed black cloths in the Aswell spring; in 1441, John Baumburgh was fined 4d for washing sheepskins in the water of Asewell; and in 1449, nine men were fined 1d by the Manor Court for daily watering their horses in the Aswell spring, 'contrary to ancient custom', thus defiling and corrupting its water 'so that the lord's tenants living thereabouts cannot have clean water for making their beer, as they are wont' (those charged include John Green, a barber, William Johnson, a butcher, and Thomas Bradley, of the noted Bradley family of Louth). The last of the above items also implies an economic importance for the waters of these springs in the medieval period, and this certainly seems to have been the case. The Aswell spring ran all along the back of the properties facing onto Walkergate, modern QUEEN STREET, which was the centre of the cloth-finishing industry in medieval Louth, with both the dyers and the walkers of this area using the waters of the spring as an essential part of their trade (walkers, or fullers, stamped on cloth in pure water to felt it and give it a smooth finish). This economic role for the Aswell spring continued into the modern period, when the spring was used to drive a fulling mill and, later, a corn mill (see further Queen Street and CHURCH STREET).

The springs clearly also had a religious role to play in the town. Not only was one of them dedicated to 'St Helen' and probably venerated as a holy spring from an early period, but there are also numerous references in the sixteenth and seventeenth centuries to relatively substantial payments being made for the dressing and cleaning of the Aswell spring in preparation for its blessing and religious usage, something which presumably continued a medieval veneration of this site. So, William Blanchard bequeathed £3 for the dressing of Aswell and other springs in the town in 1592, and payments occur in the Churchwardens' accounts in the sixteenth century and almost annually in the Corporation records from 1601–77 for the 'dressinge of Aswell' (sometimes spelt Oswell or Osewell, as in 1637 and 1664)—for example, 'ffishers wief' was paid 4s for the 'dressinge of Aswell' in 1609. This devotion was apparently primarily focussed on Holy Thursday (Ascension Day), although there are indications that the spring was prepared for other religious festivals too, as in 1559 when Mertyn Chapman was paid 12d by the Churchwardens to dress the Aswell spring for Christmas. In addition, there are also frequent accounts of large quantities of stone and timber being conveyed to Aswell in the aftermath of the Reformation, something which has been thought to indicate an unusual lavishing of attention on this area then. Some of this material was apparently being used 'for paveinge at Aswell... [and] the Raisinge of yt', as in 1621, but the quantities involved would imply that rather more substantial building works were also taking place. Although no trace of any such buildings now survive, in 1834 Robert Bayley observed that one of the much-decayed Tudor houses that persisted at Aswell to his day had 'some appearance of having been used for religious purposes', which may be significant.

Although the Gatherums and Springside area was clearly important, it only really became a significant residential area for the town in the mid-nineteenth century. This is not, of course, to say that there were no earlier buildings or residential activity around the springs. As was noted above, Bayley records the presence of several late Tudor houses 'of the worst workmanship and character' near the Aswell spring in 1834. In addition, several properties were listed here in the 1823 valuation (including the house, barn, stable and yard of James Bond, rated at £10) and there is a reference from 1717 to one Thomas Sutton paying a fat turkey at Christmas (or two shillings) for 'a Barne in the Gatherums two Cottages on Each Side his own house'. Espin's 1808 plan of the town is similarly relevant, as it not only shows buildings to the north of the Aswell pool, but also labels the area to the south of the spring (now under the KIDGATE car park) as the 'Gatherhams' and depicts buildings and gardens in that area. Nonetheless, this activity was relatively limited compared to that seen later in the nineteenth century. The expansion in residential properties in this part of town appears to have begun in the 1830s—although the 1834 plan of the town shows no change from the situation in 1808, the 1839 map depicts additional buildings to the west of the earlier buildings in the Gatherums and further buildings to the east of these too, between the channels of the Aswell spring and St Helen's spring. By the time of William Brown's Panorma—which was completed in 1847 and last updated in 1856— tightly-packed terrace housing extended along much of this area through to CHURCH STREET, both between the two springs and also on the south side of St Helen's spring, with small stone footbridges leading over the latter to afford access to the houses there. The 1889 OS map of Louth confirms the layout of these mid-nineteenth-century houses, showing two squares (one labelled Jones' Square) below what is now the Kidgate car park, and then terraces running eastwards along either side of the Gatherums and Springside footpath, with nine small footbridges crossing St Helen's spring. These houses were all demolished as slums in the mid-twentieth century and the springs are now fully culverted, with the Gatherums being maintained and developed as a landscaped, public green area by the District Council and the Gatherums and Springside Regeneration Group.

With regard to the character of this area, it would be fair to say that it appears to have been somewhat notorious in the mid-nineteenth century. So, the houses to the north of the Aswell pool, in what was known as 'Aswell Hole', included at least one brothel and a 'tramp lodging-house' in the 1840s, with the latter becoming a beerhouse briefly in the 1850s and 1860s (see ASWELL STREET for more details; the houses in Aswell Hole are discussed there, as they were usually treated as part of this road and separate to the Gatherums and Springside proper in this period). An equally disreputable character also applied to the terraced housing that lay to the south of the Aswell Pool and along the Gatherums footpath. A significant number of brothels are reported as being in business here during the 1840s and 1850s, too many to go into detail on each here. For example, one was run by Sarah Burton in 1850, who was charged with threatening her neighbour Eliza Perkins with bodily harm—Burton appears to have been still running brothels in Louth in 1879, when she was in charge of one on NORTHGATE. Another was run by Elizabeth Moncaster. This brothel is first mentioned in 1845, and in 1855 Elizabeth Moncaster and her daughter Fanny Jepson, alias Moncaster, were charged with having beaten and assaulted Lavinia Nicholson, of Welton le Wold, aged fourteen. Nicholson was apparently inveigled into the Moncaster brothel, where she then remained for ten days, stripped of her clothing and money. The girl then left the brothel, to try and 'obtain her living in a more creditable manner', and asked Jepson for her gown back, at which Jepson ran after her with a knife to stab her, and Jepson's mother, Elizabeth Moncaster, also joined in the assault! They were fined but 20s and 7s 6d, respectively, by the court, equivalent to around £100 today. A final example is the 'low brothel' in the Gatherums—a 'most notorious house of ill-fame, a resort for thieves and the very worst characters'—that was run by Ann Kime in 1857. Kime's brothel played host to a somewhat notorious local brothel-goer named William Horton (see RAMSGATE and SPRING GARDENS), whose drunken visit to her brothel in December 1857 ended with him being forcibly dragged out of the brothel at 1am by his friends, who presumably feared for the safety of both Horton and the £43 10s he had foolishly taken into the brothel with him that night (equivalent to around £3,250 today).

Of course, not every house in the Gatherums and Springside was a brothel, nor every inhabitant of the street a prostitute in the mid-nineteenth century (although on the latter question one does need to be careful—only very rarely are prostitutes marked as such in the census, and known prostitutes are usually listed under seemingly innocuous trades, such as 'laundress' or 'dressmaker'). Indeed, some inhabitants seem to have pursued reasonably respectable trades. So, for example, when a vote was taken on the question of the church rate in Louth in 1834, the inhabitants of the Gatherums included a wheelwright named William Beaumont, a stay-maker named Samuel Cant, a plumber and glazier named John Jemy, a roper named Thomas Ryall, and a tailor named Joseph Wilkinson. Similarly, on the 1851 census, the inhabitants here included an Irish lodging-house keeper named Simon Russell (described as a tea dealer in 1856), an agricultural labourer called John Hobson (whose son, Thomas, was a solicitor's clerk), a schoolmistress named Maria Barkworth, a groom named George Thomas, a journeyman painter named Cornelius Marlow, a policeman called Henry Jackson, and (as in 1834) a tailor named Joseph Wilkinson. Moreover, by the 1880s, we get the first records of shops in the Gatherums in the local trade directories, with Christopher Osbourn being listed as a shopkeeper at 24e The Gatherums from 1885–1905 and Sarah Woodliff at 12 The Gatherums in 1885 and 1889.

GEORGE STREET

George Street is, in origin, a mid-nineteenth century street, named after the George Inn on GOSPELGATE that lay at its north-east corner. It is not depicted on any of the early plans of the town, nor on the 1839 map of Louth. However, by 1844 it had clearly been laid out, as William Brown includes the street on his sketches made from the church spire in that year. At that time, George Street was undeveloped, the only properties bordering it then being those that the road ran between on GOSPELGATE and SOUTH STREET. In contrast, on the finished Panorama—first shown in 1847 and last updated in 1856—the street is depicted as lined with houses on both sides. Confirmation that the development of George Street occurred in the late 1840s and early 1850s comes from the 1850 advertisement of twelve villas being built on George Street—these were presumably the twelve terraced houses running down the western side of the road.

In 1861, George Street appears to have been a well-to-do area of town. The inhabitants of George Street then included a proprietor of houses and her son-in-law, a farmer of 60 acres (Ann Watts and Joseph

Young, number 23); a landed proprietor (Joseph Dales, number 16); a lady living off an annuity from landed property (Ann Sharpley, number 13); another landed proprietor (Mary Byron, number 29, who used to live at Broad Bank House on BROADBANK); the vicar of Utterby (Rev. Arthur Pennington, number 6); the vicar of Haugham (Rev. Henry Marland, number 8); several gentlewomen, including one from Germany (Caroline Bellevie, number 18); a master butcher (West Mawer, number 5); a rope maker employing 14 people (Luke Youle, number 27, of Youle & Suddaby's in the MARKET PLACE and on NEWMARKET); and a linen draper and silk mercer (William Askey, number 21, whose shop was in the Market Place). By the end of the nineteenth century, the various sections of back road (see LITTLE SOUTH STREET) visible on Brown's Panorama had been joined together to form a single street, crossing George Street roughly halfway along its length. Otherwise, little appears to have changed, and an examination of the 1891 census shows that the street continued to be inhabited by some of the wealthier members of Louth society: for example, Hay Sharpley, the son of John Booth Sharpley, was at 29 George Street then, living on his own means. In the twentieth and early twenty-first centuries, George Street retained much of its character, with the only real change to the streetscape being the demolition of the former George Inn on the corner of George Street and Gospelgate and its replacement with the new flats of Grosvenor Court in 1987.

GLAMIS PLACE

Glamis Place is built on land that was once part of Louth's medieval open North Field. At the end of the nineteenth century, the land here was partly occupied by George Moody's High Holme Nursery (founded 1830). A nursery remained here into the 1980s, when Glamis Place was constructed in its place, running off SANDRINGHAM DRIVE (a road established in the 1970s).

GOODWOOD CLOSE

Goodwood Close runs off LONGLEAT DRIVE. The road is absent from the 1974–6 OS map, although at least one of the properties here was constructed by 1975 and the road had been fully developed by the mid-1980s. The land it is built on was originally part of Louth's old open North Field.

GOSPELGATE

Gospelgate, also known as Goose Pool, has seen finds of fragments of Roman brick and tile, which are of potential interest from the perspective of the early origins of Louth. It is also one of the earliest recorded streets in Louth, being first mentioned in the thirteenth century. Originally, Gospelgate probably chiefly functioned as simply a medieval lane leading to the Goose Pool, one of the spring-fed pools of the town, hence its name (Gospolgat or Gosepol in the medieval period). The pool in question is believed to be the large pool depicted on the 1808 and 1834 plans of the town to the north of The Lodge on CROWTREE LANE, near to the western end of modern Gospelgate, although this may well have been only one of a number of medieval pools for keeping geese located along Gospelgate. In this context, it can be observed that traces of another, probably medieval pool have recently been found to the south of Gospelgate, during an archaeological watching brief at 9 EDWARD STREET, and a probably pre-twelfth-century pool was also discovered through excavations behind the Greyhound Inn at the eastern end of Gospelgate.

Although Gospelgate may have been primarily a lane leading to the Goose Pool(s), there was other activity here in the medieval period too. In 1317, for example, a charter of Thomas de Luda refers to the existence of a messuage—usually defined as a dwelling house with outbuildings and the site on which it stood—on 'Gospolgat', and another messuage on this road is mentioned as being given to the Parish Church of Louth by one Wilkynson in 1449–50. The nature, extent and origins of this medieval activity are, however, unclear. Certainly, excavations at the rear of the Greyhound Inn, on the corner of Gospelgate and UPGATE, indicated that this site was only occupied from the twelfth century and lay on the edge of the medieval town, with arable fields and wooded areas being located close by. Furthermore, the excavations also showed that this part of Gospelgate, at least, was largely abandoned after the mid-fourteenth century, perhaps because of the Black Death, and was only reoccupied in the eighteenth century.

Between the medieval period and the eighteenth century, there are several references to Gospelgate. Some mention the cleanliness and maintenance of the street, as in 1560 when heaps of dung were said to have been piled up on Gospelgate, or in 1634, when 3s 6d (around £400 as a labour cost today) was paid for 'mending a quicksand in Gospole'. Others refer to the presence of houses and an inn here, showing that at least part of the road was built up in the early modern period, despite the fact that the site to the rear of the Greyhound remained unoccupied until the eighteenth century. So, an inn named the Rose and Crown was located in a cottage in Gospelgate before 1624, when it is referred to as 'late' in a rental of that year, and in 1603 William Heneage Esquire, William Symcoates gent, and Widow Gersbie were all fined 3s 4d each for not sufficiently repairing and amending the footway in front of their houses in 'Gosepol' (interestingly, Heneage was actually presiding at the court at which he was thus fined!). In the eighteenth century, the extent to which Gospelgate was developed becomes a little clearer, due to the availability of Armstrong's 1778 plan of the town and Espin's 1808 plan. Taken together, these show that Gospelgate had been almost fully developed by the late eighteenth century, with buildings all along much of both sides of the street (Armstrong shows them as an unbroken run on both sides, but Espin's much more accurate plan indicates that there were still some gaps, notably on the south side of the road). A number of these eighteenth-century buildings still survive, or did so until recently. For example, 42 and 44 Gospelgate date from 1768 and The Poplars (number 15) is a late eighteenth-century building. Similarly, the former George Inn, which was run by George James Marshall in 1849 and closed in 1904, dated from the late eighteenth century—this stood on the corner of GEORGE STREET and Gospelgate and was demolished to make way for a block of flats in the 1980s.

By 1839, most of the remaining gaps in the street had been filled in by new buildings and Gospelgate was home to a number of businesses and noteworthy individuals in the nineteenth and twentieth centuries. A snapshot of the businesses on this street in the early nineteenth century is available in Pigot & Co.'s 1828–9 Directory. This lists an auctioneer named Charles Bingley operating from 'Goose Pool', along with a boot maker (Joseph Healey), a bricklayer (John Smith), a dressmaker (Elizabeth Wakelin), a baker (Joseph Edman, who continued to operate from here into the 1840s and who was also listed as one of the millers at the HORNCASTLE ROAD mill), a painter (Thomas Booth), a shopkeeper (George Cuthbert), the town crier (Richard Wakelin), a school (run by Sarah Cook), and a stone and marble mason. The latter was Thomas Ablewhite, whose yard was next door to the yard of the Greyhound Inn—his premises can be seen on William Brown's mid-nineteenth-century Panorama (first shown in 1847 and last updated in 1856), and he was the master mason in charge of the 1844 repairs to the spire of St James's Church. From 1850 through to at least 1861, the business was run by his widow, Maria Ablewhite. Over the course of the nineteenth century a number of other significant businesses operated from Gospelgate. One was Pye & Waite's, attorneys (later Waite & Son), who were based here from at least 1835 through to 1868. Others included a coach making business, run by Francis North in 1835; a porter and ale merchant, Fuller & Co., listed here in 1835 (see further NORTHGATE); and a number of schools, including the Preparatory School for Boys at The Poplars, run by Miss Carrie Surfleet and her sister (which ran from the 1890s until 1950), Miss Sarah Cook's ladies' boarding school (listed on Goose Pool in 1828–9), and Miss Mary Thorpe's ladies' school (listed in 1868).

Notable individuals living and working on Gospelgate in the same period include James Fowler, the architect and designer of numerous buildings in the town, including the 1868–9 Grammar School and Bedehouses, the latter of which face onto Gospelgate (see further SCHOOLHOUSE LANE). Fowler is listed at 12 Gospelgate (now number 24) in 1868 and is described as an architect on Gospelgate in the 1872 and 1889 directories. Just a little further down Gospelgate and set back from the road was Ivy Cottage (now number 28), the house of the bookseller J. W. Goulding and his son, Richard W. Goulding. R. W. Goulding, d. 1929, was one of Louth's most important local historians, the publisher of Goulding's Almanac, and the proprietor—after his father—of Goulding's bookshop on MERCER ROW. The most famous inhabitant of Gospelgate, however, was the woodcarver Thomas Wilkinson Wallis, who won medals for his carving at the Great Exhibition of 1851, the 1855 Paris Exhibition and the London Great Exhibition of 1862. His house was then numbered 10 Gospelgate (now number 22) and it currently bears a blue plaque: he lived here from 1851, when he bought the house for £300, until he died in 1903. Louth Museum has a fine collection of his pieces.

In the early twentieth century, Gospelgate still had a number of businesses located on it, notably a refreshment rooms, run by Sarah Campion, at 3 Gospelgate; John W. Morely's fried fish shop; Reginald Henry Fowler's architect's business; and a poultery shop, run by Edwin Swaby. However, it is now primarily a residential street, with housing developments where the former George Inn stood (Grosvenor Court, now entered off George Street); in what was once Abelwhite's Yard; in CHURCH CLOSE where there was formerly a soap factory (see further Church Close); in SOMERSBY COURT at the western end of Gospelgate (this development replaced buildings used by the Grammar School, most recently as exam halls, which were in turn built on the gardens of Westgate House); and opposite the yard of the Greyhound Inn where modern maisonettes now stand (Sarah Campion's refreshment rooms once stood here). In recent years, the St John Ambulance building at the east end of Gospelgate has closed too, because of falling membership, with it being reported in 2007 that there were moves to convert the vacant building into a house.

GOSPELGATE MEWS

Gospelgate Mews was is marked as Misdale's Row on the 1889 OS map of the town and as Capor Row on the 1808 plan and 1839 map of Louth. The origin of the name Capor Row is obscure; however, the name Misdale's Row, or Misdale Row, which was still in use in the 1980s, presumably derives from that of a former landlord or owner of this short terrace of houses. In the mid-nineteenth century, Misdale was a very rare name indeed, with all the bearers of it living in Bradford or Leeds in 1851. However, there was a Thomas Misdale living in Louth in the late eighteenth and early nineteenth centuries, whose will is dated 1812, and it consequently seems plausible that this man, or a relative of his, is the person after whom the row was eventually named. The houses of Capor Row/Misdale's Row clearly already existed by 1808, when Espin marked them and their separate yards and privies on his plan of the town, and the row can perhaps be observed, with the eye of faith, on Armstrong's less accomplished plan of 1778 too. Inhabitants of this row in 1871 included Sarah Stocks, a woman of independent means; Richard Whitton, a solicitor's clerk; William Huggard, a newspaper printer; J. W. Goulding, a printer and bookbinder (who later moved into Ivy House on

GOSPELGATE); Thomas Sedgewick, a cabinet maker; and Henry Samuel, who derived his income from houses and land.

GRAY'S ROAD & GRAY'S COURT

Gray's Road runs from CISTERNGATE down to a junction with SPAW LANE, with Gray's Court running south-west from it. Neither road is depicted on Espin's 1808 plan of Louth. However, by the end of the 1830s, the northernmost of the terraced houses that eventually ran down the western side of Gray's Road had been built, with these and a short lane being marked as 'Prospect Row' on the 1839 map of the town. This area of town seems to have developed rapidly over the next five years, to judge from William Brown's sketches of 1844. By this point, Gray's Road would appear to have come into existence, with buildings now all along most of the eastern side of what is now Gray's Road down to the junction with Spaw Lane. On the western side, buildings now extended down to the junction with Gray's Court, and the area north of Gray's Court had also been developed in this period, with some buildings to the south too.

Brown's final Panorama, first exhibited in 1847 and last updated in 1856, shows housing then all along the eastern side of the road, along with buildings and gardens to the west of the southern part of Gray's Road, an area that his 1844 sketch had left curiously blank, despite the fact that one or more buildings were actually shown here on the 1808, 1834 and 1839 plans and map of the town. On the final Panorama, the buildings depicted in this area include one with a tall chimney and a small waterwheel next to the river, at the end of Spaw Lane. Quite what this was is not entirely clear from the painting. In 1852 Brown had noted the erection of a bath house in 'Spa-lane', which the 1889 OS map marks in this position, so it may well be that the buildings, chimney and waterwheel that he paints here were associated with this—see further Spaw Lane on the baths and spa spring; it may also be relevant that the owner of this, John Harrison, is listed both as the proprietor of Louth Baths and as a machinist in the 1860s.

By the late nineteenth century, there appears to have been some remodelling of the area to the south of Gray's Court and west of Gray's Road, with at least one new house built, and this was true again in the period after the Louth Flood of 1920. In the twentieth century, the terraced houses of Prospect Row, those on both sides of Gray's Road down to the Gray's Court junction, and the houses north of Gray's Court were also all demolished—they were replaced, on the western side of Gray's Road, by flats/maisonettes and sheds associated with new housing on Cisterngate.

Aside from the spa baths at the bottom of the Gray's road (see Spaw Lane), only a handful of businesses and trades are recorded on these roads in the nineteenth century. In 1856, the only listing is for a dressmaker named Mary Ann Willman, and in 1861 and 1868 there was only Harrison's Louth Baths and a cowkeeper called Joseph Cash, who was based on Gray's Court in 1861.Another cowkeeper, named William Enderby, is listed on both Gray's Court and Gray's Road in 1872 and was still living there in 1891 (at 6 Gray's Court); Enderby apparently used to have a donkey-drawn milk cart, in which he would go off down Holmes Lane (HIGH HOLME ROAD) to milk the cows each morning. After this, no businesses or tradesmen are listed other than the baths, which continued to function into the early twentieth century. Early inhabitants of the terraced houses on these roads were, as might be expected, working class and generally poor—in 1851 there were, for example, three journeyman tailors, a bricklayer, a porter, two laundresses, a hairdresser, a dressmaker, a charwoman, an agricultural labourer, a nail maker, a pauper, and a Chelsea Pensioner living on these roads then. At the end of the nineteenth century the situation was little different, with the inhabitants in 1891 including two seamstresses (Annie Cockings and Susannah Wolfe, 10 and 18 Gray's Road), two charwomen (Catherine Crown and Francis Midgley, 3 and 4 Gray's Court), a labourer at the gas works (Charles Spalding, 4a Gray's Court), two maltsters (Cornelius Dixon and Henry Murphy, 19 and 4 Gray's Road), a carter (David Bristow, 12 Gray's Road), five laundresses (for example, Eliza Ashton and Elizabeth Parker, 14 and 6 Gray's Road), a leather tanner (George Parker, 8 Gray's Road), and a lodging-house keeper (Harriet Preston, 3 Gray's Road).

GRAYE DRIVE

Graye Drive is part of the 'Weavers Tryst' housing estate that was begun in the late 1990s. It links ERESBIE ROAD, the spine of the development, with PASTURE DRIVE, part of an earlier housing estate off of STEWTON LANE. The estate is built on land that was originally part of Louth's medieval open South Field, although most of the area had been enclosed prior to the 1801 Enclosure Act. The roads within it appear to be named after local worthies of the sixteenth and seventeenth centuries—a Milis Graye was Warden of Louth in 1562, 1563, 1570 and 1579.

GRESLEY ROAD

Gresley Road is a new residential road running north from STEWTON LANE. Up until the Enclosure Award of 1805, the land that Gresley Road stands on was still part of the town's old open South Field, and medieval ridge and furrow from this has been observed on aerial photographs of this area. In 1876, the railway line from Louth to Bardney was opened and this ran across the land now occupied by Gresley Road until 1956. In the mid–late twentieth century, factories were located on land at the eastern end of Gresley Road—after the removal of the railway, an entranceway leading to these was created where the modern entrance to Gresley Road now is. In addition to houses, Gresley Road is also the location for Keily House, the offices of the New Linx Housing Trust that manages homes in the area.

GRIMSBY ROAD

The section of Grimsby Road from FANTHORPE LANE to BRIDGE STREET is generally believed to follow the line of the ancient Barton Street, also known as Louth Street, a prehistoric and later routeway running north–south along the eastern edge of the Wolds (see further CANNON STREET). The old local name for this stretch of road was Hollowgate, referring to the steep banks either side of the road. This name was used for the road in Pigot & Co.'s directories for 1828–9 and 1835, and it is preserved in the name Hollowgate Head on Grimsby Road. It has been suggested that the place named 'the holes' that was on 'Bartonstrete' in 1433 was near to the modern Hollowgate Head—Richard Barker was fined 2d for 'digging the lord's soil' there in that year, according to the Manor Court Rolls. In the modern period, the section of the Grimsby Road north of Fanthorpe Lane (sometimes called Fotherby Road) replaced Fanthorpe Lane and Barton Street as the main routeway leading north from Louth—this route appears to be shown on Armstong's 1778 map of the Louth area, and in 1803 it became the Scartho and Louth Turnpike, with a toll-bar at Brackenborough Corner. Before the creation of this turnpike, it could apparently take two days for a cart to travel from Louth to Grimsby, because of the poor state of the roads then.

The deepest pit in Louth was the lime pit off Grimsby Road, where WOODVALE RISE now is. Chalk was extracted from this pit to burn for agricultural lime, and the lime pit here was run by Jabez Paddison and his widow, Sarah Jane Paddison, from the 1870s through to World War Two, when it was the last lime pit to be worked in Louth. In 1828–9 and 1835, this lime pit is listed as being run by William Dixon, who was succeeded by Joseph Dixon by 1842. Immediately to the south of this was St Mary's Lime Works. This belonged to George Tatam and was originally listed, in 1828–9, as being on 'Hollow gate'; however, by 1835 its directory address was given as 'Limekiln Hill' (sometimes thought to be a name for part of Grimsby Road) and in 1841 and 1852 it was listed as being simply on 'Grimsby road'. It was subsequently run by Thomas Clapham through until the end of the nineteenth century, with Clapham being listed as having both St Mary's Pit and the LONDON ROAD pit in 1872, as well as being the landlord of The Wheatsheaf on WESTGATE. In 1764, Christian Frederick Esberger mentions visiting Mr Fatchit's Lime Kiln on his way into Louth from Grimsby—Fatchit was presumably an earlier owner of one of these two pits, though which one is entirely uncertain. In 1794, the same man, or a relative of his, appears to have still been in charge of the lime pit, as a William Fatchitt is listed as a Louth 'lime-burner' in that year. Another business located on Grimsby Road in the nineteenth century was John and Robert Smith's building and bricklaying firm, listed on the road from the 1850s to the 1870s. Interestingly, they were not the only firm doing this on Grimsby Road, as George Tatam also undertook bricklaying from his Grimsby road site, being listed as a bricklayer there from 1828–9 through until 1856. Finally, there was also an inn on the west side of the road near to the lime pits, called Pelham's Pillar Arms. Whether this was the same as the beerhouse at 9a Grimsby Road that William Walkington was the tapster or innkeeper of in 1871 is, however, unclear.

With regard to the residential usage of this street, in 1808 there appear to have been a very limited number of buildings here, with most looking to be associated with the St Mary's Lime Works. The only real exceptions are two buildings either side of HIGH HOLME ROAD where it joins Grimsby road, but their occupants in that period are unknown. By the 1830s, however, the White House—or White Hall—had been built. This property was occupied by Mrs Ann Elizabeth Paddison in the mid-nineteenth century and is shown in detail on William Brown's mid-nineteenth-century Panorama. Subsequently, it was the home of Charles Goodwin Smith, of C. G. Smith & Sons (Louth Soap Works), from at least the early 1870s through to 1890—Smith traded from 26 UPGATE and had a soap factory in CHURCH CLOSE. From the mid-nineteenth century, housing also began to be developed further north on Grimsby Road. So, for example, on Brown's sketches of 1844 there were no houses beyond the one that stood on the north corner of the junction of High Holme Road and Grimaby Road, but by the time of the finished Panorama (last updated in 1856), residential properties had begun to appear in this area. By 1889, there were terraces all up the eastern side of the road and also some to the north of the lime pits on the western side. By the mid-twentieth century, there had been a further expansion of housing northwards on both sides of the road up to Fanthorpe Lane, and further north still on the west side, almost to the current junction with NORTH HOLME ROAD, with John Darke's Garage filling one of the remaining gaps on the west side by the late 1960s. By this point, houses were also beginning to be built on and around the former sites of the lime works, further south on Grimsby Road, a process completed in the 1990s (see Woodvale Rise). The period around the turn of the millennium also saw new houses built on the eastern side of Grimsby Road north of Fanthorpe Lane, filling in the last remaining gaps here too and replacing the Poultry Houses that had been located opposite the garage from at least the 1960s.

In general, Grimsby Road appears to have been a relatively peaceful part of the town in the nineteenth and twentieth centuries, aside from the occasional accident or freak weather event. For example, in 1967 a lorry demolished the iron bridge over the road at Hollowgate; in 1947, the winter was so severe that the snow drifts lay higher than the telegraph poles at the bottom of Grimsby Road; and in 1849 a house fire saw neighbours drag a five year old child to safety, only to be accused of assaulting the girl by her mother! One major exception came in 1941, when 32 Grimsby Road was destroyed by German bombs, leaving six people dead and three injured.

GROSVENOR ROAD & GROSVENOR CRESCENT

Grosvenor Road and Grosvenor Crescent form part of a large mid–late twentieth-century housing estate located to the south of KEDDINGTON ROAD. It runs from Grosvenor Road through to ADA WAY via CHARLES AVENUE, with Grosvenor Road and Crescent being the first parts of this estate to be constructed. These two roads had begun to be developed by 1950 and their northern portions are depicted on the 1951 OS map of the town; by 1959, the southern part of both roads had been laid out and they were nearly fully developed. They were constructed in a field to the west and south of the nineteenth-century Grosvenor House and take their names from it. Grosvenor House was home to William Hodson, a man of private means, in 1891, and it was probably also the unnamed property occupied by John Fanthorpe in 1871 and 1881 (a retired glass and china dealer) and Frederick Forrest in 1861 (surveyor of taxes for the Inland Revenue).

HALFPENNY LANE

Halfpenny Lane runs from HORNCASTLE ROAD through to Hallington, passing by the southern entrance to Hubbard's Hills. A large number of worked flints of Neolithic or Bronze Age date have been found to the north of this road and the east of the entrance to Hubbard's Hills, and these may represent a settlement site of that period. Another notable archaeological find from this area is a possible medieval oven or kiln, located to the south of the road near the tollhouse. Earlier names for Halfpenny Lane apparently include Hallington Beck Lane and Whitworth Hill Road. The steep eastern side of Hubbard's Hills valley, to the north of Halfpenny Lane, was originally called Whitworth Hill or Whitford Hill—it was renamed Hubbard's Hill after the tenant farmer Alexander Hubbard, who died in 1793—and the name Whitworth Hill Road must derive from this. However, it is interesting to note that the name Whitworth/Whitford Hill actually in turn derives from the name of the ford that used to be on Halfpenny Lane, where the road crossed

104

the Hallington Beck at the south end of Hubbard's Hills. This ford was still present in 1840, when James William Wilson drew the lane and showed a white chalk ford there, but had been replaced by a brick bridge by the end of the nineteenth century. It was first mentioned in 1507, when John Chapman of Thorpe Hall (LINCOLN ROAD) was said, in an inquisition post mortem, to have owned closes on the north side of 'the water having its course from Whitwath to Lowth', and the name Whitwath (Whitworth) means literally the 'white ford', from Old Norse *vath*, 'ford'.

At the eastern end of the lane is the old tollhouse of the Louth–Horncastle turnpike. The turnpike was opened in 1770, with a tollhouse on Stanmore Hill, but Stanmore tollhouse was moved to its present position in 1781 to prevent the illegal use of Halfpenny Lane. In the 1830s and 1840s, the Stanmore toll-bar took tolls averaging £222 a year, rising to £246 in the early 1860s. The small car park at the southern entrance to Hubbard's Hills is first shown on the 1968 OS map of this area, but the steep path down from the top of the eastern hills to the southern entrance is much older. In 1786, Charles Chaplin was given permission to 'enclose the Hill call'd Whitford or Hubbard's Hill from the Field of Louth', but was required to leave and grant access to 'two Roads to the Stream or Beck at the Foot of the said Hill', one of which was the path next to Halfpenny Lane. Furthermore, in 1826 the Louth Corporation contributed £5 towards the cost of making a 'foot road' around Hubbard's Hills—this is the current path along the eastern side of the valley that incorporates the steep path down to the southern entrance to the Hills. On Wilson's 1840 drawing of this end of Hubbard's Hills, the path down the hill appears well-worn, as it does on a photograph of 1900 too, by which time the top of the path had been reinforced with wooden steps due to regular use.

HARDWICK CLOSE

Hardwick Close runs off ARUNDEL DRIVE and is part of a large housing estate built to the south of NORTH HOLME ROAD in the 1960s and 1970s. The road is absent from the 1968 OS map but had been fully developed by the mid-1970s. The land it is built on was originally part of Louth's old open North Field.

HAREWOOD CRESCENT

Harewood Crescent runs off CHATSWORTH DRIVE and is part of a large housing estate built to the south of NORTH HOLME ROAD in the 1960s and 1970s. The road is shown as complete on the 1968 OS map, with houses on both sides. The land it is built on was originally part of Louth's old open North Field.

HARRINGTON WAY

Harrington Way runs westwards from HARVEYS LANE and is part of an early twenty-first-century housing estate developed off an eastern extension to MONKS DYKE ROAD. The land that it is built on was originally part of Louth's old open East Field, before this was enclosed under the Enclosure Act of 1801, and medieval ridge and furrow has been observed from this area on aerial photographs.

HARVEYS LANE

Harveys Lane runs north-west from the far eastern end of MONKS DYKE ROAD. In the early twenty-first century, the eastern end of Monks Dyke Road was extended and a new housing estate was developed here, with Harveys Lane being one of the new residential streets of this development. The land that it is built on was originally part of Louth's old open East Field, before this was enclosed under the Enclosure Act of 1801, and medieval ridge and furrow has been observed from this area on aerial photographs.

HAVELOK CLOSE

Havelok Close is located off HAWKER DRIVE, which runs south from STEWTON LANE. This area was fields up until the late twentieth century, when the housing estate here was built. These fields were already enclosed at the start of the nineteenth century, but they had once been part of the old South Field of the town—medieval ridge and furrow from this has been observed on aerial photographs of this area. Havelok Close is presumably named from Havelok the Dane, who appears in medieval tales written in Lincolnshire, the earliest dating from the twelfth century.

HAWKER DRIVE

Hawker Drive was built in the late twentieth century as a new estate on top of the fields that used to be to the south of STEWTON LANE. These fields were already enclosed at the start of the nineteenth century, but they had once been part of the old South Field of the town— medieval ridge and furrow from this has been observed on aerial photographs of this area.

HAWKSMEDE WAY

See SWALLOW DRIVE.

HAWTHORNE AVENUE

Hawthorne Avenue is a residential street running between HIGH HOLME ROAD and CHARLES STREET. In 1844, to judge from William Brown's sketches of that year, Charles Street was simply the access to the brickyard, and the site of Hawthorne Avenue was a field, with a hedgerow and trees to the west. However, by the time that Brown had completed his Panorama (first exhibited in 1847 and last updated in 1856), Charles Street had been laid out and new factory buildings, with a tall chimney, had been built on the high bluff where Hawthorne Avenue meets Charles Street. This was new ironworks of John Sanderson (or Saunderson). Known as New Bridge Hill Iron Works, this iron foundry and agricultural implement maker appears to have still been operating in 1891, although John Saunderson is listed as retired, aged 82, in 1901 and the ironworks had been demolished by 1906, to be make way for the southern part of Hawthorne Avenue.

On the 1906 OS map, only the northernmost and southernmost portions of Hawthorne Avenue are depicted, with only the latter actually marked as Hawthorne Avenue and 'Allotment Gardens' located in the area between the two sections of road. However, the street had clearly been completed by 1911 at the latest, as the terraced houses in the middle section of the street appear in the census of that year. Inhabitants of the street in 1911 included Richard and George Dales, a newspaper compositor and an apprentice motorcycle mechanic, respectively (number 5); Frederick Jarris, a railway engine driver (number 4); Charles Lowis, the caretaker of Hubbard's Hills and an army pensioner (number 10); Arthur Hotchin, a grocer's assistant, who lived with his wife, Sarah Anne, and a boarder named Frank Shaw, a master baker (number 14); Albert Trevor, a foreman in a coalyard (number 22); Thomas Cheetham, a railway locomotive fitter (number 24); and William Trafford Stevenson, a fruit merchant (number 34). At this point, Hawthorne Avenue was only really built up on the eastern side of the street, with mainly open ground shown on the western side of the street in the 1950s, aside from numbers 1–9 at the south end on this side: these appear to have been amongst the first houses built on this road, being present on the 1906 OS map. By the 1960s, however, the gaps on the eastern side began to be filled in with modern bungalows, a process completed by the end of the century.

HAZEL GROVE

Hazel Grove runs south-west from SYCAMORE DRIVE, which is the spine of a late twentieth-century housing estate to the south of WOOD LANE. Each road in this estate is named after a different type of tree.

HIGH HOLME ROAD

High Holme Road was formerly known as Holmes Lane, and it has been suggested that this street-name derives from 'The Houlmes', the name of 'one pasture in the north field of Louth' that John Bradley bequeathed to Francis Bradley, his wife, in 1590. The old North Field of the town lay to the north of Holmes Lane and the road appears to have been largely undeveloped until the 1830s, probably consisting primarily of rough pasture land and allotments, aside from a couple of buildings located at or near the junction with GRIMSBY ROAD. The 1830s saw this beginning to change, with the construction of the new Union Workhouse on Holmes Lane, at the top of BROADBANK, in 1837. Built at a cost of £6,000, it was intended to house up to 300 paupers, although there were only 132 inhabitants in 1841 and 179 in 1851. The workhouse closed in 1935 and reopened as the County Infirmary in

1938; its buildings now form part of Louth Hospital. The 1834 plan and the 1839 map of the town indicate that the same period also saw building activity to the south of Holmes Lane between Broadbank and Grimsby Road, along with the foundation of UNION STREET there.

To the east of the Workhouse, the 1839 map of Louth shows a windmill and buildings in a plot to the east of the Union Workhouse. William Brown's sketch from the spire of St James's Church similarly depicts a tower windmill, buildings and gardens of some sort on this site in 1844 (although Brown shows the structures closer to the road than they appear on the 1839 map). Positioned near the top of Broadbank, this was presumably the mill on Broadbank that is listed in the 1841 directory as belonging to the Topham family, whose bakery was on EASTGATE. By 1856, this windmill and its associated buildings had gone, replaced by a large, magnificent house called High Holme, with a walled greenhouse at the end of a long garden. This was the residence of Henry Hynman Allenby, landed proprietor and Justice of the Peace (d. 1869), and it was later used by the Misses Anne and Caroline Chappell, who ran a ladies' boarding school here from the 1870s through until the early twentieth century. The road eventually became known as High Holme Road due to the presence of this building here, although the building is now long gone—it looks to have been demolished in the 1970s, with its site currently functioning as a staff car park for Louth Hospital. Further east still was George Moody's nursery, founded in 1830. Later also known as Louth Nursery and High Holme Nurseries, it was located where MILL LANE now is, with the house originally standing to the east of the junction between this road and High Holme Road. Visible on both Brown's sketches of 1844 and his final Panorama of 1856, George Moody's High Holme Nurseries was still listed here in the 1937 directory and continued to be marked as a nursery on the OS maps of the 1950s. By the end of the 1960s, however, the original nursery grounds had been built over by new housing along Mill Lane and the new HOLMES CLOSE. Also depicted on Brown's sketch and his finished painting is what appears to be another nursery at the east end of the road, by the junction with NEWBRIDGE HILL; certainly, this is what was there in 1889. Finally, in the 1850s John Walmsley had a famously smelly bone crushing mill on Holmes Lane—in 1857, he was charged by the residents of Holmes Lane and the neighbourhood with 'causing a nuisance injurious to health, by boiling bones and offal upon certain premises belonging to him, situate in Holmes-lane.' Walmsley had to enter into sureties of £200 in response to this charge, and promised to abate the nuisance as much as possible.

In addition to these businesses, Brown's sketch of the road also depicts a small number of what look to be residential properties on Holmes Lane east of the Workhouse. In 1844, these were all on the south side of the road, but by 1856 residential properties had started to appear on the north side with the erection of High Holme. By the late nineteenth century, there was an increasing scatter of residential properties along both sides of the road, although there were still large undeveloped areas—one of these was used as the club field by Louth & District Athletic Club in 1868, and Louth United Football Club had a ground on Holmes Lane from 1869. By 1906, the process of house building along this road had accelerated still further. The nursery on the south side of the road at its eastern end had gone, to be replaced by a long terrace of houses, with some new houses built on the northern side of the road opposite these too and more new terraces at the western end of the street, between High Holme and Mill Lane. The aftermath of the Louth Flood of 1920 saw another of the fields on High Holme Road developed, when it was given over to house the refugees from the flood, first in 'Canvas Town' and 'Hut Town' and then, from 1930, in the houses of THE CRESCENT. By the 1960s, there was housing along almost the entire road, with the new High Holme Road Secondary School (now Cordeaux School, see NORTH HOLME ROAD), opened in 1956, positioned behind these on the north side.

Aside from problems involving the bone crushing mill, High Holme Road appears to have been a reasonable peaceful part of Louth in the mid-nineteenth century, perhaps because of its still predominantly agricultural character then. There were, however, a couple of exceptions to this. One occurred in 1851, when a certain Joseph Hutton, tailor, and Thomas Dowse, groom, were both charged with indecently exposing their persons in Holmes Lane 'with intent to insult some female children'—they were both sentenced to hard labour as rogues and vagabonds. Quite what was happening here is not entirely clear. Other flashers of this period in Louth tended to operate on their own, not in pairs (see BRIDGE STREET, for example). Moreover, Joseph Hutton was a 40 year old married tailor with three children on Eastgate in 1851 and Thomas Dowse was probably the 30 year old unmarried man of that name who was staying with family on MONKS DYKE ROAD in 1851, making a youthful prank seem less likely. Another curious incident was reported in 1850. This involved an alleged assault on a shoemaker from WALKERGATE named Edward Rowson. He was apparently fond of spying on 'the proceedings' of couples taking moonlight walks in quiet places in the town, and decided to turn his hand to blackmail with one couple, saying he would 'tell all the town of... the proceedings of the two lovers' if they did not pay him. Quite what he had seen is left unsaid, but the man he tried to blackmail reportedly became so indignant that he thrashed Edward Rowson severely. The court decided to discharge the defendant, William Fallow, due to the reprehensible conduct of Rowson.

HILL RISE

Hill Rise runs east from GRIMSBY ROAD and is a late twentieth-century residential close built after the 1990 OS map was surveyed. The site was previously occupied by Poultry Houses from at least the 1960s through to the 1980s.

HILL TERRACE

Hill Terrace runs east from LINDEN WALK and is a late nineteenth-century development. In 1891, inhabitants included Elizabeth Duncan Jones, from New South Wales—who was of independent means and employed a governess, Bessie Gallaher, for her three children—and George Ranshaw, draper. The first boarding house for the Girl's Grammar School was located on Hill Terrace until 1908, when it moved to The Limes on WESTGATE.

HOLMES CLOSE

A mid-twentieth-century road, laid out on land previously used by High Holme Nurseries (off HIGH HOLME ROAD). Holmes Close is depicted on the 1968 OS map, by which point it was fully developed.

HORNCASTLE ROAD

Horncastle Road was administered as part of the Louth to Horncastle turnpike from 1770, with the tollhouse for this stretch of turnpike originally on Stanmore Hill, before it was moved to its present position on the corner of HALFPENNY LANE in 1781 to prevent the illegal use of this road. The line of Horncastle Road ran past old enclosures and through the open South Field of the town before the 1805 Enclosure Award. As such, it is unsurprising that traces of both medieval ridge and furrow and enclosure boundaries have been observed on both sides of the road—for example, medieval ridge and furrow was recorded by an earthworks survey on land to the rear of numbers 10–18 Horncastle Road, and medieval ridge and furrow, an enclosure and a boundary were seen near to the water treatment plant on aerial photographs. This primarily agricultural character of the area around Horncastle Road remained apparent into the nineteenth century and beyond. On both the 1839 map of the town and William Brown's 1844 sketch, made from the spire of St James's Church, Horncastle Road appears almost entirely devoid of buildings, the only exceptions being a single building on the south side of the road and a five-sail windmill and associated buildings on the north side. Little had changed by the time of Brown's finished Panorama, first exhibited in 1847 and last updated in 1856, which shows those parts of Horncastle Road visible from St James's spire to be still entirely surrounded by fields, aside from the above buildings.

With regard to the windmill, this is believed to have functioned from the 1820s through until 1910. In 1835 and 1841, it was run by Edman, Griffin & Pearson, presumably the Joseph Edman, John Griffin and William Pearson who had bakeries on GOSPELGATE and EASTGATE at that time. In 1851 John Chatterton was the miller here, and in 1861 the mill was being run by a journeyman miller named John Dobson, who was recorded as a miller on RIVERHEAD in 1851 and 1871. In the mid-1870s, William Scarborough took over the windmill on Horncastle Road, having previously worked from the watermill on Maiden Row (CHURCH STREET). Another major nineteenth-century feature of Horncastle Road is the reservoir, located to the south-west of the windmill, which was established here in 1872–3 and so post-dates Brown's Panorama. This was built by the Louth Water Works Company to supply water to the town using gravity, with the water being pumped up to the reservoir from the waterworks that had been established near the watermill on CROWTREE LANE.

On the 1889 OS map, Horncastle Road still appears largely undeveloped, as it does in 1906 too, although there were a few new properties established along the road by that time, such as Thorpe View and The Bungalow on the south side. The real development of Horncastle Road as a residential street only really begins in the mid-twentieth century, however, when houses were established on both sides of the road from the junction with EDWARD STREET down to the former site of the windmill. By the late 1960s, the housing on the south side had been developed further, with the establishment of VANESSA ROAD, HUNTER PLACE and LINDA CRESCENT, along with tennis courts, a playing field and a pavilion to the south of these that belonged to King Edward VI Grammar School. The same period also saw the establishment of the water treatment plant at the southern end of Horncastle Road, opposite the old tollhouse. The succeeding decades saw continued, if less extensive, development in places along the road, although there are still significant green areas on either side of it, with fields along a large proportion of the south side of the road still and the golf course, reservoir and Grammar School fields on the north.

The availability of large open areas on Horncastle Road led to it being fairly frequently used for shows and similar events in the past. The Lincolnshire Show, before it purchased its own site to use as a showground in 1958, moved around the county, and in 1909 it was held in fields off Horncastle Road. Indeed, this was not the first time that the fields here had been used for the Lincolnshire Agricultural Show—the show was held here in 1899, 1889 and 1878 too, in four fields belonging to Joseph Cusworth (a grocer and Justice of the Peace based in the MARKET PLACE) that lay adjacent to Horncastle Road. In 1878, a procession of ornamental flags and banner poles and triumphal arches led the way from the railway station on RAMSGATE through to the showground on Horncastle Road, and the town was reported to have been 'very prettily decorated'. In general, Horncastle Road appears to have been relatively peaceful in the nineteenth century, although it was one of the places that suffered from the noted Louth flasher, William Hopper. In 1851, Hopper—a bricklayer who was described as 'a disgusting brute in human shape'—indecently exposed his person on Horncastle Road twice in one week. Hopper seems to have had some sort of compulsion relating to this, as this was the third time he had been convicted of the offence (see BRIDGE STREET and EASTGATE), and on the previous occasion he had been flogged and sentenced to one year of hard labour. For his offences on Horncastle Road, Hopper was sentenced to another flogging and another year on the treadmill of Louth House of Correction (on Eastgate), and he was an inmate there at the time of the 1851 census. Even this didn't persuade him to desist, however, and by 1858 he was once again up in front of the court on a charge of indecent exposure.

HUNTER PLACE

Hunter Place is a street of residential housing that runs off VANESSA ROAD, to the south of HORNCASTLE ROAD. Established by the late 1960s, the housing here was built on what had previously been agricultural land. From the mid-twentieth century, tennis courts, a playing field and a pavilion were located to the south of this road for the use of King Edward VI Grammar School—these were accessed by a footpath from Horncastle Road that passed by the eastern end of Hunter Place. The Pavilion there has since been demolished.

HURTON'S YARD

See PAWNSHOP PASSAGE.

IRISH HILL

Irish Hill was laid out as a road between 1808 and 1834 and runs from WESTGATE up to CROWTREE LANE. In 1834, Bayley depicted two L-shaped blocks of buildings on the west side of the street on his plan of Louth. One of these lay on the corner of Westgate and Irish Hill, and this block is shown remodelled and more extensive on the 1839 map of the town, when it is labelled as a foundry (a label also present on William Brown's 1844 sketch of these buildings). On Brown's finished Panorama, first exhibited in 1847 and last updated in 1856, this block of buildings is marked as the works belonging to William Grounsell. He was first listed as a iron founder and machine maker on Westgate in 1835—although the entrance to the works was actually at the bottom of

114

Irish Hill, where there is now a driveway—and his firm of agricultural implement makers continued to be listed on Westgate through until 1861 (William Grounsell died in 1859 and the iron foundry and works on the corner of Irish Hill and Westgate had been demolished by the time of the 1889 OS map). It is possible that this is also where John Saunderson, an iron founder and machine maker listed on Westgate in 1828–9, had his works. Certainly, there is no other iron foundry marked on the nineteenth-century maps of Westgate, nor is any other obvious on Brown's Panorama. On the other hand, Saunderson was still listed as a machine maker on Westgate (though not an iron founder) in 1835, when Grounsell was also listed there as a machine maker and iron founder. Furthermore, in 1841 Saunderson was no longer listed, but there was now a John Hill listed as an iron founder on Westgate in addition to Grounsell. The implication would seem to be either that there was another iron foundry and machine maker's on or just off Westgate, whose location is unknown, or that Grounsell and the others shared the same site in this period, something which might account for its apparent expansion between 1834 and 1839.

The site of the block of buildings depicted further south on Irish Hill in 1834 also looks to have been completely redeveloped by 1839. Previously it had been simply an L-shaped block, but by 1839 it took the form of two rows of cottages facing each other across a narrow lane that ran westwards from Irish Hill. These cottages are labelled as Westgate Cottages on the 1839 map and were identified as such throughout the nineteenth century. These were cheap working-class houses, and in 1841 the fourteen cottages here were inhabited by two journeyman blacksmiths (Richard Malim and Henry Andrews), a dressmaker (Kezia Fox), a carter (James Harrison), five labourers (John Broomhead, John Crowson, George Bromby, William Luddington and Thomas Reetham), a journeyman bricklayer (Thomas Hill), a journeyman miller (John Jekyll), and an 80 year old living on her own means (Ann Dring). It is worth noting that all but one of the inhabitants of Westgate Cottages in 1841 were said to have been born in England (the sole exception being the wife of Richard Malim, who was born in Scotland), and that almost all of these were, in fact, born in Lincolnshire (the exceptions here being the wife and family of Thomas Hill).

In 1851, there was a similar mix of working-class people living in Westgate Cottages, including a significant number of labourers (especially farm labourers), a groom, a joiner, two journeyman blacksmiths, two housekeepers and a beggar. However, six of the families living there then were recorded as Irish in origin, including those of Bridget Money (a widow whose son, Michael, was an agricultural labourer), George Curran (a farm labourer who headed a household of ten people) and Thomas Reany or Rainey (a farm labourer who headed a household with fifteen people living in one cottage). Furthermore, seven of the nine families living in the cottages were listed as Irish by 1861, and by 1871 this had increased to nine out of twelve families in the terraces here, with fourteen of the inhabitants then listing 'agricultural labourer' as their occupation. This increasing domination of the cottages by Irish families led to the adoption of the name Irish Hill for the road here. The cottages were demolished in the mid-twentieth century, with new houses subsequently built both on their former site and along the opposite side of the road, which had previously remained undeveloped (it is shown as a nursery associated with a house fronting onto Westgate on Brown's finished Panorama of 1856, and was apparently once run by George Tuxworth).

The inhabitants of Irish Hill made occasional appearances in the local courts during the mid-nineteenth century. For example, in 1851 John Fitzpatrick, James Rainey and Thomas Haggleton, all labourers living in Westgate Cottages, were charged with being drunk and disorderly and resisting the police in SPRING GARDENS. More serious were the events of November 1856. Then, Irishman Martin Monaghan, of Westgate Cottages, was charged by 'a fellow-countryman and neighbour' John Gibbons, with a 'most brutal and unmanly assault' that saw Monaghan bite off the whole of Gibbons' lower lip. The appearance of the victim in court was described as 'horrible', with the whole lip torn away. Apparently, Gibbons had been drinking in 'Pat Kaye's beer-shop in Aswell-hole' (see ASWELL STREET), when Gibbons struck him. Later, when back in Westgate Cottages, he and Monaghan met outside the houses and Monaghan challenged him to a fight, during which he took hold of Gibbons' lip with his teeth and bit it off. Monaghan fled to Hallington, where he was apprehended by the police. He was fined 30s for the injury to Gibbons (equivalent to around £109 today), which he paid and so avoided a short prison sentence.

116

JAMES STREET

James Street (or James' Street) runs from EVE STREET through to RAMSGATE and has its origin in the eighteenth century. James Dunn, a local bricklayer, was leased land in Northgate in 1793 by the Louth Corporation in return for an agreement to spend £1,000 in building 'the new intended road from Padehole [NORTHGATE] to the Navigation'. James Street was the main result of this agreement, being named after James Dunn and labelled as James' Street on the 1808 and 1834 plans of the town, with Eve Street representing the final section of the 'new intended road' that linked the new James Street through to Northgate.

The new road passed close by Louth's recently-constructed carpet factory on its way to Ramsgate and the RIVERHEAD. The carpet factory had been built in 1787 and spanned the River Lud, being powered by two waterwheels. It was first rented to Richard Brumfitt, a carpet manufacturer from Leeds, but in 1790 Adam Eve took over the lease, buying it from Brumfitt for £180 in partnership with two Leeds merchants. This partnership was dissolved in 1799, and in 1801 Adam Eve gained full control of factory, which employed sixty people, including women and children, working on twenty machines. A steam engine was introduced in 1834 and the carpets produced here were highly commended at the 1867 Paris Exhibition. The carpet factory finally closed in 1883, due to competition from steam-powered looms. It was subsequently used by a timber merchant, cabinet maker and chair maker named William Frederick Hoggard, whose firm made all types of chairs and could reportedly construct a Windsor chair every seven minutes. On the 1906 OS map, the building was labelled 'Saw Mill', with a timber yard on the north side, and the firm was still here in 1920, when tree trunks were washed out of Hoggard & Co.'s timber yard into WELLINGTON STREET by the Louth Flood. The carpet factory was still standing in 1956, but by 1968 the part that spanned the river had been taken down. Now nothing remains of the carpet mill aside from footings, and both the former wool warehouse on the north side of James Street and the carpet weaving rooms that lay opposite it on the south side of the street are private dwellings.

James Street, as a planned road, was already well developed on both sides of the road by 1808, fifteen years after Dunn agreed to built it. Of particular note are the cottages that were then located at the eastern end of the street, which were built by Adam Eve for his workers in the carpet factory, and the large house on the south side. This was Ivy House, the home of Adam Eve and his wife from 1794—not only was it surrounded by gardens, but it also had stabling for six horses and a brewhouse of its own. Nonetheless, although it was already extensively developed by the early nineteenth century, James Street has seen significant changes over the succeeding two centuries. For example, the Technical School on James Street was constructed on the former gardens of Ivy House in 1897. This was the first home of the Girls' Grammar in 1903, before it moved to WESTGATE, and Monks' Dyke School used the Technical School as an annexe from 1929 onwards, in order to meet the demand for places. Indeed, in World War Two, 140 pupils used this site after the arrival of the evacuees from Leeds and other Yorkshire towns; the building currently houses the Town & Country Kiddies nursery. Even more noticeable is the run of new, later twentieth-century buildings found all along the northern side of the street, from the supported housing of Maxey Court at the western end (on the site of a number of buildings including Charles Court, which ran north from James Street to the Lud) through to the new James Street Family Practice building— behind a short, mid-twentieth century terrace—and James Court (opposite Ivy House and built in 1982). Moreover, it is worth remembering that James Street was also affected by the Louth Flood of 1920. In particular, the workers' cottages that lined the southern side of the eastern end of James Street were destroyed by the flood, and the housing that was built to replace it here was constructed on an entirely different alignment and facing onto Ramsgate.

With housing down both sides of much of the road, James Street was a major residential area in the nineteenth century—for example, in 1861, over 330 people were living here on the night of the census. They included, unsurprisingly, a number of carpet weavers (seven households), along with paupers (in some quantity), labourers, shoemakers, bricklayers, joiners, bonnet makers, dressmakers, butchers, lodging-house keepers, cabinet makers, and tea dealers, although there were also carpet manufacturers, wine merchants, corn merchants and landed proprietors here too. However, James Street wasn't simply a residential area in the mid-nineteenth century, it was also where a number of businesses were based in addition to the carpet factory. So, in the 1828–9 directory, James Street was the trading location for a bricklayer (Richard

Dyas, who was still working from here in the 1860s), a butcher (Mary Barnes, whose business survived into the 1850s), a plumber (David Scott), and four shopkeepers (Richard Dyas again, Hugh Norton, John Palmer and Thomas Wilson). In 1835, a number of these were still trading from James Street, and they had been joined by a baker (Timothy Topham, who was later based on EASTGATE), a cooper (Charles Tattershall), and a patten maker (William Freeman; pattens were under-shoes of wood and metal designed to be worn strapped beneath the shoes to raise the wearer out of the filth of the streets). There were also three beerhouses listed on James Street in 1835 (run John Hurst, Hugh Norton and Joseph Willman), and the street had gained another one by 1841. By 1856, the commercial aspect of the street had developed still further, with two schools (Ellen Nicholson's and Nathaniel Thomas's) and a poulterer (John Mitchell) amongst the new enterprises on the street, although the number of beerhouses had declined from four to just one (Thomas Dunham, based at number 58).

In the late nineteenth and early twentieth centuries, James Street continued to be a significant residential street within the town, although there was around a sixth fewer residents at the time of the 1891 census than there were a generation earlier. Despite this relative decline, there was still a similar mix of people living on the street then, the major exceptions being the near-absence of carpet weavers—the carpet factory closed in 1883 and only Thomas White's house at 48 James Street still housed people pursuing this trade in 1891—and the absence of people described as paupers. Inhabitants of the street in 1891 included Arthur Johnson, an accountant's clerk (number 103); Robert Drewell and his aunt Ann Cole, a plaster and a bonnet maket (number 69); Catherine Borman, a washerwoman (number 40); Richard Garbutt, a ratter (number 71); John Brader, a railway guard (number 62); Charles Sharpe, a postman (32 James Street); Charles Cotton, a milkman (number 45); Harry Taylor, a butcher (number 46); Charles Harrison, a building contractor (Brook House); Thomas Smith, a bird-scarer (number 50); and a significant number of dressmakers (for example, Christina Donner, number 64) and people 'living on their own means' (for example, Elizabeth Lill and her stepdaughter, number 80, and Elizabeth Eve at number 70). In the same period, the 1889 directory continued to list a number of businesses and tradespersons as operating from James Street. So, Thomas Darnill & Son, who had the brickworks on CHARLES

STREET, operated from 31 James Street in 1891, as did William Frederick Hoggard's chair-making business in the old carpet factory, a builder named Richard Ingram (number 77), two shopkeepers called Ann Nortcliff and Robert Whitton (numbers 30 and 66), and a grocer named Francis Porter (number 22). There was also still a single beer retailer on the street, Job Robinson at number 2. This building had been the place of business of a furniture broker named Thomas Hobbins in 1868 and 1872, but by 1885 it was listed as a beerhouse under the control of Job Robinson (it was also listed as such in 1872, but there are reasons to think that this was a mistake). Robinson was formerly the landlord of the Prince of Wales at 146 Eastgate in 1881 and the keeper of a beerhouse on Northgate in 1882, and by 1891 he had moved his place of business again, this time from 2 James Street to 6 Eve Street, where he remained into the twentieth century.

James Street also makes a number of appearances in the surviving court reports from the mid-nineteenth century. For example, begging seems to have been widespread in mid-nineteenth-century Louth and beggars were fairly frequently apprehended on James Street. In January 1848, one such beggar on James Street was Timothy McGarry, a native of Secunderabad, Hindostan (India), who had a child with him. It was reported that 'the poor fellow... appeared to be a novice at the trade, and quite broken down by misfortune,' to the extent that he managed to elicit sufficient sympathy from the court that he was discharged by the Mayor and given relief from the poor box. Prostitution was also present on James Street around this time, with at least one brothel reported to be operating on James Street in 1851. This had been apparently lately opened 'in a court in James'-street', presumably Charles Court (now the site of Maxey Court). James Street likewise saw its share of thieves in the 1840s and 1850s. For instance, in 1847 two carpet weavers—Henry Smith and George Edwards—were charged with stealing 10d from the till of Jane Brown, a grocer on James Street. Similarly, in October 1856 John Jackson of Nottingham—'a hawker of obscene books and publications'—was charged with stealing a half-crown from Ann Greenfield's grocer's shop on James Street by sleight of hand.

Finally, there are also reports of fights involving the inhabitants of James Street in the mid-nineteenth-century. For example, in August 1850 Simeon Boss and Jonathan Edwards, both of James Street, were charged with stabbing and wounding William Sugden. Sugden claimed that he and Boss were scuffling, when Edwards handed Boss an object with which Boss then stabbed Sugden in the head. Boss denied this, and upon investigation it emerged that Boss and Sugden had quarrelled 'about their wives' and that a 'fair stand up fight' had ensued, during the course of which Sugden had his head knocked 'against the tiles of a hog-stye', with no evidence to support the charge of stabbing. In consequence, Edwards was discharged and Boss was merely required to pay his own costs. The nature of the quarrel between Boss and Sugden 'about their wives' is not stated, but two things are worth noting with regard to this. First, the presence of Jonathan Edwards at the fight between Boss and Sugden is readily explicable, given that Simeon Boss appears to have married Jonathan Edwards' sister, Mary Ann, in June 1849—as such, a quarrel about Boss's wife would also have been one about Edwards's sister (on the Edwards family, see further MONKS DYKE ROAD, where they had a brickyard). Second, Simeon Boss was described in the 1850 court report as a 'Jew hawker of James-street', which marks him out as unusual within a town that appears to have had few non-Christians living in it in the mid-nineteenth-century.

It seems likely that Simeon Boss of James Street was not simply a lone 'Jew hawker' living in Louth, but rather a member of a Jewish family that had settled in the town during the 1840s. Certainly, there was a 'well-known Jew' named Herman Boss, a silversmith and jeweller, living on VICKERS LANE in Louth in the 1840s and 1850s. Herman Boss was born in Berlin and lived in Louth with his wife, Augusta, also born in Berlin. He is first mentioned in 1844 and again in 1848—when he was accused of knowingly receiving stolen goods, with his religion and residence being mentioned in the second court report—and he also appears in the 1851 census on Vickers Lane. Similarly, 'a Jew' named Louis Boss is mentioned in Louth in November 1847, when he was charged with knowingly receiving a stolen silver watch, the property of Thomas Smith of Fulstow (he was found not guilty). As such, we would seem to have evidence for at least one Jewish family in the town in the mid-nineteenth century.

In the 1850s, this family suffered some misfortune, with the death of Simeon Boss in late 1850 and the death of Herman Boss in 1853. Simeon's widow, Mary Ann Boss, returned to live with her parents and was still living there with her brother Jonathan Edwards in 1861 (by which time they lived on Eve Street); she remarried in 1867. Herman's widow, Augusta, appears to have returned to Hull—where Herman Boss had lived before he moved to Louth—to marry Jacob Cohen in March 1857, who was born in Prussia and presumably also a Jew, given his name. In 1861, Jacob and Augusta Cohen were living at 7 NORTHGATE in Louth, along with Nathan Boss (probably Augusta's son from her marriage to Herman, born in 1850), their young children and a German servant, and they ran a watchmaking and jewellery business from this property for a number of years—see further Northgate. It is worth noting that there was one other possible member of the Jewish Boss family in Louth in this period too. This was Morris Louis Boss, who was a jeweller lodging on Walkergate (QUEEN STREET) in 1861 and who lived at 1 SPOUT YARD from 1881. Although his religion is unstated, he too was born in Prussia (around 1835), was a jeweller, and had clearly been in Lincolnshire for some time, as he was father to a boy born in Saltfleet in the 1850s according to the 1881 census, and it consequently seems likely that he was a member of the Boss family discussed above. Morris Louis Boss remained at 1 Spout Yard until his death in 1913, having become a naturalized British citizen in 1895.

JENKINS CLOSE

See ANTHONY CRESCENT & AMANDA DRIVE.

JUBILEE CRESCENT

Jubilee Crescent is located east of BRACKENBOROUGH ROAD and currently contains 117 homes. A small-scale council housing project was completed here in the inter-war years, its name associating it with the Silver Jubilee of George V in 1935. Such council housing projects in Louth had hot water, bathrooms and (from 1930) electricity, and were criticised by some contemporaries as 'workmen's palaces'. The land that Jubilee Crescent was built on was originally part of Louth's old North Field, before the Enclosure Commissioners assigned it (along with the land to both the north and the south) to William Stephenson and William Wright in 1805.

JULIAN BOWER

The name Julian Bower was applied to the crown of the southern hill above Louth from at least the sixteenth century and is thought to refer to a medieval turf maze of some sort that was located on the hilltop there, rather than a Druidical alter of the type imagined by R. S. Bayley in 1834. The first mention of Julian Bower is in relation to the events of the 1536 Lincolnshire Rebellion, when the rebels of Louth mustered at Julian Bower cross on 4 October of that year, suggesting that this site was already a notable landmark. The fact that there was a cross there is also interesting—this would appear to have been a physical cross that was located at Julian Bower, as it is mentioned again in 1544–5, when 3s were paid for the making of a new cross at 'Gelyn Bowar' (equivalent, in terms of a labour cost, to around £750 today). Moreover, another early reference to the site, from 1568–9, refers to the Churchwardens paying for 'Gilian bower' to be dressed (cf. the GATHERUMS & SPRINGSDE for the dressing of the Aswell spring in this period). Taken together, these references suggest that Julian Bower was of some importance to the town in that period.

There are a handful of references to Julian Bower in the following centuries, although many or all of these may be using the name Julian Bower as simply a term for the southern hilltop, rather than referencing any turf maze or cross there. For example, in 1639 a certain Walker was paid 6d for watching at 'Jillion Bower' for the coming of the Earl of Lindsey, and in 1603 it was ordered that 'all whose grounds abut upon the common sewer in Spittle hill laine [probably meaning UPGATE/LONDON ROAD, as modern SPITAL HILL is a nineteenth-century street] leading as far as Gillyon Bower' need to cleanse and flush the sewer that lies against their property. This suggestion that the name Julian Bower ceased to refer to a specific site and instead was used of the whole hilltop is certainly supported by the nineteenth century references to Julian Bower, which saw the name Julian Bower being applied then to the hilltop on both sides of London Road–Upgate.

So, on the one hand, Robert Bayley marked Julian Bower on the eastern side of the road on his 1834 plan of Louth, to the north of where the London Road Cemetery would be later established and to the south of the accessway from that road through to the bottom of BOWLING

GREEN LANE. Similarly, William Brown marked the wooded hilltop on the east side of London Road–Upgate, south of the lime quarry, as Julian Bower on his 1844 sketch of the town; the limeworks on the eastern side of the road were known as the Julian Bower Lime Works in the nineteenth and twentieth centuries; and the site of the London Road Cemetery was known as Julian Bower Hill in the 1850s. On the other hand, the 1889 OS map marks both 'Julian Bower' and a residence called Julian Bower House on the western side of the London Road–Upgate, and this was certainly where the Julian Bower windmill was located, which was run by John Bush Cox in 1849—indeed, the road here was called Julian Bower Road in the nineteenth and twentieth centuries (see below). Equally, a footpath running south from HORNCASTLE ROAD was known as Julian Bower Footpath at the time of the Enclosure Award of 1805. In light of this apparent usage of Julian Bower for the entire crown of the southern hill, it is unclear whether the original Julian Bower maze and cross were located on the west side or the east side of London Road–Upgate, although Bayley's 1834 plan may be the best guide to any surviving local tradition with regard to its location, given that he discussed Julian Bower and its cross in the book that his plan was published in.

The road currently known as Julian Bower, which runs west from what is now the northernmost end of London Road, was known by several different names in the nineteenth century. In 1805, it appears to have been known as Pig Closes Road, but on the detailed 1889 OS map of the town it is marked as Mill Lane. Moreover, it is listed in the local directories as Julian Bower Road from 1872 through into the twentieth century, and in 1849 and 1856 the address of the windmill that was located on this road was given simply as 'Julian bower'. This windmill was already in place at the time of the Enclosure Act of 1801 and it is shown on both William Brown's sketch of 1844 and his final Panorama of 1847–56. It was run by John Bush Cox in 1849, William England in the 1850s and 1860s (who had moved from his bakery on EASTGATE to Julian Bower Hill by 1861), and Samuel Adlard Lowis in 1872. It is also probably the mill that John Holland is recorded as operating on 'Quarry hill' in 1828–9 (he had previously been a miller at the BRIDGE STREET watermill). By 1889, however, the mill was marked as 'disused'.

At the end of the nineteenth century, the only buildings on Julian Bower Road were those associated with the former windmill, Julian

Bower House to the south, and Briar Cottage near to the junction with London Road. Although it hasn't seen significant development since this point, a handful of other properties were constructed on the road in the twentieth century, primarily at its eastern end. Louth Open Air School for sickly children was also based at Julian Bower from June 1922, after the original JAMES STREET premises of this school were damaged in the 1920 flood (it had initially moved to Hubbard's Hills after the flood). This school continued to educate children, up to the age of 11, into the 1930s and 1940s—in 1939, a Miss Bond taught here, and the school finally closed at the end of October 1947. More recently, tennis courts belonging to the Grammar School were constructed in a field bordering onto Julian Bower Lane in the mid-twentieth century, and the allotment gardens to the south of the entrance to the road first appeared on the 1968 OS map.

KEDDINGTON CRESCENT

Keddington Crescent is a mid-twentieth century housing estate, located to the north of KEDDINGTON ROAD, which was completed by the time of the 1951 OS map. The road known as LIME GROVE, which runs north from Keddington Road, was originally part of the Keddington Crescent, but was renamed in the 1970s when the area to the west of Keddington Crescent began to be developed. Previously, this area had been partly occupied by the nineteenth-century Eastfield House (known as Elm Court in the 1960s), but this was demolished in the 1970s and new houses were built on its site, facing onto what was now known as Lime Grove. The area on the west of Lime Grove that lay to the north of the site of Eastfield House was a caravan park in the mid-1970s, but had become housing by the end of the 1980s—see BEECH GROVE.

KEDDINGTON ROAD

Keddington Road (or Keddington Lane) runs east from NEWBRIDGE HILL and HIGH HOLME ROAD, continuing the line of High Holme Road. It was first recorded at the time of the Enclosure Act of 1801 and is very likely to have been well-established by that point, as it forms the main route eastwards from Louth to Keddington and Alvingham. Before enclosure, it ran through the open fields of Louth, and traces of medieval ridge and furrow field systems have been observed to both the north and the south of the road from aerial photographs. Enclosure saw two major changes, aside from the ending of the open fields and their replacement with fields and allotments belonging to single owners. The first was that the junction where Newbridge Hill, High Holme Road, Keddington Road and BRACKENBOROUGH ROAD all met was altered, so that the last of these started around 200 metres to the north-east. The second was that a kink in Keddington Road was introduced at the point where it left Louth parish, as the Enclosure Commissioners for the two parishes assigned slightly different alignments to the road.

Initially, Keddington road would have had an almost entirely agricultural character along its length, with only two households on the road in the 1841 census, both those of market gardeners (Thomas Sleight and Charles Walker; note, a nursery is marked on this road on the 1824 OS map). William Brown's sketch of the road, made in 1844 from the spire of St James's Church, shows this character well, with the road being nearly entirely devoid of buildings and lined by fields. The only exceptions are a single, large building depicted on the north side, just beyond the post-enclosure junction with Brackenborough Road, and two buildings either side of the far end of the road, just before the parish boundary. The first of these was Eastfield House, which had been built in a subdivision of one of the new allotments of land at some point before 1844—this was the home of Edward Cartwright from the 1840s through to the 1860s, a farmer and landed proprietor who had previously been a butcher on EASTGATE in 1841. By the early 1870s, Eastfield House had become Samuel Bateman's classical boarding school, which prepared pupils for Oxford, Cambridge and the Civil Service at a cost of 24 guineas per year. In 1871, seventeen pupils were staying in Eastfield House, all of whom were born in Lincolnshire and aged between twelve and sixteen, aside from one who born in London and another who was only seven. The school was still located there in 1885, but had moved to WESTGATE by 1889 and Newbridge Hill by 1896, with Eastfield House being the private home of a draper, Joseph Vere, in 1891. The other two buildings depicted in 1844 were Eastfield Lodge and probably Lyndon Lodge, which are discussed below.

Little had changed on Keddington Road east of the junction with Brackenborough Road by the time that Brown had finished his

126

Panorama (it was first exhibited in 1847 and last updated in 1856). However, to the west of this junction there had been dramatic changes, primarily brought about by the coming of the railway to Louth in 1847–8. In particular, the railway station and a goods yard had been established immediately to the south of Keddington Road, on land that had been bought by Edward Blyth at the time of enclosure. The first train ran between Keddington Road and Grimsby on the 17 September 1847, with the line being opened to passenger traffic in March 1848 (see further RAMSGATE). The route the track took northwards is still visible from Keddington Road, as is the restored signal box next to the road—this was built for the Great Northern Railway in 1886, with a timber-frame on a red-brick base. The road itself was also affected by these developments, with a new railway crossing established here for the line from Grimsby as it entered the goods yard and station. This was a busy crossing at which one could get delayed, and to save time it was apparently customary to walk down the track directly to the station, rather than take the road route along Newbridge Hill. In December 1856, the Rev. William Mason, vicar of Bilsby, was killed doing this after he accidently stepped in front of an engine. In 1869, VICTORIA ROAD was opened to the south of Keddington Road in order to relieve the pressure on the Keddington Road railway crossing.

Keddington Road remained largely undeveloped, aside from around the railway, right the way through the nineteenth century. In 1861, only 26 people were listed in the census as living on this road (28 if we include the Railway Gatehouse), including ten at Eastfield House, and the situation wasn't too dissimilar in 1891, to judge from both the census and the 1889 OS map of Louth. To the west of the Brackenborough Road junction, through to Newbridge Hill, there were two railway cottages and two gatehouse cottages (inhabited by railway workers), along with the Rose Nursery to the south between the railway and Victoria Road. The latter was where Henry Norton grew roses commercially from at least 1881 through until the early twentieth century; the nursery fronted onto Keddington Road and then stretched down the western side of Victoria Road. Moreover, the road to the east of the Brackenborough Road remained virtually empty of buildings—the 1889 OS map shows just Eastfield House, Lyndon Lodge and two small dwellings to the east of this on the north side, and Grosvenor House and Eastfield Lodge to the south, along with the Elms, which had a driveway that opened onto Keddington Road in this period, although it was located considerably to the south of the road, near the RIVERHEAD (see ELM DRIVE). Eastfield Lodge was the home of Thomas Hague, Esq. in the 1870s, a JP for the West Riding of Yorkshire, and Richard Thomas Bord in 1891, a man of private means—it was also one of the two buildings visible at the far end of Keddington Road on Brown's Panorama and sketch. Lyndon Lodge was the home of Amy G. Robinson, the daughter of the rector of Thorganby, from at least 1889 through until after World War One, and before that it appears to have been the home of James Nell, corn merchant, in 1871, and perhaps John Burke, a market gardener, in 1861. Lyndon Lodge is also probably the other building visible on Brown's Panorama at the far end of the road in the 1840s and 1850s. Grosvenor House, in contrast, was not depicted by William Brown—in 1891, it was home to William Hodson, a man of private means, and it was probably the unnamed property occupied by John Fanthorpe in 1871 and 1881, a retired glass and china dealer, and Frederick Forrest in 1861, surveyor of taxes for the Inland Revenue.

By the time of the 1906 OS map, however, Keddington Road had begun to see significant changes. Keddington House and an associated nursery had been constructed on the north side of the road by this point, between the railway line and Brackenborough Road, whilst Norton's Rose Nursery on the south side had disappeared, its site being built on by properties fronting onto both Keddington Road and Victoria Road; the Spar shop on Keddington Road currently occupies one of these new buildings. Terraced and semi-detached housing had also begun to appear on the street east of the Brackenborough Road junction, up to Eastfield House. By the early 1950s, there were further developments. The northern side of Keddington Road between the railway and the Brackenborough Road junction now had housing on it too, and to the east of Eastfield House there was now the large KEDDINGTON CRESCENT housing estate, which joined through to JUBILEE CRESCENT beyond. On the southern side of the road, GROVESNOR ROAD & GROSVENOR CRESCENT had also begun to be developed in the field to the west and south of Grosvenor House by 1950, along with further properties on the northern side of the road opposite Grosvenor House and south of Eastfield House (for example, BOWERS AVENUE).

By the late 1960s, Grosvenor Road and Crescent had been completed and the estate on the south side had extended into CHARLES AVENUE too. The same period also saw the further development eastwards along Keddington Road, with the establishment of the ELM DRIVE housing estate (including DAVID DRIVE, ADA WAY and STAINESWAY) on the south side, opposite Lyndon Lodge, on land that had previously belonged to The Elms, along with new housing to the east of Lyndon Lodge. In the 1970s, Eastfield House (then known as Elm Court) was demolished, to make way for new houses facing onto Keddington Road and Keddington Crescent, with the straight section of the latter that lead north from Keddington Road being renamed LIME GROVE. Further east, LYNDON WAY & LYNDON CRESCENT were laid out and developed by the mid-1970s, these roads being named after the nineteenth-century Lyndon Lodge that lies to the west of the entrance to these roads, and the land of Eastfield Lodge was encroached upon. By 1990, Eastfield Lodge had been demolished and replaced by new houses and SWALLOW DRIVE had been laid out to the north of Keddington Road—the latter was joined to the new FULMAR DRIVE (off Brackenborough Road) during the course of the 1990s. The final undeveloped field on Keddington Road was developed in the late 1990s to form KESTREL DRIVE.

KENWICK CLOSE & KENWICK GARDENS

Both Kenwick Close and Kenwick Gardens are residential streets that run east from KENWICK ROAD. Kenwick Close was built around 1960 and appears on the 1967–8 OS map of the town, whilst the four houses of Kenwick Gardens were built by the end of the 1980s. The land that these roads occupy was once part of Louth's old open South Field until the 1801 Enclosure Act and remained agricultural land through until the mid-twentieth century.

KENWICK PASTURES

The modern Kenwick Pastures appears on the 1889 OS map as a short, unnamed road running west from LEGBOURNE ROAD corner, where the latter road and KENWICK ROAD meet. In 1889, the road was largely undeveloped, aside from some buildings at its western end. By the

129

1960s, however, there was more activity there, and the last two decades have seen further dwellings erected on this road.

In 1805, a private road known as Gibbet Road ran west from Legbourne Road corner right the way through to LINDEN WALK, but was said by the early twentieth century to have been 'improperly annexed'. Its name, Gibbet Road, probably indicates that a gibbet was present somewhere here in the past, from which criminals could be hung and their bodies displayed in irons. Certainly, one local tradition is that the corpse of John Keal, a woodcutter, was displayed in a gibbet at the corner of Kenwick Road and Legbourne Road (although there are conflicting reports on the truth of this matter). Keal was convicted of brutally murdering his wife and baby son in 1731, chopping off the child's head and stabbing his wife in the throat and chest, and the judge at the time apparently commented on his lack of remorse. Keal's gibbet cage is now in Louth Museum and Keal's ghost was said to haunt this part of town for many years. J. E. Swaby reported that the customers of a public house that once stood on the opposite corner of the road—The Fox & Hounds, see Legbourne Road—played a joke on one of their number, persuading him one night to take a bowl of broth outside to the ghost of John Keal. As the man stood outside in the darkness with the bowl, one of the pranksters, concealed by the hedge, groaned "It's ower 'ot" (over hot), whereupon the bowl-carrier threw the contents towards the voice, crying "Then blow on it!"

KENWICK ROAD

Kenwick Road ran through the old open South Field of Louth, past the Saturday Pits (which were used as a temporary market in the seventeenth century, see below), and traces of medieval ridge and furrow have been noted near to it. It is thought that the ancient Barton Street, a prehistoric and later routeway running from Barton on Humber southwards along the eastern edge of the Wolds, ran along the line of Kenwick Road before continuing on to Cawthorpe and Muckton, and a handful of interesting archaeological finds are known from the vicinity of Kenwick Road. One is a small scatter of Neolithic or Bronze Age flints, including an arrowhead, found just to the east of Kenwick Road near to the Saturday Pits. Another is a potential Romano-British enclosed farmstead on the western side of the road, to the south of Southfield House. In the late eighteenth century, Kenwick Road was administered as part of the turnpike from Louth to Withern and Saltfleet, under the Louth Turnpike Act of 1770, and it is marked on Armstrong's 1778 map of the Louth area with the toll-bar at the junction of the Withern and Saltfleet roads (now a roundabout at the end of the LOUTH A16 BYPASS).

In the mid-nineteenth century, Kenwick Road was primarily agricultural in character, as can be most readily seen on William Brown's 1844 sketch from St James's spire and his finished Panorama of 1847–56: both show a road dominated by fields, with just a handful of properties present on it. There were, nonetheless, some noteworthy sites on the road then. One was the junction where Kenwick Road met Legbourne Road. This was Legbourne Road corner, which local tradition holds to be the site of a gibbet where criminals could be hung and their bodies displayed in irons, a usage supported by the fact that Gibbet Road ran west from this corner in 1805 (see KENWICK PASTURES). A second was Southfield House. This was a large house built on the plot of land that was awarded to Thomas Julian in the Enclosure Award of 1805, and from the 1840s through into the 1870s it was home to the grocer and soap maker Benjamin Hyde (see CHURCH CLOSE), who, in 1851, lived there with his wife and five servants—a coachman, a footman, a cook, a housemaid and a lady's maid. It was subsequently the home of William Hyde, solicitor and farmer of 1000 acres, in 1881.

A third notable site was the Saturday Pits, located at the southern end of Kenwick Road. This was used as a temporary market site in 1631, when plague forced the market to be moved out of the centre of town. The people from the surrounding villages would get no closer than shouting distance to the townsfolk, and would only retrieve their money once it had been washed in vinegar and 'every spell and flourish of exorcism' had been performed over it. In the mid-nineteenth-century, whiting (whitewash for houses) was manufactured from chalk at the Saturday Pits, and the cottages for the manager and workers here are visible on both Brown's sketch and his Panorama. A final interesting site on the mid-nineteenth-century Kenwick Road is the property that Brown depicts on the west side of the road, just to the south of STEWTON LANE. This would seem to be the White Horse public house, given its position and the fact that this was the only building on this part of the road in 1889, and it must have been constructed after 1844, as Brown did not include it on his preliminary sketch of the area.

131

Whether it was a beerhouse from its first construction is unknown, but it was certainly one by 1861, when Robert Smith was recorded as a beer seller at the White Horse (indeed, he appears to have been based here from at least 1856). In the 1870s and 1880s, George Pridgeon ran the White Horse, followed by Thomas Maxey and, in 1896, Joseph B. Kitching.

At the end of the nineteenth century, little had changed on Kenwick Road south of the junction with Legbourne Road. The Saturday Pits were still marked as a whiting works (run by Hurley & Co.), and the only significant properties on the road were the houses by the Saturday Pits and Southfield House, although just to the south-east of the Saturday Pits the buildings later known as Kenwick Thorpe Farm were already marked present in 1889. This lack of development continued into the early twentieth century—by 1906, Southfield Villa had been established on the west side of the road and Kenwick Thorpe Farm is named, but otherwise the road was still dominated by fields along its entire length. However, new housing had been developed all down the eastern side of the Kenwick Road from the Legbourne Road junction through to Southfield House by the middle of the twentieth century, with SOUTHLANDS AVENUE (which runs eastwards from the northern end of the road) also established in this period. By the 1960s, the houses between Southfield Villa and Southfield House on the west of the road had been constructed too, as had KENWICK CLOSE, leaving only KENWICK GARDENS to be built, which it was by the end of the 1980s.

The area of Kenwick Road that lies between Legbourne Road and the NEWMARKET–Stewton Lane junction was usually treated as separate to the southern part of Kenwick Road before the twentieth century, being variously referred to as Alford Road, Legbourne Road and Newmarket in the nineteenth century. This stretch of road had seen a degree of development by the end of the nineteenth century. The White Horse was still there, and fields still predominated, but by 1889 the former had been joined by a short row of terraces on the eastern side of the road, to the north of Legbourne Road corner. The late nineteenth century had also seen structural changes to this part of Kenwick Road. In 1876, the railway line from Louth to Bardney was opened—this line ran along the north end of Kenwick Road and was crossed by a bridge, which required alterations to the road here. As with the southern section of Kenwick Road, however, the major changes came in the mid-twentieth century, with the development of MAYFIELD CRESCENT and FLORENCE WRIGHT AVENUE on the east side of the road and the establishment of housing down most of the eastern side of the street too. The western side of the road also saw activity then, with a new row of houses running north from the junction with Legbourne Road by the middle of the century. However, the major development on the western side came in the late twentieth century, with the construction of the ALBANY ROAD and BARTON GATE housing estate, which was fully developed by the end of the 1980s.

KESTREL DRIVE

Kestrel Drive is a residential street that runs north from KEDDINGTON ROAD. The street and its houses were developed in the late 1990s in the final undeveloped field off Keddington Road. The land Kestrel Drive is built on was originally part of Louth's old open North Field, before the Enclosure Act of 1801, and traces of medieval ridge and furrow have been observed from aerial photographs in the field immediately to the north of the road. The same field has also seen finds of medieval pottery, including green, brown and black glazed wares, and a scatter of Mesolithic–Neolithic/Bronze Age worked flints, including a possible microlith blade or core.

KIDGATE

Kidgate is first mentioned in the Louth Manorial Court Roll for 1442 and its western half was probably originally a back access road for the long, thin medieval tenements that faced onto MERCER ROW and ran back to Kidgate. The rear sections of these tenements are likely to have been undeveloped in the medieval period, with the tenants practicing their business at the Mercer Row frontage of the tenement and using the sections near to Kidgate for other activities, such as keeping livestock or small-scale vegetable growing. Certainly, the modern Mawer's Yard, located between Mercer Row and Kidgate and away from the Mercer Row frontages of the medieval tenements, appears to have seen little activity in the medieval and early modern periods, with the only pre-modern find made during an excavation here being a single sherd of mid-thirteenth- to mid-fourteenth-century glazed pottery.

Despite its origins, Kidgate had developed into a residential and commercial street in its own right by the modern period. In 1778, Armstrong's plan of Louth shows buildings on both the north and the south side of Kidgate west of ASWELL STREET, and on Espin's more accurate plan of 1808 there were a significant number of buildings all along the north side from UPGATE to Aswell Street and a number on the south side of here too, including part of the terrace of houses that lies to the west of the ASWELL STREET junction. By 1828–9, a flour dealer (John Petchell), a cabinet maker (Richard Foster), two shoemakers (Joseph Procter and William Russell), a tin-plate worker (John Parker), a dressmaker (Elizabeth Brown), a straw hat maker (Harriet Dales), and two tailors (John Willey and John Arliss) all had their places of business listed as Kidgate, and there was also a school there then, run by Matilda and Susannah James.

By 1835, the number of schools listed on Kidgate had increased to two, run by Vigesima Proctor and Mary Taylor, and Susannah James's school was also probably still on the street then despite its absence from the 1835 directory, as it was certainly listed on Kidgate in 1841. The mid-1830s also saw the appearance of William Lison's store and William Rysdale's beerhouse on Kidgate. Indeed, the 1834 plan of Louth and the 1839 map indicate that there had been a significant increase in the number of buildings on the western half of Kidgate since the early nineteenth century, with structures shown along almost all of the south side of the street from UPGATE to Aswell Street by the end of the 1830s. Some noteworthy buildings and sites were located here too. One was the Wool Market that was built for the Louth Corporation on Kidgate and opened on 18 June 1825—this is located on the south side of the street, on the western corner of LEE STREET, and wool markets were held here from 1825 through to 1843; it is currently operated by John Taylors as The Wool Mart Auction Rooms. On the opposite side of the road were a pair of warehouses that are both now part of the Joseph Morton pub (previously known as Scarfe's Wine Bar and Kai's Bar), the smaller of which bears a date stone indicating that it was built in 1674 and rebuilt in 1818 and the larger of which probably dates from the early nineteenth century. To the west of these is an open area facing onto Kidgate that is currently part of Hurton's Yard, but which was once apparently known as Mawer's Square. It was here, according to C. S. Carter, that all the fights of the 1840s between the Grammar School boys ('the Tigers') and the boys of Roger's school at The Priory ('the Bull Dogs') took place, and any quarrel that progressed far enough in nineteenth-century Louth is said to have led to a cry of "let's hev it out in Mawer's square." Finally, on the opposite side of Mawer's Square were warehouses that apparently served as the barracks for French prisoners during the Napoleonic War and also for 'the Yeomanry', perhaps the Louth Independent Volunteer Yeomanry Cavalry, which fought in the Napoleonic War and is recorded from 1797. They probably also functioned as the barracks for Colonel John Henry Loft's regiment, the 'Royal Louth Volunteers', in 1794 and 1795, as these were said to be in Kidgate.

If the western half of Kidgate was medieval in origin and well-developed by the first half of the nineteenth century, the same cannot necessarily be said for the eastern half that lies beyond the modern junction with ASWELL STREET. Although this section of Kidgate was at least partly in existence by the late eighteenth century (a small part of it was depicted on Armstrong's 1778 plan of Louth), the early plans of the town show only eighteenth- and nineteenth-century property boundaries on this stretch of road, which might indicate a post-medieval origin for it. Furthermore, the 1808 and 1834 plans of the town depict very few buildings on Kidgate between Aswell Street and CHURCH STREET in the early nineteenth century, in contrast to the situation on the western half of the street (see further below). A distinction between the eastern and the western half of Kidgate is also apparent in the fact that the 1808 plan only applies that street-name to the road from Upgate to Aswell Street, with the road from Aswell Street to Church Street being instead labelled Kit Cat Lane. This is not the only instance of the section of road east of Aswell Street being known by a name other than Kidgate, either. The 1834 plan of Louth labels this eastern section of road as Cat Lane, and from at least the mid-nineteenth century it also appears to have been known as Paradise Lane or Paradise Hill. For example, in 1840–1 the British School—now Kidgate School—was built on a piece of land said to be in Paradise Lane, according to David Robinson, and this stretch of road was reportedly known to many local people as Paradise Hill, rather than Kidgate, in the early twentieth century.

In the first half of the nineteenth century, the eastern part of Kidgate appears to have been dominated by a market garden and nursery that covered a significant proportion of the area to the south of the road, to judge from its depiction on William Brown's mid-nineteenth-century Panorama. The first certain tenant of this market garden was Morgan Jones, who rented it from the Louth Corporation and was listed here in Pigot & Co.'s 1835 and 1841 directories; subsequent tenants included John Mitchell. In 1840–1, a part of this market garden, known as Paradise, was cleared to allow for the building of the British School (Kidgate School) on the section of road from Aswell Street to Church Street—twenty-four apple and nineteen pear trees were removed to make way for the school, along with current bushes, gooseberry bushes and plots of rhubarb. Morgan Jones was paid £67 15s in compensation for his loss, and he continued to use the remainder of the site all around the school as a market garden, as can be seen on both Brown's 1844 sketch of the area and his finished Panorama of 1847–56. Costing around £1,000 to build, the British School was intended to accommodate 160 boys and 150 girls. The first headmaster was James Seller Forster, and the school was improved and expanded in 1855—by 1857 it had 252 boys and 217 girls on its roll, though the number declined significantly over the later nineteenth century (in 1898, there were, on average, only 170 boys and girls and 85 infants attending the school). Up until 1929, pupils stayed in the school until 14, but in that year the senior pupils, aged 11–14, were moved to the new Monks' Dyke Senior School—see MONKS DYKE ROAD.

By the end of the nineteenth century, Kidgate was not only fully developed along its western half, but there was activity along much of its eastern section too. For example, the buildings between Aswell Street and the British School were established in the mid-late 1830s, and in the 1860s one of these was Charles Ross's pipe factory (number 46). In 1868, the classroom of the British School was filled with smoke caused by the factory burning old tobacco pipes, and Ross had to be persuaded by the Superintendent of Police, William Roberts, not to do this during school hours. Ross's pipe factory was located on Kidgate from at least 1861 through until the 1880s. The northern side of Kidgate from Aswell Street to Church Street had also seen significant development by the time of the 1889 OS map, with terraced houses present all along its length. One of these had been the place of business of John Bradshaw, boot and shoe maker—in the 1860s and 1870s, his address was listed as Kidgate (number 63), although in 1856 it had been given instead as Paradise Lane. There had also been houses built on the south side of the road and to the east of the British School, although there were still large undeveloped areas here in 1889. By 1906, there had been some infilling of these gaps, but the eastern end of the south side of Kidgate would not be fully developed until the mid-twentieth century, by which point the Kidgate car park had also been erected on the north side of the street, over the former site of some of the houses of the GATHERUMS.

Turning at the western half of Kidgate around the start of the twentieth century, there were a number of interesting businesses present there then. One of these was Mawer Brothers, who were builders, contractors, carpenters and monumental masons. This firm was established in 1874 and operated out of Kidgate from at least the 1880s until well into the twentieth century, with as many as sixty carpenters on Mawer Brothers' books before World War One. Mawer Brothers had, at one point, a showroom on the northern side of the junction between Kidgate and Upgate, and their main premises off Kidgate encompassed the Wool Mart, the Joseph Morton pub, and the group of recently built shops opposite this, hence the local name of Mawer's Square for this area (see above). Another notable late nineteenth- and early twentieth-century business on this part of Kidgate was a beer retailer at 2 Kidgate, on the corner of Update and Kidgate. Run by Henry Dabb in 1871, Walter James Jones in 1881 and 1885, William Jacklin and his wife in the 1890s and 1900s, and subsequently Benjamin Hempstock, this was the Eagle Inn according to the censuses—it is marked in this position on the 1889 OS map, although in the 1901 directory the Eagle was listed on Upgate rather than Kidgate for some reason. A final interesting business premises on the western part of Kidgate was Strawsons' banana ripening store. The Strawsons had a fruiterer business in town, with shops at 30 Aswell Street and 12 MARKET PLACE, from the 1880s into the mid-twentieth century, and the family's banana ripening store was just to the east of the current entrance to the Golden Fleece yard. The unripe, green fruit was imported from Liverpool or London and then placed in this building, where a humid heat was applied to it in order to assist the ripening process. The banana ripening store has now been demolished, with its site occupied by late twentieth-century residential buildings. Other areas that have seen significant demolition and rebuilding along this part of Kidgate include the buildings on either side of the road near to the Upgate junction, such as the Eagle Inn, and the buildings that used to stand in and to the east of Hurton's Yard/Mawer's Square.

KILN LANE & KILN LANE PATHWAY

Kiln Lane runs both south from NORTHGATE and east from BROADBANK and is named from the malt kilns that were once based in this part of town. The earliest malt kiln here was on the current Co-operative supermarket site. A three-storey malthouse and hay or corn stacks are visible here on both William Brown's 1844 sketch of the town, made from the spire of St James's Church, and his final Panorama (first exhibited in 1847 and last updated in 1856). This malt kiln belonged to John Hallam in the mid-nineteenth century, who was described in 1851 as a maltster, an ironmonger and a farmer of 56 acres, employing three men—his beerhouse faced onto Northgate and was known as the Malt Shovel (now the Miller's Daughter). Whether Hallam was the first to have a malthouse on this site is unknown, but there were certainly maltsters on Northgate before him. For example, Thomas Fuller is listed as a maltster, brewer and porter merchant on Northgate in 1841, and in the 1820s and 1830s Thomas Bogg had an ale and porter brewery, a malt kiln and a drying kiln on Northgate (he retired due to ill health in 1835). Hallam's business was subsequently run by his widow, Sarah, and, in the 1880s, by his daughter and her husband (Esther and William Barton). The other malt kiln off Kiln Lane was on the site of the Kiln Lane car park, where a large malthouse is depicted on the 1889 OS map. This may well have started life as the beetroot distillery built east of Broadbank House in 1857, which apparently had 'a good season' in 1858 (Brown's Panorama of 1847–56 shows only fields here, which were reached by a brick bridge over the Lud). This malt kiln was long-lived: in the twentieth century, it was owned by the Newark-based Gilstrap Earp and later Associated British Maltsters, and it survived until the mid-1970s, when it was demolished to make way for the car park.

Malt kilns and beetroot distilleries are not the only businesses to have been based on Kiln Lane—there was also a tannery marked on the 1889 OS map here, located to the south of the Lud on the eastern side of the road, and the same area now houses the Co-operative supermarket and its car park. The latter was constructed in the late 1980s (initially branded as a Leo's) and as part of this development a new road entrance into KILN LANE was constructed from Broadbank. Kiln Lane is also the home of The Warple Press printing works, housed on the north bank of the Lud, opposite to where the ABM malt kiln and granary stood and on a site that was once part of the garden of Broadbank House. The late twentieth and early twenty-first centuries have also seen the construction of a number of residential properties on the southern half of Kiln Lane, most recently on the western side between the Broadbank entrance to the road and the river.

With regard to the origins of Kiln Lane, this street is not shown on either the 1808 or the 1834 plans of the town—indeed, relatively little appears to have been present in this part of town then. Archaeological work undertaken immediately to the west of Kiln Lane and south of the Lud (where an abattoir was based in the twentieth century) indicates that this area, at least, was originally a periodically inundated floodplain of the Lud, which required deliberate and substantial dumping during the nineteenth century in order to raise the ground level here by a metre or more, drying the area out and so making it suitable for building. Consequently, the relative paucity of early nineteenth century development is perhaps hardly surprising. By the 1840s, however, this part of town does appear to have been increasingly developed, with Brown's sketch and Panorama showing a brick bridge across the Lud and substantial buildings present to the east of Kiln Lane. In the next decade, the area to the north of the Lud also appears to have been developed, first as the site for a distillery and later as a malt kiln (see above). As such, it seems credible that Kiln Lane had its origins in the 1840s and the 1850s, serving this new development and activity.

On the north side of the Lud, the line of Kiln Lane is continued by Kiln Lane Pathway, also locally known as Brewer's Lane. A small lane or path is shown here on both the 1889 and the 1906 OS maps of the town, joining the northern end of Kiln Lane to HIGH HOLME ROAD. In the late nineteenth and early twentieth centuries, Kiln Lane Pathway was undeveloped; however, a small number of buildings were established on this route in mid-twentieth century, and the houses constructed in CEDAR CLOSE in the 1970s backed onto it. Most recently, the path has been the subject of an access dispute, with a local resident erecting a fence across it, reportedly in order to prevent vandalism of his property.

Discussions over whether the path ought to be designated a right-of-way were ongoing in 2012.

KILN YARD

Kiln Yard runs south from the eastern end of QUEEN STREET. Its name, current from at least 1841, derives from the malt kilns that were located in this yard—for example, a large malthouse of the 'Maiden Row Brewery' (see CHURCH STREET) formed the eastern side of Kiln Yard at the time of the 1889 OS map. These buildings are visible on the 1808, 1834 and 1839 plans and maps of the town, and in the twentieth century the maltings here have seen several uses after brewing ended on the Maiden Row site in 1902. For example, Strawson's jam and pickle factory, Luda Works, was located in the former malt kilns in Kiln Yard until the late 1950s. By 1939, it had become one of the largest preserve-makers in the county, and Mr E. Strawson was said to always attend the mixing of the firm's special Christmas puddings—only after he died was it realised that only he knew the recipe! The buildings here have subsequently been used as a tannery, processing leather and suede skins.

In the nineteenth century, Kiln Yard was home to a significant number of people. In 1841, thirteen households were based in Kiln Yard, including those of a pauper (Robert Coupland), a laundress (Elizabeth Caldecot), three agricultural labourers (Thomas Stones, William Clark and John East), a carpet weaver (John Wilkinson), a labourer (William Wakelin), a brickmaker (William Danner), a tailor (Richard Farver), and a blacksmith (Richard Bellamy). The situation in 1861 was similar, though in that year residents of Kiln Yard included the brothel-owner Elizabeth Moncaster (aged 49, whose occupation was listed as 'formerly laundress'; she lived here with two teenage daughters and a boarder—see further GATHERUMS & SPRINGSIDE on Moncaster), a fishmonger (George Day), and a malt maker (James Wilson). By 1881, however, only two households were listed in Kiln Yard: that of Charles Paddison, agricultural labourer, and that of John Fawn, maltster's labourer.

Some of the inhabitants of Kiln Yard occasionally found themselves featuring in the court reports of the regional newspapers during the mid-nineteenth century. For example, in 1848, a Jane Everitt of Kiln Yard was charged with brawling, making use of 'most disgusting language', and causing a nuisance and annoyance in the neighbourhood (she was fined 5s and costs). In 1850, Edward King, a hawker of caps, got himself drunk and deliberately set fire to the chimney of his house in Kiln Yard by ripping up a straw mattress and stuffing it in the fireplace—his neighbours fetched the police 'in great alarm' to stop him, and King was fined 10s and costs for his trouble. Finally, in 1855 William Moncaster and 'a female named Martha Arliss, who lives with him as his wife', had a narrow escape after stealing a fowl from James Harrison, beerhouse keeper of Walkergate (Queen Street), only avoiding conviction because Harrison in the end declined to identify the bird for some reason.

Other interesting events in Kiln Yard during the mid-nineteenth century included a public meeting of the Total Abstinence Society, which apparently took place in the yard and saw Richard Horn of Leicester give a lecture there. Most intriguing of all, however, was a case brought by a resident of Kiln Yard called William Stote Manby to the Vice-Chancellors' Court in 1855, which was reported widely in the regional and national press, including in *The Times*. Despite the fact that his father, William Manby, was 'a very weak and silly person'—who 'became utterly imbecile' and was known locally as 'Silly Billy'—and his grandfather was an illiterate who suffered a brain injury from a horse and lived in a mud hovel in Keddington, William Stote Manby was actually the distant, dispossessed heir of the £50,000 per year estate in Northumberland of Dorothy Windsor, his grandfather's cousin (d. 1756, formerly Dorothy Stote, daughter of Sir Richard Stote). In 1855, Manby, described as both a pauper and a gardener, attempted to recover the inheritance in court, alleging that fraud, enabled by his grandfather's mental incapacity, had deprived him of his rightful estates. However, the action was unsuccessful, because of the amount of time that had passed and the difficulty in proving that the dispossession had been due to fraud. Manby brought the case to Vice-Chancellors' Court again in 1857, having obtained proof of his relationship to Dorothy Windsor, but the action was again dismissed. William Stote Manby was living in Kiln Yard in 1851, when he was listed as a manure merchant, having previously been listed as a gardener living on MONKS DYKE ROAD in 1841; by 1871, he was living off Aswell Street and working as a shoemaker. He died in Louth in 1872.

LABURNUM CRESCENT

Laburnum Crescent runs north-east from SYCAMORE DRIVE and then around to the southern end of the latter, which is the spine of a late twentieth-century housing estate located to the south of WOOD LANE. Each road in this estate is named after a different type of tree.

LACEY GARDENS

Lacey Gardens runs south from EASTGATE. It was constructed as a new council housing estate in the inter-war years, and the council houses here were amongst the first to be built in Louth. The estate is named after Alderman Lacey, a former mayor and councillor. Lacey Gardens Junior School, at the back of Lacey Gardens, was established in the 1960s to cater for the population of the new ST BERNARDS AVENUE estate; it also took on the older pupils from the former Holy Trinity Parochial School on the corner of RIVERHEAD ROAD and EASTFIELD ROAD, leaving only the infants there. In 1979, the infants moved to the new site too, in buildings adjacent to the junior school, with this new school being known as the Eastfield Infants' School.

LANGLEY CLOSE

Langley Close is part of the 'Weavers Tryst' housing estate that was begun in the late 1990s. It runs north-east from ERESBIE ROAD, the spine of the new development, up to the rear of houses facing onto STEWTON LANE. The estate is built on land that was originally part of Louth's medieval open South Field, although most of the area had been enclosed prior to the 1801 Enclosure Act. The roads within it appear to be named after local worthies of the sixteenth and seventeenth centuries—a Nathaniel Langley was Warden of Louth in 1632, 1638 and 1639.

LEAKE'S ROW

Leake's Row (or Leak's Terrace) runs north from KEDDINGTON ROAD, next to the former line of the Grimsby–Louth railway line. The road is absent from William Brown's 1844 sketch of the town but is present on his final Panorama of 1847–56. In the second half of the nineteenth century, the row of houses here was called Leak's Terrace and they were treated as an extension of NEWBRIDGE HILL in the censuses. Inhabitants in 1861 included an agricultural labourer (Eardley Fenwick), a wood turner (Frederick Hoggard), a railway engine driver (John Poole), a railway porter (James Bellamy), and a minister at the CANNON STREET Independent Chapel (William Herbert). In 1881, there were eighteen properties on Leak's Terrace (numbered from 28 Newbridge Hill) and the inhabitants then included seven or eight people who were employed by the nearby railway and four maltsters. The latter may well have worked at the large maltings that lay at the northern end of Leake's Row, next to the railway, according to the 1889 OS map of the town. This malthouse eventually burned down in 1972, and in the twentieth century it was owned by Gilstrap Earp and later Associated British Maltsters. The southern end of Leake's Row was undeveloped in the late nineteenth century and shown as the site of allotment gardens in 1906. It had, however, seen some development by the middle of the twentieth century and was marked as a depot into the late twentieth century, before North Holme Court sheltered housing was built on the site in 1987.

LEE STREET

Lee Street runs from KIDGATE to NEWMARKET. In 1808, this area of town consisted of fields and gardens, but by 1834 Lee Street had been laid out and was already lined with cottages and properties on both sides. The road itself is said to be named after Robert Lee of Thorpe Hall (Town Clerk in 1762 and Warden in 1776), who had a large garden here.

The Methodist Sunday School opened on Lee Street in 1812 and was used for services whilst the 1835 enlargement of the EASTGATE chapel was underway, as well as for prayer meetings. In 1848, a special showing of William Brown's Panorama was put on for 'juvenile teetotallers' in the Wesleyan Schoolroom on Lee Street. Subsequently, the Louth Free Methodist Church took over the Sunday School on Lee Street, using it as a place for meetings, services and a Sunday School after their expulsion from the Wesleyan Methodist community in 1852. From 1856, the Church of England Free Evening School, supported by voluntary subscriptions, operated from the former Wesleyan and Free Methodist

Sunday School, for the benefit of those adults and youths who had been taken too early from school and so needed tuition in reading, writing and arithmetic. In 1861, the attendance was said to be 120 adults and 120 youths, and the free library attached to it contained 400 volumes. This venture was so successful that £1,000 was spent on a new building on NORTHGATE for the school in 1863; this is now the British Legion Hall. A number of other schools were also located on this street in the nineteenth century, including Misses Annison and Beeton's young ladies' boarding school in the 1820s and the 1830s (it was later listed on UPGATE in 1841 and on Northgate in 1849 and 1856); Mrs Gray's boarding school and Mrs Lawrence's day school, both listed on Lee Street in 1856; and the Nicholsons' ladies' school at 8 Lee Street, listed here in 1861 and 1868. The latter was subsequently run by Sarah, Annie, Judith and Emma Holden (or Houlden) in 1872, who continued to run a private school at number 8 right into the early twentieth century, although by 1911 Sarah Holden had died and the remaining two sisters were listed simply as music teachers. Finally, also relatively long-lived was the preparatory or day school at 41 Lee Street—first listed under Miss Eliza Jackson in 1872, this was still running after the First World War, when Miss Kate Walker was in charge of it.

Lee Street continued to be developed into the mid-nineteenth century (for example, the new terrace of houses at the southern end of the street bears the date 1856), and by the end of the century it was fully developed all along the road. In 1861, 142 people were listed as living on Lee Street, ranging from a professor of music (Charles William Kew, number 37) through to a Free Methodist minister (Edwin Wright, number 18), a cowkeeper (Elvin Would, number 20), and a baker (William Dobbs, number 36). In 1891, there were 151 people recorded on this road, including the Holdens at number 8 (teachers and schoolmistresses), Frances Bingham at number 20 (a lodging-house keeper), Frederick Grounsell at number 5 (an agricultural implement maker whose business was based on Northgate), George Barnard at number 19 (a police constable), and Sarah J Paddison at number 22 (a lime burner, who was still living there well into the twentieth century—see GRIMSBY ROAD).

In addition to schools, there were a number of other businesses based on Lee Street in the nineteenth and early twentieth centuries. For example, in 1828–9 Lee Street was listed as the place of business of

Haywood & Colam, bricklayers, plasterers and lime burners, and of a coach proprietor named William Cartwright, though by 1835 the latter had moved to Northgate and the former to SPITAL HILL and Upgate. In 1856, William Dobb's bakery was located here, which was first listed on Lee Street in 1849 and still run by members of the Dobbs family from 36 Lee Street in the late 1890s; it was subsequently run as a bakery by Edward Hallifield in the early twentieth century and as a shop by George Morgan Hempstock in 1919. Also listing Lee Street as their place of business in 1856 were a bricklayer, William Crow, and a horse and gig letter, William and Richard Major (also spelled Mager)—the latter business was still on Lee Street in the 1860s, when the pair were described as livery stables keepers, and Richard Mager was letting horses here in 1868. In the late twentieth century, Ayscough Hall was built on Lee Street, and this has since been the venue for a large range of community activities on the street, including dances, talks and clubs. This hall was built on the site of Pool's Cottages, which were demolished in the mid-twentieth century.

LEGBOURNE ROAD

Legbourne Road currently runs from KENWICK ROAD through to a roundabout at the end of the LOUTH A16 BYPASS, which was once the location for a toll-bar established under the Louth Turnpike Act of 1770 for administering the roads to Withern, via Legbourne, and Saltfleet. In the nineteenth century, the section of road from Legbourne Road corner (the current junction with Kenwick Road) through to NEWMARKET was sometimes also counted as part of Legbourne Road, and the Leckeburngate recorded in 1317 has been considered to be the original name for Newmarket. At the start of the nineteenth century, Legbourn Road was known as Legburn Low Road and ran across land that was once part of Louth's medieval South Field, with mainly open fields to its south and old enclosures to its north. Under the Enclosure Act of 1801, the remaining open fields here were enclosed and the pre-existing road (shown on Armstrong's 1778 map of the Louth area) was planned out as a twenty-four feet bridle road by the Enclosure Commissioners.

Legbourne Road is probably the site of Haregarths, first recorded in the fourteenth century. This area of land was said to be in the South

Field of the town and the modern Agarth House probably preserves the name Haregarths—the building bearing this name is currently located on Legbourne Road, but in the late nineteenth century it was located a little further towards Legbourne and set back from the road, behind the buildings of Agarth Farm. In 1317, a charter of Thomas de Luda mentioned one or more strips of land at Hargarth, and other early references include one from 1529, when the Churchwardens gave the bellman a penny for warning people to keep their cattle, swine and sheep out of this place. In 1540, the Churchwardens' accounts mention Haregarths again, when they paid 4d to two men for bringing into Louth the corpse that had been found in Haregarths in the 'great snow'. The proceeds from the sale of the bells and other items from St Mary's Church (see BRIDGE STREET) were used in 1553 to pave ASWELL STREET and dyke and hedge Haregarths in the South Field.

In the mid-nineteenth century, Legbourne Road was largely undeveloped—certainly, on both William Brown's 1844 sketch of the road and his finished Panorama (1847–56), it appears to be almost entirely surrounded by fields, aside from a small number of properties. The most distant of these, on the south side of the road, looks to be where South Field Farm is now located. A closer property, on the north side of the road, is marked as being that of 'Elvin' on Brown's 1844 sketch. In the 1851 census, a John Elvin, aged 71, is listed as a gardener with an address of 'South Field', which is appropriate for this site, especially as John Elvin was definitely active on this road in the 1850s (see below). The same census lists a number of other households as 'South Field', but it is unclear if any of these were on what is now Legbourne Road too. The only probable exception is the property inhabited by William Barker—this is listed between Elvin's property and another South Field property, but is actually assigned 'Legbourn Road' as its address. The final property is only present on Brown's Panorama, not his earlier sketch, and so presumably post-dates 1844. This property is located on the south side of the road, near Legbourne Road corner, and it may be the Horse & Hounds (later the Fox & Hounds) public house, which was located in this area in the nineteenth and twentieth centuries. The Horse & Hounds is first mentioned by name in 1861, when John Elvin (then 81) was listed as the beerseller here, but Elvin had previously been listed as a beerseller at an unnamed beerhouse on Legbourne Road in 1856, which was probably the same site. In 1872, the keeper of this beerhouse was John Barned (listed as Barnard), and he and his wife, Ann, remained in charge of the public house now known as the Fox & Hounds until 1908 (John died in 1892). The local hunt apparently met at the Fox & Hounds every Boxing Day for drinks and food.

Legbourne Road continued to be sparsely populated and primarily agricultural all the way through the nineteenth century. By 1889, there were a handful of properties at the western end of the road, including the Fox & Hounds, but only on the north side and only between Legbourne Road corner and the vicinity of the late twentieth-century ERESBIE ROAD. Moving eastwards towards Legbourne, Agarth House and associated farm buildings were located on the north side, South Field Farm was on the south, and there were then a small number of cottages on the road itself, such as Bar Field Cottage—otherwise, however, fields dominated. In the twenty-first century, the road continues to see a significant degree of agricultural activity along its length, although there have been two significant developments since the end of the nineteenth century. One was the establishment of a garage and Louth Garden Centre on the road just to the east of the Agarth Farm. The garage—now two car dealerships—came first, established in the mid-twentieth century (it was present by the late 1960s), with Louth Garden Centre moving onto its current site in the late twentieth century (it was previously on WOOD LANE). The other was the increase in residential properties on the road, especially at the western end. This development really began in the mid-twentieth century, with housing established all along the south side of the road and on part of the north side (eastwards from where Eresbie Road now runs) by the early 1950s, with the garage on the south side of the road established by the 1960s. The final major expansion came at the end of the 1990s, when the 'Weavers Tryst' housing estate was established to the north of Legbourne Road, entered via the new Eresbie Road.

LIME GROVE

See KEDDINGTON CRESCENT.

The Lincoln Road (the B1200) runs west from WESTGATE and ST MARY'S LANE towards Lincoln and South Elkington. In 1765, this road was termed Thorpe Hall Lane (in the *Journals of the House of Commons*), and it had previously been known as 'Schepe brygge lane' in 1446, presumably referring to an earlier incarnation of the bridge across the Lud at the western end of Westgate. Lincoln Road currently begins at the junction with St Mary's Lane, with the section of road running south-west from this towards the Lud and the centre of town usually being classed as part of Westgate, although the medieval name for the road and the nature of the reference to it in the fifteenth century suggest that it originally extended at least down to the bridge over the Lud. From 1765, Lincoln Road was administered as part of the Dexthorpe Turnpike, with a tollhouse erected between Thorpe Hall and the Elkington fork, and the trustees of the Turnpike took control of the bridge too, rebuilding it in 1789–91.

The most important building on Lincoln road is, of course, Thorpe Hall. Thorpe Hall is usually dated to the late sixteenth century, with the present west front said to date from 1584, although there is also much seventeenth-century material inside the present building. However, we ought not to confuse the date of the present building with the origin of Thorpe Hall itself, as there was definitely a Thorpe Hall in existence long before the late sixteenth century. For example, the 1459 will of John Louth, the keeper of Louth Wood, shows that he was the owner of Thorpe Hall when he died, 'having bought it to my great and notable cost', something which implies that he had purchased an already existing property. Similarly, in the reign of Henry VII, John Chapman was the owner of Thorpe Hall and he was succeeded in turn by another John Chapman. The latter owned the property in 1499 and was a merchant and generous contributor to the building of the spire of St James's Church—when he died in 1505, he left the ownership of Thorpe Hall to his infant son, yet another John Chapman (d. 1564). Interestingly, although Thorpe Hall is currently situated in the parish of South Elkington, in 1547 it was described as 'Thorp hall within the pariche of louth'.

In the late sixteenth century, Thorpe Hall came into the hands of Sir John Bolle (d. 1606), and it stayed with this family into the eighteenth century. It is to Sir John Bolle that the famous Green Lady story is attached. The Green Lady is believed to be Donna Leonora Oviedo, who Sir John Bolle met during the Siege of Cadiz in 1596. Supposedly, she sent jewels and a portrait of herself in green to Sir John, hence her nickname, and she is said to haunt the gardens of Thorpe Hall, though sometimes she has apparently been seen leaving through the coach entrance at the back of the hall and running across the road in the direction of Deighton Close. In the period after the Second World War, a man reportedly saw a woman run in front of his car by Thorpe Hall and was so convinced that he hit her that he actually called the police, but no trace could be found of any accident or woman, and this experience was apparently repeated with a female driver in the early 1960s. Since it passed out of the hands of the Bolle family, Thorpe Hall has had a number of owners, for example John Fytche, who lived there in the second half of the nineteenth century with his family and eight or nine servants—including a coachman, a cook, a butler, a gardener and a lady's maid—and Captain Julius Tennyson, nephew of the Poet Laureate. During the Second World War, Thorpe Hall was used at first for evacuees and later as the HQ for the Grenadier Guards, who were garrisoned in Louth in the latter stages of the war.

On the north side of Lincoln Road are Thorpe Hall Farm and Deighton Close. Thorpe Hall Farm is marked on the 1889 OS map and was occupied by Tom Haywood, a farmer of 121 acres, in 1881 (he lived there with his wife, niece and three servants) and John Appleby, farmer, in 1891—the latter was still there in the early twentieth century. Deighton Close, slightly nearer to the road, was built around the start of the twentieth century and was the home, from at least 1901, of Joseph Bennett, timber merchant, who had five servants living in the house in 1911. The Bennett family timber business was based in Grimsby and Joseph Bennett died aged 100 in 1955. The house was subsequently bought by the council in 1964 and used from 1967 as a special school for boys with emotional and behavioural difficulties; this school closed in 2003, and provision for these special educational needs in the local area was moved to Spilsby.

LINDA CRESCENT

Linda Crescent is a street of residential housing that runs off HUNTER PLACE, to the south of HORNCASTLE ROAD. Mostly established by the late 1960s, the housing here was built on what had previously been agricultural land. From the mid-twentieth century, tennis courts, a playing field and a pavilion were located to the south of Hunter Place and Linda Crescent for the use of King Edward VI Grammar School— these were accessed by a footpath from Horncastle Road that ran alongside the eastern properties of Linda Crescent.

LINDEN WALK

Linden Walk runs south from NEWMARKET and has been known by a number of names since the start of the nineteenth century. In 1805, at the time of the Enclosure Award, it was a private road, giving access to old enclosures in the former open field, named Keal Closes Road. By the mid-nineteenth century it was known as Green Lane and Bull Piece Lane, and after the opening of the cemetery between LONDON ROAD and Linden Walk in 1855 it was known as Cemetery Lane (or Cemetery Road). Only in the early twentieth century did the name Linden Walk become current.

On William Brown's 1844 sketch of the town, Linden Walk appears almost entirely undeveloped. From the mid-nineteenth century, however, this began to change. Thomas Ashley's ironworks apparently first began in a small way on Linden Walk, before they moved to CINDER LANE as trade increased, and in 1889 Newmarket Iron Works was marked on the eastern side of the road, opposite QUARRY ROAD. The buildings this business occupied were almost the only structures on the road at the time of William Brown's finished Panorama (1847–56) and they were presumably also where Ashley's ironworks began. In the 1860s, the Newmarket Iron works was run by William Watkinson, an agricultural implement maker and iron founder who employed sixteen men and three boys, and he appears to still have been there in the 1880s. From the early twentieth century, it was run by Evan William Macdonald and made steam traction engines and road rollers, and the firm of Macdonald's Engineers (founded 1911) is still in business in the twenty-first century.

In the latter half of the nineteenth century, Linden Walk became not only one of the access roads to the new town cemetery, hence its name then, but also a significant residential street. Inhabitants in 1881 included the iron founder Thomas Ashley, who then employed 54 people in his business and lived at 8 Cemetery Lane; Joseph Coulson, a grocer (number 30); Joseph Smith, a steam plough cultivator who employed five men (number 14); William Watkinson, an implement maker employing six men (number 23); John Sudbury, a pawnbroker (number 25); and Charles Bradstock, a railway gate house keeper, who managed the railway crossing which then existed at the south end of Linden Walk (where the Louth–Bardney line ran from 1876–1956). In 1889, the OS map of that year depicts houses on both sides of 'Cemetery Road' down to HILL TERRACE, with then a handful of properties located to the south. One of these looks, from both the 1889 and 1906 maps, to be a market garden, presumably that of the North family. In 1851, 'Green Lane' was home to two market gardeners, William North and Joseph Brown, but by 1861 only William North appears still to have been there—the road was then termed Bull Piece Lane and the only households were those of William Watkinson, the implement make and iron founder, William North, the market gardener, and a groom named Samuel Chapman. The North family market garden continued to be based on this road well into the twentieth century, when it was run as J. North and Son (Jesse North was the son of William North). At the southernmost end of the road, beyond the railway crossing, was a brickyard—this belonged to Peter Dickie, a Scotsman, in the nineteenth century. He is listed only as a travelling linen and woollen draper in the 1850s and 1860s, but in the 1870s and 1880s he was also listed as a brick and tile maker.

By 1906, further housing had been built at the north end of Linden Walk, and in the late 1920s TENNYSON ROAD was constructed to the south of Hill Terrace. In the late twentieth century, the SEYMOUR AVENUE housing estate (off Newmarket) was constructed on the land that lies to the east of Linden Walk and the south of Tennyson Road, including the area once occupied by J. North & Son's market garden.

LINDSEY WAY

Lindsey Way runs west off HAWKER DRIVE, which in turn runs south from STEWTON LANE. This area was fields up until the late twentieth century, when the housing estate here was built—Hawker Drive and HAVELOK CLOSE were built first, with Lindsey Way developed in the 1980s. These fields were already enclosed at the start of the nineteenth century, but they had once been part of the old South Field of the town—medieval ridge and furrow from this has been observed on aerial photographs of this area.

LINK, THE

The Link runs east from ST BERNARDS AVENUE through to VIRGINIA DRIVE and is part of the large, post-World War Two St Bernards Avenue council housing scheme, this element of it being laid out after the time that the 1956 OS map was surveyed. A Methodist chapel was established on the corner of The Link and Virginia Drive in 1960; this closed in 1977, due to falling membership and a difficulty in providing ministers. The land it stands on was originally part of Louth's old open South Field.

LITTLE CROWTREE LANE

Little Crowtree Lane was a new road laid out under the Enclosure Act of 1801. The Enclosure Commissioners laid out twelve plots of land here, to be assigned to people who had the right to only a small plot under the 1805 Enclosure Award—for example, William Dixon, a lime burner (see GRIMSBY ROAD). A barn is recorded as being erected by John Tatam 'next the Little Crow Tree Lane' in 1825 and a windmill is visible here on both William Brown's 1844 sketch of the town and his finished Panorama (first exhibited in 1847 and last updated in 1856). The lane remained otherwise undeveloped through the nineteenth century and into the mid-twentieth century. By the 1960s, however, development had begun to occur on both sides of the lane, and this continued into the late twentieth and early twenty-first centuries.

LITTLE LANE & MOUNT PLEASANT

Little Lane originally encompassed both the road now bearing this name and at least the eastern part of MOUNT PLEASANT, which was laid out by the 1805 Enclosure Award as a new road with 21 plots of land along it. In the mid-nineteenth century, the names Little Lane and Mount Pleasant appear to have been used somewhat interchangeably—for example, in 1861 only Mount Pleasant occurs in the description of the relevant enumeration district, not Little Lane, but the census pages themselves actually use Little Lane throughout, never Mount Pleasant. Similarly, households assigned a Mount Pleasant address in one census were given a Little Lane address in another—for example, the household of William Bradley, a groom, is the first property listed on Mount Pleasant in 1851 and also the first property listed on Little Lane in 1861, whilst what had been 34 and 35 Little Lane in 1861 were 34 and 35 Mount Pleasant in 1871. By the late nineteenth century, however, a clear distinction appears to have emerged, with both Little Lane and Mount Pleasant appearing in the censuses then and the 1889 OS map labelling the north–south portion of the road as Little Lane and the east–west part Mount Pleasant, as now.

The northern end of Little Lane, off MONKS DYKE ROAD, is depicted on the 1808 and 1834 plans of the town, with slightly more of this part of the road visible on the 1839 map of the town. The 1808 plan shows buildings on the western side of the junction between this lane and Monks Dyke Road, and the 1834 plan and the 1839 map add one on the eastern side of the junction and a handful further south along the road too. However, Little Lane doesn't appear to have been a particularly developed part of the town at this point. In contrast, by the time of William Brown's 1844 sketch of the area and his final Panorama of 1847–56, things had moved on somewhat. Housing was present then along a significant proportion of the western side of the north–south stretch of Little Lane and there was a market garden and a number of buildings on the eastern side too, although the east–west stretch of Little Lane (modern Mount Pleasant) appears to have been largely devoid of buildings at that time and dominated by a nursery. The situation had changed little by the end of the nineteenth century on modern Little Lane, to judge from the 1889 OS map, although modern Mount Pleasant had seen the development of a number of properties by the time that this map was surveyed, including Beaconsfield Terrace, just to the west of the junction with Little Lane.

In 1861, around 170 people were living on Little Lane/Mount Pleasant, including dressmakers (for example, Ann Smith and Elizabeth Adlard, numbers 3 and 11); bricklayers (for example, George Clark, number 5); a builder (James Harrison, number 14); a printer (William Hussard, number 22); labourers (for example, David Elvin, number 28); and gardeners, notably William Donington, at number 35, and William Staples, at number 34. In the 1856 directory, a William Dunnington—the same man using his normal spelling of his name—is listed as a gardener and seedsman on Little Lane, and he was still listed as having his place of business on 'Mount Pleasant, Little Lane' in the 1872 directory (he is also said to have had a base in the Market Hall then) and on Mount Pleasant in 1889. William Dunnington continued to live on Little Lane/Mount Pleasant until at least 1891, and he presumably made use of the market garden on the east side of the road in the second half of the nineteenth century. By 1896, the business was run by Jesse Dunnington, who was still based here in 1901 and 1905, although by 1909 he was listed on STEWTON LANE. Whether William Staples, gardener, had a separate business or worked under or with his neighbour William Dunnington in 1861 is not clear, but by 1872 he too was listed separately as a gardener with a base in the Market Hall and a house on Little Lane, and in 1889 and 1896 he was listed a market gardener on Mount Pleasant. He was still listed as a market gardener living here in 1901, although by 1911 he had moved to QUEEN STREET. The Dunnington and the Staples nursery businesses were not the only ones listed on Mount Pleasant by the late nineteenth century either—in 1896, John Bee and Thomas Robinson were both listed there too. Thomas Robinson was a son of William Robinson—owner of a long-established nursery to the south of Mount Pleasant, off NEWMARKET (established on land awarded to the family under the 1805 Enclosure Award)—who appears to have run his own nursery business on Mount Pleasant from the 1890s through to World War One, moving into 18b Little Lane by 1901 and 2 Moss Side, Mount Pleasant, by 1911. John Bee, previously a maltster, lived at 27 Mount Pleasant in 1901 and was still listed as a market gardener here after the First World War.

The 1906 OS map shows an expansion of the nursery businesses to both the north and the south of Mount Pleasant when compared to the situation in 1889, along with an increase in the number of properties at the western end of this road. A major development here came in the inter-war years, when a small-scale council housing project—MOUNT PLEASANT AVENUE—was completed to the south of Mount Pleasant, with the new houses being provided with hot water, bathrooms and electricity. In the mid-twentieth century, there was additional development on both Mount Pleasant and Little Lane, although there were still large areas of nursery on the former in the late 1960s. Further major changes came in the late twentieth century with the establishment of the large ROBINSON LANE housing estate to the south of Mount Pleasant, built on top of the former Robinson family nursery there.

LITTLE SOUTH STREET

Little South Street runs south from SOUTH STREET before turning west to meet GEORGE STREET, and a similar loop of road runs from George Street westwards before turning south to join South Street once again. The latter stretch of road is not marked as part of Little South Street on early or modern maps, but forms a clear pair with it: it is presumably the 'Little George Street' that is mentioned immediately before Little South Street in a list of roads in Louth that were 'not repairable by the Local Authority' in 1902 (*Sessional Papers of the House of Lords*). These roads provide access to the rear of the properties fronting onto George Street and short sections of them are visible on William Brown's Panorama of 1847–56—by the end of the nineteenth century they had been joined together to form a single loop of street that crossed George Street roughly halfway along its length. The name Little South Street is marked on the eastern stretch of road by the 1889 OS map and there were buildings fronting onto this street at that time. In 1911, a number of households were listed here, including those of Charles Hargraves, a farm labourer (number 1); Robert Taylor Cook, an agricultural mechanic (number 3); Charles Forman, a joiner working for the railway (number 4); Joseph Garbutt, a baker (number 5); and Charles Coates, a domestic groom (number 7). The road saw a small number of additional buildings constructed on it in the mid–late twentieth century.

LONDON ROAD

London Road currently runs southwards from UPGATE, beginning next to the London Road Cemetery and the junction with JULIAN BOWER. Previous to the late nineteenth century, however, it appears that at least part of the southern section of Upgate, between the junction with NEWMARKET and the Cemetery, was also sometimes considered to be part of London Road. So, for example, Bowling Green House—located on the above stretch of road and the home of West Larder, lime burner (see BOWLING GREEN LANE)—was classed as part of London Road in the 1860s and 1870s, but by the 1880s it was instead treated as lying on Upgate (as number 89); there was a lime works listed on London Road that was run by Thomas Haywood in 1841 and Thomas Clapham in 1872 (on Clapham, see GRIMSBY ROAD), which must have been in one of those pits marked on the southern part of Upgate on the 1906 map of the town; and in 1849, George Thompson's Plough beerhouse, located on the south side of the junction between modern Upgate and Newmarket, was listed on London Road, as was Charles Scott's Lion beerhouse, which was located on the opposite side of the same road.

London Road was also known as Spilsby Road in the nineteenth century and was part of the Dexthorpe Turnpike, as was the road that ran west from WESTGATE to Market Rasen. This turnpike was established by an Act of Parliament in 1765 and the south-bound toll house was at Kenwick Bar, just beyond the LOUTH A16 BYPASS roundabout (see further below). The turnpike trust was responsible for the improvement of the road and the London Road causeway by 'Hungry Spot' was probably its work, as was the cutting through Julian Bower Hill, made to lower the gradient of the turnpike (this was completed in 1839). Before it became part of the Dexthorpe Turnpike and known variously as the Spilsby Road, London Road and Upgate, the road south from Newmarket was probably known as 'Spittle hill laine', after the medieval leper hospital that used to be located at Spital Hill on the western side of road here (see SPITAL HILL). In 1603 it was ordered that 'all whose grounds abut upon the common sewer in Spittle hill laine leading as far as Gillyon Bower [Julian Bower]' needed to cleanse and flush the sewer that lay against their property. The modern street that is named Spital Hill is a post-1808 development and, as such, the section of road that led up to Julian Bower and which was called Spittle hill laine in 1603 cannot have been this—rather, Spittle hill laine must be the early seventeenth-century name for that section of modern Upgate/London Road which ran south to at least Julian Bower.

The most important development on the section of road currently called London Road is, of course, the town's cemetery. This was opened here in 1855, with a mortuary chapel for the Anglicans and one for the

Nonconformists. This new site replaced the over-full cemetery at St Mary's, off BRIDGE STREET, which in turn had replaced the medieval cemetery around St James's Church. The final cost of the new cemetery was around £2,700—equivalent to approximately £250,000 today—and it opened for Nonconformists in March 1855, with the Anglican portion consecrated in December after some delay and argument. Interestingly, the cemetery site appears also to have been used as a burial site in the sixth century: a skeleton accompanied by an Anglo-Saxon cruciform brooch of that period was found buried 18 inches below the ground surface at the London Road Cemetery. Another significant development on London Road was the establishment of sports grounds here. Louth Cricket Club arrived first, opening a new ground and pavilion on London Road in 1869. Louth previously had cricket grounds on Hallington Walk (presumably near Hubbard's Hills), where Louth played the Stamford club in July 1838; on Elkington Cow Pasture, where Louth played the All England Eleven in 1850 (see Louth A16 Bypass); and 'near to the railway station', mentioned in 1851 (presumably on the two and a half acres of pasture known as Cricket Close that was located in the triangle between HIGH HOLME ROAD and NEWBRIDGE HILL—this belonged to Adam Eve, of the JAMES STREET carpet factory, in 1831). In the late twentieth and, especially, the early twenty-first centuries, the London Road cricket ground saw significant redevelopment, with around £1.5 million spent on the new pavilion and pitches here in 2007–09, including two new adult football pitches and a new cricket oval. In the late twentieth century, Louth Athletics Club also set up a track across the road on the former site of town waste tip, which had in turn replaced allotment gardens in the mid-twentieth century. Finally, new allotment gardens were established by the 1960s on the west side of London Road, south of Julian Bower, which still exist today, and in the early 1930s a specialist Tuberculosis Hospital was founded on the western side of London Road, to the south of Julian Bower, where Luda Lodge is.

At the south end of London Road was the toll house at Kenwick Bar, just beyond the Louth A16 Bypass roundabout. In 1844, the toll house was occupied by Jacob Gainsley and his wife. On the evening of Thursday, 30 May 1844, a man named William Markham (a former baker's apprentice in Louth and a keeper of Lincoln Lunatic Asylum) asked for a drink and a biscuit, which Mr Gainsley supplied him with in his house. Markham examined the brace of pistols old Gainsley had on the wall and asked him what they were for—he replied 'to protect myself from robbers', at which Markham took one down and shot at the old man. Missing his aim, he took a heavy hammer out and beat Mr Gainsley around the head with it, doing the same to Mrs Gainsley when she entered the room and attempted to stop him (he also bit off part of one of her fingers). The Gainsleys' son then entered the room and was shot with the second pistol, although the ball lodged in his arm and he was then able to wrestle the hammer from the attacker and use it upon him. Whilst they fought, the old man recovered enough to retrieve his sword-stick, which he unsheathed and then stabbed the assailant with several times. The three struggled together until they were all too weak from loss of blood to continue, the toll house being reportedly completely besmeared with it. Meanwhile, old Mrs Gainsley got out of one of the windows to raise the alarm—on discovering this, Markham took out a razor and threatened to slit his own throat unless he was allowed to flee, which the men apparently let him do. He was eventually tracked down to Bilsby, near Alford, where he slit his throat upon hearing the police enter his lodgings. A surgeon managed to sew up the wound up again, but he ripped it open once more when he was left alone. Despite this, William Markham survived. He had apparently intended to avenge himself on Gainsley for informing on his brother for riding on the shafts of his wagon three years previously. His defence was that a recent epileptic fit had left him of unsound mind, but he was nonetheless found guilty of shooting with intent to kill; Markham was transported on the Hyderabad (with 249 other convicts) to Norfolk Island, between Australia and New Zealand, on 15 October 1844. He was subsequently transferred to Port Arthur on Van Diemen's Land (now Tasmania) in 1847, and he died there on the 26 Dec 1882.

LONGLEAT DRIVE

Longleat Drive runs south-west from ARUNDEL DRIVE. The road is absent from the 1974–6 OS map, although at least three of the properties are recorded as constructed by 1970; the road had been fully developed by the mid-1980s. The land it is built on was originally part of Louth's old open North Field.

LOUTH A16 BYPASS

The Louth A16 Bypass was opened in 1991 with a party and carnival organized by the Rotary Club of Louth. The campaign for a bypass began in the 1960s, but work only started on it in 1988, with the final road costing £6.6 million (equivalent to around £11 million today). The new bypass followed one of the more expensive of the proposed routes, to the west of Hubbard's Hills, after a local campaign against the cheaper options that would have seen the bypass cut across Westgate Fields and the Golf Course off CROWTREE LANE.

There are a handful of interesting sites and find-spots close to the bypass. For example, a large scatter of Neolithic/Bronze Age flints was recovered from a site between the bypass and Brock a Dale plantation, in Raithby cum Maltby parish (between the HORNCASTLE ROAD and the LONDON ROAD roundabouts). There has also been a find of an odd, silver ancient Greek coin of around 500–250 BC from the area of the northern end of the bypass. The coin could be a modern copy, but if it is genuine then it would be an intriguing find—other early Greek coins from Lincolnshire include a third- to first-century BC coin from Heckington and a fourth-century BC coin of Philip II of Macedon from Tupholme. The Bypass also passes through Elkington Cow Pasture to the west of Louth (north of the LINCOLN ROAD). This was the site of much sporting activity in the nineteenth century. It was used frequently for fox hunts (by, amongst others, Lord Yarborough's Hounds) from at least the 1820s, and also for steeple chases. Moreover, there was a cricket ground here—first mentioned in 1849, the cricket ground at Elkington Cow Pasture was the site of the match between Louth and the All England Eleven, including Alfred Mynn, which was played on the 23–25 September 1850. The match was watched by up to 1,500 spectators, and the All England Eleven won the match in one innings.

LOVE LANE

Love Lane runs between CROWTREE LANE and WESTGATE. It is marked on the 1808 plan of Louth but appears to have been entirely undeveloped throughout the course of the nineteenth century, with houses only being constructed off this road during the twentieth century—Riverdale was built first, apparently in the mid-twentieth century, with Westgreen coming later.

LUDGATE & HEALEY'S COURT

Modern Ludgate lies to the east of the original Ludgate. The latter was cleared to make way for the old Telephone Exchange, which was first constructed in 1965–6 and subsequently extended, and what is now Ludgate was actually the historical Healey's Court.

Ludgate (occasionally termed Ludgate Hill) ran north from CHEQUERGATE and probably had its origins in the first half of the nineteenth century, given that it appears to be absent from both the 1778 and 1808 plans of the town, but is labelled on William Brown's 1844 sketch of the town and is identifiable on the 1839 map of Louth. In 1828–9, the only business listed on Ludgate was the coach works of Stephen A'Court. In 1835, there were more businesses listed on Ludgate, including two coach makers (Paul Strawson and Henry Walkington), a coach smith (George Dyas) and an Infants' School (run by John and Mary Shefford). By 1841, however, the only coach maker on Ludgate was Esberger & Co., with Henry Walkington no longer listed and Paul Strawson then being based on Walkergate, modern QUEEN STREET. The coachsmith and the school were similarly absent in that year (the Infants' School was on Enginegate—BROADBANK—in 1841 and run by William Rodgers). Esberger & Co.'s carriage and coach builders, later Esberger & Son, was said to be founded in 1818 and continued to trade from Ludgate into the early twentieth century, although they were taken over by another firm before World War One. William Brown's final Panorama of 1847–56 depicts Esberger's works, including part-built coaches in the yard. The other significant business on Ludgate from the mid-nineteenth century was a posting house and livery stables. This was run by George Smith in the 1870s and 1880s, by Emma Smith (George Smith's widow) in the early 1890s, and then by Isaac Thorn from at least 1896 onwards. Thorn's livery stables diversified into a motor garage in the early twentieth century and supplied carriages and cabs to meet every passenger train at the railway station off RAMSGATE; it also ran a charabanc service to Mablethorpe in 1930s. Finally, Chequergate Iron Works was based on the eastern corner of Ludgate and Chequergate. This is depicted on the 1889 OS map of the town and was presumably where James Turner, agricultural implement maker, engineer and machine manufacturer of Chequergate was based (he is listed as such in the 1885 directory and in the 1891 census).

In addition to businesses, Ludgate was also home to a quantity of residential properties, mostly low-quality, one up-one down terraced houses, which were already there by the time of Brown's 1844 sketch of the street. In 1861, inhabitants of Ludgate included Frederick Esberger, master coachbuilder and employer of seven men and five boys (number 10); Elizabeth Medley, aged 75, a pauper (number 8); Henry Grounsell, a millwright (number 19); John Jackson, an agricultural labourer, and his son Newel, listed simply as 'insane' (number 1); John Jenney, a plumber and glazier (number 13); and Bratley Smith, a butcher (number 22). In 1891, there were a similar range of people represented, including Emma Smith, a livery stable keeper (number 24); George Andrew Muck, a house painter (number 19); and Annie Kirman, a charwoman (number number 23). The houses here, along with the other buildings, were demolished in the mid–late twentieth century as a result of the redevelopment of this site.

With regard to Healey's Court, this does appear to have been present on the 1808 plan of the town, unlike Ludgate. The cottages here were of even lower quality than those on Ludgate and the inhabitants appear to have been poorer too—in 1861, five of the households here were headed by paupers (ranging in age from 41 to 86), and there were three washerwomen, two charwomen, several labourers and a dealer in old clothes living here. The early terraced housing here—which is visible on the 1808 plan of Louth, Brown's sketch and his Panorama—was demolished by the early 1930s, as part of the general slum clearances of that period. More recently, Healey's Court was renamed Ludgate and it has seen new development along it, including the SPOUT YARD park at its northern end.

LYNDON WAY & LYNDON CRESCENT

Lyndon Way runs north from KEDDINGTON ROAD, with Lyndon Crescent running off it. Both were laid out and developed by the mid-1970s on land that was originally part of Louth's old open North Field, before the Enclosure Act of 1801, and traces of medieval ridge and furrow have been observed from aerial photographs in the field immediately to the north of these road. The same field has also seen finds of medieval pottery, including green, brown and black glazed wares, and a scatter of Mesolithic–Neolithic/Bronze Age worked flints, including a possible microlith blade or core. Lyndon Way and Lyndon Crescent are named after the nineteenth-century Lyndon Lodge that lies to the west of the entrance to these roads. Lyndon Lodge was the home of Amy G. Robinson, the daughter of the rector of Thorganby, from at least 1889 through until after World War One, and before that it appears to have been the home of James Nell, corn merchant, in 1871, and perhaps John Burke, a market gardener, in 1861. Lyndon Lodge is probably also visible on William Brown's Panorama of 1847–56 at the far end of Keddington Road.

MAPLE CLOSE

Maple Close runs north-east from VICTORIA ROAD and is a residential housing estate built in the late twentieth century. The land it stands on was once part of the old open North Field of Louth and medieval ridge and furrow has been identified to the south of this road.

MARJORIE LANE

Marjorie Lane runs north-east from NEWMARKET. A lane in the vicinity of Marjorie Lane appears on the 1889 OS map of Louth, when it ran through to a small, unidentified building in a field. The building had gone by the mid-twentieth century, and by the end of the 1960s this lane appears to have been shortened and realigned, starting slightly further south on Newmarket, with a large warehouse constructed at its eastern end. This warehouse was subsequently developed into a substantial factory, which was in turn demolished to make way for the houses off GRESLEY ROAD. The properties to the south of Marjorie Lane appear to date from the second half of the twentieth century, after the realignment of the lane.

MARKET PLACE & CORNMARKET

It is likely that there was a market of some sort in the area of the present-day Market Place and Cornmarket from an early period, associated initially with the Middle Saxon minster (monastery) of Louth. In the latter half of the eleventh century, the centre of Louth was remodelled by Remigius, Bishop of Lincoln, in order to attract burgesses to the town that his predecessor had bought for £160. This remodelling laid out long burgage tenements (which can still be traced today to the south of MERCER ROW) and the medieval market place to the north of these tenements. This medieval market place probably originally extended from the south side of Mercer Row right across to the north side of the Cornmarket, without any interruption. This large, open area was at some point divided up into three separate areas via the construction of the two blocks of buildings that currently form the north side of Mercer Row, the south side of the Cornmarket, and the west side of the Market Place. These buildings appear to have their origins in the butchers' stalls of the medieval market place, which had been converted into two permanent blocks of buildings by the early seventeenth century at the latest (see BUTCHER LANE & LITTLE BUTCHER LANE).

There are a number of references to Louth's market place during the medieval period. The market place was, for example, the site of the medieval chapel of St John. This was first mentioned in 1311, when Roger of Louth, son of William de Lekeburne, granted his brother Master Thomas de Luda some property in the market place that lay next to the chapel of St John. In 1450, thirteen butchers were fined for leaving large piles of stinking offal at the east end of the chapel of St John, and the chapel was probably located on the west side of the medieval market place, that is, on the west side of either modern Butcher Lane or the Cornmarket (see further Butcher Lane). The chapel was demolished under the 1547 Chantries Act of Edward VI and its site passed through several hands before the Corporation of Louth finally bought it in 1567. The medieval market place was also the site of the Holy Trinity Bedehouse ('Trinitye beid house'), which provided housing, fuel and board for six poor men or women. This Bedehouse was originally supported by the Guild of the Holy Trinity until its dissolution during the Reformation, and it was apparently located on the north side of what is now the Cornmarket. The Trinity Bedehouse continued to function here until 1766, when it was united with Our Lady's Bedehouse and replaced by the apartments for Bedewomen in SCHOOLHOUSE LANE. In 1699, Mrs Gabell, a widow, paid 22s and 2 bottles of claret in rent for a chamber over the Bedehouse in the Butcher Market

(Cornmarket). There was also an 'Old Hall' somewhere 'in the markit place', which was used by the town's Corporation before the Town Hall was built in the late sixteenth century (see below on this). This continued to be used into the seventeenth century, with 21s 6d being spent on 'mending the old Hall' in 1635 and two chambers 'in the markit place called the old Hall' being leased for 41 years in 1658. Furthermore, in 1685, a shop in Mercer Row was said to be 'parcell of the Old Hall'. Taken together, these references suggest that the Old Hall was probably located somewhere around the junction of Mercer Row and the modern Market Place.

Other notable and early features of Louth's market place included the pillory—a wooden structure with holes for the head and hands, into which criminals were locked. This was first mentioned in 1274–5 and was said to be in the common market in 1428. In 1499, it was ordered that anyone tethering horses or mares around the 'Pyllore' (pillory) on market day should forfeit 2d to the lord of the manor for each offence. In 1566, Henry Totie, carpenter, was paid for significant works on the pillory, including 74s 4d for 'timbr to the pillorie'. Further payments for work on the pillory are mentioned in the sixteenth and the seventeenth centuries, through until 1677. The stocks (into which the feet of a criminal were locked whilst they were in a sitting position) were presumably also in the market place—they are referenced in 1447, when a thief was placed in them before being taken to Lincoln gaol, and a number of payments concerning them are recorded from the sixteenth and seventeenth centuries, as in 1637 when 2s was paid for mending the irons of the stocks. Whether the whipping post, mentioned three times in the seventeenth century, was also in the market place is unclear. However, there was a public water-supply in the market place from an early period. A well 'in the markitstede' was mended in 1516–17 at a cost of 6s 8d, and a new pump of lead was erected in the market place in 1597. There continued to be a water-supply here into the nineteenth and twentieth centuries, with a new pump and pillar set up in the Market Place in 1821 using part of the money subscribed for the demolition of the late sixteenth-century Town Hall.

A number of references are made to events occurring at the market in Louth during the medieval and early modern periods. Some of these mention violence or thievery. For example, in July 1442, a gang from outside of town, led by John Towes of Kelstern and Robert Chatterton of Thoresway, assaulted a servant of Thomas Fitzwilliam in the market place of Louth with carleaxes, swords and staves. In 1447, 'a certain thief whose name is at present unknown' (that is, he must never have given his name and was unknown in the town) stole, in the common market at Louth, a pair of knives from Thomas Randolue of Skamulby (Scamblesby) and another pair from Master Alan Barton, chaplain (he was the individual mentioned above who was placed in the stocks; he subsequently died in Lincoln gaol). Others mention the practice of forestalling. Forestalling was the making of excessive profits by buying goods before the market opened—signalled at Louth by the ringing of a bell, with the Churchwardens paying Robert Odlyng 20d for setting up the bell in the market place in 1550—and then selling them on at a higher price, to the detriment of ordinary market-goers who could otherwise have bought the goods more cheaply. For example, in 1450 the bailiff reported that a stranger had brought some salmon to market—a luxury fish—and Thomas Brygge and John Wryght, butcher, had bought it before it was offered at the market so that they could then sell it at a higher price, which they did 'taking excessive gain'. Similarly, John Styrcroft was accused of buying sieves at market in 1447 from William Syver of Langwath and then reselling them at a small profit 'to the prejudice of the lord and the detriment of his market' (this was regrating, which was like forestalling but done whilst the market was running). Yet more references mention fraud in the market place—for example, in 1602, William Camplymd and Walter Ramerley of Marshchapel sold salt in Louth Market Place 'by illicit measures, to the great damage of the subjects of the lady the queen'.

Entertainments and other notable happenings are also recorded as occurring in the market place during this period. For example, in 1557–8 a payment of 16d was made to the schoolmaster, Mr Goodall, in order to reimburse him for money spent on the furnishing of the Corpus Christi play that was put on in the market place the previous year. The market place was also probably the site of bull- and bear-baiting then. The former activity was first mentioned in Louth in 1430–1, and bull-baiting usually took place in or near to market squares and near to slaughtering areas, making Louth's market place a good candidate for the site of this medieval and early modern spectator sport (the butchers' stalls were in the west of the medieval market place and butchers are said to have slaughtered livestock in the Butcher Market, modern Cornmarket, as late as the mid-nineteenth century). The last reference to the baiting of bulls with dogs in Louth occurs in 1641. With regard to bear-baiting, this is mentioned three times in the 1530s and 1540s (for example, in 1537-8 the Churchwardens paid 20d to the servants of the queen's grace for a bear), and whilst no location is specified, the market place is once again a credible candidate. More seriously, in 1537 the market place was used to hang six men for their part in Lincolnshire Rising. Their executions were delayed until market day, Saturday 10 March, so that the people of Louth could assemble and witness the deed, and in this context it is important to note that the market place had functioned as a gathering place for the people of Louth at the start of the Lincolnshire Rising too, when a crowd had assembled here to burn the books of John Franke, or Frankishe, the Registrar of the Bishop, in October 1536.

Turning to look specifically at the modern Cornmarket, this has been known by a number of names in the post-medieval period: the Cornmarket, from at least the early eighteenth century through until the present day; the Butcher Market, from at least the late seventeenth century through until the late nineteenth century; and the Beast Market, from at least the early seventeenth century through until the early nineteenth century. With regard to the name Butcher Market, this is the name used on the early plans of the town and in some of the nineteenth-century censuses, and it was also used in a rental of 1699 which refers to the Trinity Bedehouse as being in the Butcher Market. This name, like Butcher Lane and Little Butcher Lane, probably derives from the use of this part of the medieval and early modern market place by butchers' stalls, with these being converted, at some point, into two permanent blocks of buildings that now form the southern side of the Cornmarket. Indeed, the small shops on the south of Cornmarket are said to have been used almost exclusively by butchers (who slaughtered livestock in front of them) until the mid-nineteenth century.

The early name Beast Market is even more interesting. This name was still in use for the Cornmarket in 1815, when the New Guild Hall of 1815 (located on the site of the mid-nineteenth-century Corn Exchange in the Cornmarket, now the modern Halifax building) was described as being 'on the North-West Corner of the Beast Market in this Town'. It was more commonly used in the seventeenth century, however—so, for example, in 1670 the 'Trinity Beadhouse', which was apparently located on the north side of what is now the Cornmarket (see above), was described as being situated 'in ye beast Market', and in 1603 either Butcher Lane or Little Butcher Lane was described as running 'from the Beast Market to the Mercer Row'. This is particularly interesting from the perspective of the question of where Louth's livestock market was located in the medieval and post-medieval periods. Edward VI's charter of 1551 established a new weekly beast market in the Quarry (see NEWMARKET). However, the use of the Quarry for this new beast market, held then on a Wednesday, appears to have been short-lived, for the Warden and the Six Assistants were clearly petitioning for permission to move the market from the Quarry by the early seventeenth century, apparently on the grounds of convenience—presumably the Quarry, located beyond the edge of the town, was inconvenient as a site for a weekly market. They received this permission in 1605 from King James I, who agreed that they could henceforth move the weekly market 'of oxen, sheep and swine' from the Quarry to 'a certain place within the town aforesaid [Louth], called the Beast Market', or to 'any other convenient and fit place within the town, or the precincts thereof'.

There are two important implications to be taken from the above. The first is that the Warden and the Six Assistants wished to move the weekly beast market to a place called Beast Market which lay in Louth— in other words, they wished to move it to the modern Cornmarket, which was called the Beast Market in contemporary documents. How long they kept this 'market of oxen, sheep and swine' in the centre of town is not entirely clear from our surviving evidence. In 1785, however, it was resolved that the 'Sheep and Pig Markett' would in future be kept in the 'New Markett Place in Upgate, and nowhere else in Louth'. Although it isn't stated where the sheep and pig market was being moved from, the Beast Market or Cornmarket seems the most plausible solution. Not only was it where the Corporation moved it *to* in the early seventeenth century, but the new site on Upgate is also termed the 'New Markett Place', which carries overtones of it replacing the old Market Place in the centre of town, and the statement that the sheep and pig markets will henceforth be held 'nowhere else in town' suggests that they had been held within town up to that point (the Quarry, it should be noted, was still very much beyond the borders of the town in 1785, as can be seen from Espin's map of 1808, which shows it to have been then separated from the town by fields). The 'Market for Sheep and Pigs' was eventually moved back to the Quarry in 1802 (specifically, to 'some place

167

in the Quarrell to be set out by the Corporation for that purpose'), though whether the cattle market returned to the Quarry before or after the sheep and pig market moved there is not entirely clear. In 1817, it was resolved that 'a Market for the sale of fat and lean cattle be holden in the Quarry in Louth in Louth on Friday the 18th day of April Instant and on every Friday fortnight afterwards.'

The second implication is that at least part of Louth's market place had been used for a beast market at some point previous to 1605, as otherwise that fact that the Cornmarket area was already 'called the Beast Market' in 1605 (and, indeed, in 1603) is difficult to explain. Given that Louth's weekly market for oxen, sheep and swine had been based at the Quarry from 1551 under the provisions of Edward VI's charter and that the Warden and the Six Assistants had to petition for permission to move it from here, the suggestion must be that the name 'Beast Market' for the Cornmarket area had its origins in a pre-1551 usage of at least this part of the medieval market place. In other words, it is likely that the Corporation wished to move the weekly market to the site in town where beasts had been traditionally sold before 1551. In this context, it may well be relevant that there is a reference from 1529 to a tenement in town that was situated in the 'Sheip-markytsted' (Sheep-marketstead), which was presumably a variant form of 'Beast Market'.

With regard to the buildings and businesses of the Cornmarket in the modern period, a couple of sites are particularly deserving of comment. One is the site in the north-west corner of the Cornmarket, now occupied by the Halifax bank. A theatre was built here by Edward Blyth, merchant, in around 1790, and this was the venue for the first performance of 'True Patriotism: or, Poverty ennobled by Virtue', which was apparently met with 'universal applause' and printed by J. Jackson of Louth in 1799. The lower part of building was also used by the bankers Abraham and Challis Sheath of Boston as a banking house. The Theatre was bought and converted into the town's 'New Guild Hall' in 1815, after the demolition of the Town Hall that stood in the Market Place (below). Subsequently, the Theatre continued in a small building behind the Guildhall, which is depicted on Bayley's 1834 plan of the town. The theatre here is mentioned in 1830 and was the cause of some controversy in 1836. The *Hull Packet* reported in December 1836 that 'the *Liberal* town-council of Louth, who consist of Dissenters, have refused permission to Mrs W. Robinson to open the Theatre there, on account of the wickedness of theatrical entertainments!' The Theatre had finally closed by 1845 and the new Corn Exchange was subsequently built on the site of the Guildhall and Theatre. The foundation stone for the Corn Exchange was laid in 1853 by the Mayor, and the building was built for a contract price of £2,110 by John Levitt of Louth, who was also a stonemason. The very detailed Italianate frontage of the new, three-storey building weathered extremely badly, because the stone it was made from had been incorrectly cut, and it was said to be 'like a rotting cadaver' by Pevsner in 1964. It was demolished in 1974 and replaced by the Halifax building in 1981, with the old statue of Ceres put on plinth over ROSEMARY LANE, until it had to be taken down due to its continued decay in 1993.

The sites either side of the Halifax are also of interest. That to the east is the Masons Arms Hotel. The three-storey front range of the Masons Arms probably dates from the eighteenth century, although it was extensively remodelled in the mid-nineteenth century and around 1900, whilst the part of the Masons Arms behind the front unit, the rear bar, may be seventeenth century in origin. This inn is first mentioned in the eighteenth century, when it was called the Bricklayer's Arms. The earliest reference appears to come from Christian Frederick Esberger's journal for 1764, where he refers to putting his horse up in 'the Briklayers Arms' in Louth in July of that year. There were subsequently a number of references in newspapers to the Bricklayer's Arms from 1780 to 1800, and it also appears in the 1782 licensing list. In around 1800, the Congregationalists, or Independents, met in a loft near to the north entrance of the yard of the Bricklayer's Arms (their chapel was subsequently built on CANNON STREET), and in 1801 the proprietor of the Bricklayer's Arms was Rebecca Wilson, who also provided a postal service. The inn was renamed the Masons Arms in 1801 and has continued to trade under this name ever since. On the opposite side of the Halifax building, to its west, is the HSBC bank. This was the premises of the Lincoln & Lindsey Banking Co., which had opened a branch in Mercer Row in 1833, but quickly moved to its permanent site in the Cornmarket (it was there by 1841). This bank was amalgamated with the Midland Bank in 1913, which was in turn acquired by the Hongkong and Shanghai Banking Corporation in 1991. The Louth branch was renamed the HSBC in 1999.

Turning to look at the modern Market Place, this was home to some significant buildings. Perhaps the most interesting of these were the Market House and the Town Hall, both products of the late sixteenth century. The Market Hall was begun in February 1580, when £58 2s 11d was paid by the Warden towards 'the making and new building of the market howse w'in the market place of lowth', and even larger sums were spent on the 'markett howse standing in the market place' in 1581, including paying for carrying loads of stone from the old Louth Park Abbey for use in its construction. The Town Hall was begun in 1585 and completed in 1597, and it functioned as a town hall, session house and lock-up for over two hundred years. In 1714, the roof of the Town Hall was so decayed and out of repair that it had to be removed and replaced, and 'a good large Town Clock' was erected upon the new roof. In 1769, the cage and dungeon that took up the lower part of the Town Hall were converted into two shops, with a new cage and dungeon created under a set of steps constructed on the outside of the hall at that time. The Town Hall in the Market Place was eventually demolished in 1815, with the Theatre in the Cornmarket being purchased in that year and converted into the 'New Guild Hall' to replace it; shortly before its demolition, a drunken soldier imprisoned in the cage set fire to his straw bed there and so lost his life.

With regard to the location of the Town Hall of 1585, it has recently been suggested that this was erected in the south-east corner of the modern Market Place, where there is currently a pedestrian island opposite the former Woolworths store. However, this is almost certainly wrong. A Corporation record from 1815 is quite clear that the sixteenth-century Town Hall ('the Old Guild Hall'), which had been 'lately taken down', was 'in the South West Corner of the Market Place', not the south-east. Furthermore, both the 1805 Enclosure Award plan and Espin's original 1808 plan of Louth clearly mark the town hall in the south-west corner of the Market Place—indeed, it is shown half in the south-west corner of the Market Place and half in the middle of Mercer Row, partly blocking that street and leaving only two narrow accessways from Mercer Row through to the Market Place (to the north and to the south of the Town Hall). This odd and inconvenient position for the Town Hall of 1585–1815 is confirmed in volume nine of John Britton's *The Beauties of England and Wales* (London, 1807), which states that Louth's 'town-hall is an old plain building, standing at the end of the principal street leading to the market place. By dividing a part of the street into two narrow lanes, it becomes offensive to the eye and a nuisance to the inhabitants.' If the Town Hall therefore wasn't located in the south-east corner of the Market Place, but rather in the south-west, there may still have been something in this corner, not least because possible footings were observed here when the pedestrian island was constructed. What these might have been from is uncertain, but one possibility is that they could relate to the 'markett howse standing in the market place' of 1580–1.

Moving forward into the modern period, the Market Place saw the erection of another new Market Hall in 1866–7, the Market House of 1580–1 having apparently disappeared by the nineteenth century. The new Market Hall—still used as a market hall until the late twentieth century but now occupied by the Yorkshire Trading Company—was built on the northern side of the Market Place at a cost of £7000, and a number of properties had to be demolished to make way for it, including one of the 'great houses' of Louth. The latter was first mentioned in 1621, when it belonged to George Smith, and again in 1624, when it belonged to his sister, Frances, the widow of Abraham Blanchard. The 'great house' on the north side of the Market Place was also where John Naull entertained William Cobbett, the radical campaigner, in 1830. Another of the properties lost during the building of the new Market Hall was the New Reindeer Inn. This was first mentioned in 1782 and its landlord in 1861 was Dickinson Lewis, innkeeper and brewer. In September 1858, there were two complaints of billiards being played at late hours in the New Reindeer Inn, to the annoyance of the neighbours—Dickinson Lewis, the licensee then too, promised to be more circumspect in the future. On the opposite side of the Market Place was another lost inn, the Fleece. The Fleece Inn was on the site of the former Woolworths—now a discount store—on the south side of the Market Place from at least 1755, when it is first mentioned in newspaper advertisements. It changed its name to the Golden Fleece in the early twentieth century and the old hotel frontage in the Market Place was bought by Woolworths, with the present Golden Fleece then being erected in the old inn yard; the current Market Place entrance to the store on this site dates from the mid-twentieth-century, but the original Fleece Inn frontage survives above ground level. During World War

One, members of the Scottish Horse Regiment were billeted at the Golden Fleece, with their horses stabled in the inn yard.

Other interesting buildings and businesses in the Market Place include, on the south side, the current Spar store, next to the former Fleece Inn, which has an elaborately decorated Victorian frontage above the twentieth-century ground floor of the building. On the east side of the Market Place, the street is dominated by the impressively high frontage of the Oxfam charity shop. This was originally the new printing premises of J. and T. Jackson, which was opened on New Year's Day, 1844, although the Jacksons' printing business had been based here since the late eighteenth century: J. Jackson printed 'True Patriotism: or, Poverty ennobled by Virtue' in 1799; J. & J. Jackson printed 'Poems by Two Brothers', by Alfred and Charles Tennyson, in 1827; and the Jackson firm was the agent for the *Hull Packet* newspaper from at least 1800. Finally, mention ought to be made of Eve & Ranshaw on the north side of the Market Place. This firm has its origins in the latter half of the eighteenth century, with Adam Eve trading as a mercer and grocer on the western part of the Market Place site from 1781. The imposing Market Place frontage and plate glass windows of this store apparently date from the 1880s, shortly after the name of the store was finally established in its modern form. By 1890, the millinery and dressmaking department of Eve & Ranshaw alone employed 40 women.

Lying at the centre of town, the Cornmarket and the Market Place were often the scenes of criminal activity, violence, drunkenness and other curious happenings in the nineteenth century, just as they were in the medieval and early modern periods. For example, in 1848 Robert Baker, poulterer, was charged with being drunk and disorderly in the Butcher Market at the time that prisoners were being taken from the gaol into the sessions court for trial (the sessions court was presumably being held in the Guildhall at that time). In 1855, a gardener of Louth named William Donnington—see LITTLE LANE & MOUNT PLEASANT—was charged with creating a great disturbance on Saturday night in the Market by 'beating his wife in a most unmanly manner because she would not give him money to buy more drink': this was his seventh conviction for similar offences, and he was fined 20s and costs. In 1847, James Wilson, a resident in a brothel in Louth, was charged by Robert Wood, toy-dealer, with stealing five brooches, some earrings and other articles from his shop in the Market Place—Wilson apparently crept into the shop after seeing that no-one was in it, holding the bell so that it wouldn't ring, but was observed doing this by some boys who informed the police. In 1851, two men attached to an American circus that was performing in Louth were charged with stealing a silver spoon from the Fleece Inn, where they were staying with the circus horses (they were apprehended in Alford, where they had travelled on to with the circus). In 1849, James Brewster, aged twelve, was charged with picking the pocket of Miss Emma Hunt in the Market Place and was sent to prison for three months 'as a rogue and vagabond'. Finally, in 1842 there was a case of wife-selling in the 'open market' at Louth, when an unnamed man sold his wife to another for 5s, 'receiving 6d back for luck'.

MARTIN CLOSE

See SWALLOW DRIVE.

MAYFIELD CRESCENT

Mayfield Crescent runs east from KENWICK ROAD and had been largely developed by the early 1950s, although the properties in the central area of the crescent are slightly later in date. The land that Mayfield Crescent stands on was part of the town's old open South Field, and medieval ridge and furrow has been observed on aerial photographs of this area.

MEADOW CLOSE

Meadow Close runs north from TUDOR DRIVE and both are part of the SEYMOUR AVENUE housing estate, which was constructed off NEWMARKET in the late twentieth century. Meadow Close is built on land that was once part of the old open South Field of Louth, although a more immediate predecessor was J. North & Son's market garden off LINDEN WALK. This market garden was first recorded in the mid-nineteenth century and still appeared on OS maps into the mid-twentieth century; the houses on the western side of Meadow Close are constructed on its former grounds.

MERCER ROW

The centre of Louth is believed to have been remodelled after 1066 in order to create burgage tenements, with 80 households of burgesses established in the town by 1086. The early, pre-1100 forms of such tenement plots in towns are generally very long and narrow, running back from the main street, whilst those of the twelfth and thirteenth centuries tend to be less elongated. Once established, the boundaries of these plots are usually extremely long-lived features in towns and traceable into the modern period, and this appears to be the case in Louth too. Here the late nineteenth-century Ordnance Survey maps of Louth and its property boundaries clearly show long and narrow, early-style plots fronting onto Mercer Row, and it is a reasonable conclusion that this road preserves on its south-side the original tenement boundaries created by the late eleventh-century remodelling of the town. As to what lay to the north of these tenements in the medieval period, the answer is almost certainly the town's market place. This probably originally extended from the south side of Mercer Row right across to the north side of the CORNMARKET, without any interruption. This large, open area was at some point divided up into three separate areas via the construction of the two blocks of buildings that currently form the north side of Mercer Row, the south side of the Cornmarket, and the west side of the MARKET PLACE. These buildings appear to have their origins in the butchers' stalls of the medieval market place, which had been converted into two permanent blocks of buildings by the early seventeenth century at the latest (see BUTCHER LANE & LITTLE BUTCHER LANE).

In the medieval and early modern periods, the people engaged in commerce and industry on this street probably practiced their business at the Mercer Row end of the tenements and used the southern sections away from road for other activities, such as keeping livestock or small-scale vegetable growing (see further KIDGATE). In terms of the commercial activities and trades taking place here, it is likely that at least some of the bakers, vintners (wine merchants), carpenters, painters, smiths, bookbinders, tailors, cap-makers, leather dealers, bell-makers, wool merchants, tipplers (tavern-keepers), barbers, parchment-makers, doctors, saddlers, cheesemongers and the like who seem to have lived in the medieval town were based here, along with the mercers—dealers in textile fabrics—after whom the street is named. There are also a number of references to Mercer Row in the medieval and early modern periods. For example, in 1450 thirteen men were fined for placing offal in 'the common way' at the south end of the butchers' stalls, which was probably Mercer Row, and in 1550, Thomas Spenser, a draper (a dealer in woollen cloth), gave a shop on Mercer Row, with a chamber over it and a little house to its rear, to the Churchwardens of Louth. The yearly rent of the above property, which was around £4, was to be used by the Churchwardens to support the poor of Louth.

The conversion of the butchers' stalls of the medieval market into a permanent block of buildings forming the north side of Mercer Row— probably at some point between the mid-fifteenth century and the end of the sixteenth—was obviously a very significant development in the history of Mercer Row. Another was the erection of the New Town Hall in 1585–97. This was situated half in the south-west corner of the Market Place and half in the middle of Mercer Row, partly blocking the street and leaving only two narrow accessways from Mercer Row through to the Market Place (to the north and to the south of the Town Hall). In 1807, John Britton wrote that the Town Hall stood 'at the end of the principal street leading to the market place' and that, 'by dividing a part of the street into two narrow lanes, it becomes offensive to the eye and a nuisance to the inhabitants.' The sixteenth-century Town Hall remained in this inconvenient position until 1815, when it was demolished. The 'Old Hall' that the 1585 Town Hall had replaced as a public hall may also have been situated at this end of Mercer Row, where the road runs into the modern Market Place. The 'Old Hall' was said to have been 'in the markit place' in 1658 and a shop in Mercer Row was said to be 'parcell of the Old Hall' in 1685—taken together these references imply such a location, and quantities of dressed stone have been found in this area, behind 32 Mercer Row, currently Shoe Zone (see further Market Place & Cornmarket on both of these buildings).

Looking into the modern era, there are a number of significant buildings on Mercer Row. One was the New King's Head inn, at the western end of the street, now the King's Head Hotel (for the 'Old King's Head', see NEW STREET). This inn is first specifically mentioned in the mid-eighteenth century. In 1747, for example, a cock fight at 'the New King's Head at Louth' was advertised in the *London Evening Post*. The event was to last three days (Tuesday 12 May–Thursday

14 May) and 53 cocks were to take part, the highlight being a match between the cocks of the Duke of Ancaster and George Heneage, Esq., with a prize of 20 guineas a battle. Cock fighting at the New King's Head is mentioned again in 1755, when fights were scheduled to take place there each morning of the Louth Races, with a prize of five guineas a battle (Thomas Taylor is listed as the landlord then). The New King's Head was one of the 'better' inns in town, and was not the scene of significant and regular disturbances, unlike some of the public houses in the town. It was, for example, used for auctions, property sales and bankruptcy cases in the eighteenth and nineteenth centuries, and it provided accommodation for travellers; functioned as a posting house; hosted the South Wold Hunt Ball supper in the 1840s and 1850s (which was attended by local luminaries, with the dancing held at the Mansion House on UPGATE); and was used for the festivities surrounding the laying of the foundation stone of the new Town Hall in 1853.

One notable visitor to the King's Head was the Duchess of St Albans, Harriet Mellon. She was a famously beautiful former actress who had married a wealthy banker, Thomas Coutts, and later the 9th Duke of St Albans, William Beauclerk. Large crowds apparently lined the streets on her arrival in town in 1828, forcing her carriage to travel at walking pace, and constables had to be employed to keep the crowds outside of the New King's Head when she arrived there. In response, the 'rabble' outside lifted each other up to try and spy at her through the windows, whilst others lined the upper windows of a facing grocer's house in order to gaze into the inn. When the Duchess went shopping in Louth, she was reportedly followed by the ladies of Louth from store to store, with her every purchase observed through the shop windows. The Duchess, on leaving Louth, apparently vowed never to visit the town again, a verdict that the *Stamford Mercury* wholeheartedly approved of, deploring the 'rudeness' of the folk of Louth. *The Times* of London, however, rather acidly observed that if the Duchess wished for privacy, then she might usefully reconsider her fondness for public exhibition and ostentatious displays of munificence.

The current Gothic frontage of the inn was completed in 1839 and was designed by the landlord at that time, George Rivis Willoughby, who was a trained architect. The King's Head continued to be one of the major inns in Louth through the nineteenth and twentieth centuries—selling around 64,000 pints of beer each year, along with 200 gallons of spirits, in 1929—and it has recently reopened after a major refurbishment. It was not, however, the only drinking establishment on Mercer Row. Immediately opposite the King's Head was the Old Reindeer Inn, which stood on the site of the Yorkshire Building Society. This was first mentioned in 1782 and continued to function through into the early twentieth century; it was demolished in 1931 and replaced by the present Reindeer Buildings. Another significant building was located just to the east of the King's Head, where Peter Rhodes now is to be found. This was Kelsey House, which was occupied by Edward Stainton in 1613, and previously Mr Simcotes and Richard Rigges (Edward Stainton was Warden of Louth in 1618 and 1633, the year of his death). Opposite this building was the Public Building, which was built in 1833 and used by the Louth Mechanics' Institute from 1834–52, when it moved to the Mansion House on Upgate. Classes were offered in subjects such as chemistry, drawing, and botany, and lectures were provided here on a wide range of subjects.

Further east along Mercer Row is W. Boyes & Co.'s general store. This was once the site of the drapery emporium of Sutton & Oldroyd, which burnt down on 3 January 1863, with damages estimated between £16,000 and £20,000 (equivalent to around £1.2–1.5 million today) and the premises and stock being only partly insured. Twenty people who lived at the back of the shop escaped, but the old Louth fire engine proved inadequate and by the time those of Alford, Boston and Grimsby had arrived, the front wall had fallen inwards. This disaster stimulated the Corporation to establish a proper fire brigade in town. To the east of Boyes are numbers 18 and 20 Mercer Row, which stand to the west of PAWNSHOP PASSAGE. These were occupied by John Marshall, apothecary, in the early eighteenth century, and Thomas Wetherell, apothecary, after John Marshall's death in 1759. The property was then divided up around 1790, with the eastern part (number 20) becoming a home to a printer and bookseller, run first by Robert Sheardown—who had previously operated from a low thatched building at 15 Mercer Row, which had been a bookseller's from at least 1700—and later as J. W. Goulding and Son (J. W. Goulding died in 1922 and his son, Richard Goulding, in 1929). The last owner of Goulding's Bookshop was Vernon Guy Knight, who disappeared in 1964, leaving his Jaguar car at the Randolph Hotel in Oxford, and the shop ceased trading as a bookshop after this; it is currently Chuzzlewits Tea Rooms. Finally, it is worth

177

mentioning that the Boots pharmacy and chemist shop at 26 Mercer Row is a modern building, actually built in the mid-1950s for the company.

As one of the main streets in the town, Mercer Row saw a significant amount of criminal activity, violence and drunkenness in the past. For example, in May 1848, Matilda Weldon—'one of the most notorious disorderly prostitutes in this town'—was charged with behaving in an indecent manner on a Saturday night in Mercer Row. As she was of a notoriously bad character and had several previous convictions, she was sent to jail for three months. In April of the same year, a butcher named John Robinson, who kept a stall in the Market Place, was charged with being drunk and indecently exposing himself on the footpath of Mercer Row, for which he was fined 1s. In September 1854, Joseph Chapman, a fruiterer who similarly kept a stall in the Market Place, was charged with brawling and using 'disgustingly obscene language' in Mercer Row. And in January 1857, 'a poor lost creature' named Elizabeth Clarke, of North Thoresby, was charged with being drunk and disorderly in Mercer Row—she was only 15 and had about a month previously 'commenced her dreadful career of vice... in a low brothel kept by a woman named Ann Kime' in the Gatherums (see GATHERUMS & SPRINGSIDE). There were also a large number of cases involving beggars on Mercer Row. In June 1851, John Brown, a labourer from London and a discharged soldier, was charged with being drunk and begging at night time in Mercer Row. Likewise, in January 1852 Edward Hurley, an Irish labourer, was charged with begging in Mercer Row and sentenced to fourteen days—he reportedly replied 'Arrah, now, yer worship's honor that's not a bit of use to me at all; could not yer worship jist be after sending me for three months now, then it would get me the winther over nately', to which the Mayor responded in the negative. Finally, Mercer Row was occasionally the scene of punishments, notably in July 1731, when Mary Wright was found guilty of stealing goods from William Thorpe and John Prideon: she was sentenced to be stripped to the waist and whipped the length of Mercer Row, from the Town Hall to the Blue Stone, which lay at the junction of Mercer Row and Upgate (see further Upgate).

MERIDIAN VIEW

Meridian View forms the spine of a late twentieth-century housing estate running west from UPGATE. The houses here were constructed in the 1990s on land that was once part of Louth's old open South Field—medieval ridge and furrow has been identified in this area from aerial photographs.

MICHAEL FOALE LANE

Michael Foale Lane runs south-east from KEDDINGTON ROAD. It is an early twenty-first-century housing estate, houses here being sold as new builds in 2003 and 2004. The road is named after Colin Michael Foale, the British-American NASA astronaut who was born in Louth on 6 January 1957. The land that the road was built on was once part of the G.N.R. Engineering Works in the late nineteenth century, and it continued to be marked on maps as such into the mid-twentieth century.

MILL LANE

Mill Lane runs north from HIGH HOLME ROAD, and was known as High Holme Mill Lane in 1889. The corn mill after which the road is named belonged to the Topham family, whose bakery shop was based on EASTGATE. This six-sail windmill was in existence by 1872 and was eventually demolished in 1910. How long it had been here before 1872 is unclear, although the Topham mill was on WESTGATE in 1856 and both the mill and Mill Lane are absent from William Brown's Panorama of 1847–56. Aside from the mill, the road was largely undeveloped in the nineteenth century, with George Moody's High Holme Nursery (founded 1830) being the dominant feature on both sides of the road, especially the east. This situation continued into the twentieth century, although some of the nursery land on the western side of the junction between Mill Lane and High Holme Road had been replaced by housing, facing onto the latter, by 1906. By the end of the 1960s, however, the nursery land to the east of the road had been built over both by new housing fronting onto Mill Lane and by the new HOLMES CLOSE, which ran east from Mill Lane. A nursery did continue to operate on the western side of the road into the 1980s, but Mill Lane also saw continued development then, with WELBECK WAY established running west from Mill Lane in the 1970s and housing built on the final nursery grounds by the end of the 1980s (see GLAMIS PLACE). The site of the former corn mill currently lies under one of the playing fields of Cordeaux School (see NORTH HOLME ROAD).

MILLERS COURT

Millers Court is a modern road that runs north from Charles Street, immediately to the west of a lane that led to Charles Street Mill and Dyas Row in the latter half of the nineteenth century. The mill here was a six-sail windmill, located at the north end of this nineteenth century lane, and it was built on the site of a probably demolished, earlier mill—the latter was present at the time of the Enclosure Act of 1801, but it is not marked on the 1839 map of Louth, William Brown's 1844 sketch of the town or the Panorama of 1847–56. John Allison is listed as a miller and baker on Charles Street from 1861 to 1872 and presumably worked out of this mill. From 1885, Hall Brothers are listed as millers here, their windmill surviving the fire that burnt down the adjoining Crown Roller Mills in 1905. Bryan Hall's milling business subsequently moved to the RAMSGATE water mill, and no windmill is marked on 1932 OS map of this area.

With regard to the lane leading up to mill, this is present on the 1889 map of the town, as was Dyas Row, or Dyas Terrace, running north-east from the northern end of the road. In 1891, the 74 inhabitants of Dyas Row included a railway brakeman (Barton Holt, number 4), a washerwoman (Millicent Rushby, number 14), a police sergeant (George Pridgeon, number 7), a blacksmith (Elven Dixon, number 7), and a flour miller (John Lutty, number 2). By the mid-twentieth century, the windmill here was long-gone, but there were houses developed to the south of Dyas Row, on the east side of the lane. In the 1990s, a new road immediately to the west of the old lane was established, leading to four new properties—it is this that bears the name Millers Court.

MILLGOOD CLOSE

Millgood Close is a small, late twentieth century housing development that runs south-east from MONKS DYKE ROAD. The houses here were built in the 1970s.

MINSTER DRIVE

Minster Drive runs west from SPIRE VIEW ROAD and forms part of a late twentieth-century housing development off WOOD LANE. The land it is built on was once part of Louth's old open South Field.

MONKS AVENUE

Monks Avenue runs south from EASTGATE. It was formerly an accessway to the rear of the nineteenth-century Priory Terrace and Casswell Villas that front onto Eastgate, running between them and then along their back side. Immediately to the south of this lane was an open area and large pit in 1889, which was the former brickworks of Bellamy & Co. (see Eastgate). By 1906, an iron foundry had been established here which seems to have continued into the mid-twentieth century, and Monks Avenue may have provided access to this. Certainly, by 1932 there appears to have been an extension southwards of Monks Avenue into this area, along with the establishment of a handful of residential properties off Monks Avenue. By the late 1960s, the iron foundry had gone and the area to the south of Monks Avenue was a Builders Merchant's Yard and Public Works Contractor's Depot, with the latter accessed via this lane; more recently, the houses of PRIORY CLOSE were constructed on this land in the late twentieth century.

MONKS DYKE ROAD

Monks Dyke Road (sometimes Monks Dyke, Monk's Dyke Side or similar) runs east from CHURCH STREET. The earliest evidence for human activity in this area of Louth is a Bronze Age barbed and tanged arrowhead found on the field of Monk's Dyke School (approximately where St Michael's Primary School now stands), which is probably indicative of local hunting activity. The road itself is named after a later feature, the medieval Monks' Dyke. This channel was cut by the monks of Louth Park Abbey, founded in 1139, in order to supply their abbey with water from the Aswell and St Helen's springs in Louth (see

GATHERUMS & SPRINGSIDE). At the eastern end of the Monks' Dyke, the channel divided, with one arm sweeping around the east side of the abbey, serving two fish ponds, and the other flowing around the western side and then turning north to join the Lud. The first references to this channel come from the thirteenth and fourteenth centuries. According to a charter of 1315, the monks had originally paid a rent of 4d a year for the right to channel water from the two springs through to Louth Park Abbey, until John Siadeway discharged them from this obligation, and the monks' right of way here is first mentioned in a document of 1235–53. The importance of this water-supply to the monks is demonstrated by a general excommunication issued by the bishop in 1510 for all those who polluted or diverted the Monks' Dyke. By the early nineteenth century, only St Helen's spring still flowed down the dyke, with the Aswell spring having been diverted at some point to run a water mill (see CHURCH STREET). The Monks' Dyke nonetheless remained a significant feature well into the twentieth century, running alongside the road, with one motorist reversing into it by mistake in August 1929.

With regard to the road that ran alongside the dyke, this was a private carriage way at the time of the Enclosure Award of 1805, and Monks' Dyke Head—at its western end, where it joins Church Street—was mentioned in 1603. In that year, Richard Varley was ordered to 'repair the foot-way below his close at Munck dikes heade' before the first day of August, or face a fine of 3s 4d. Only a small proportion of Monks Dyke Road is visible on the 1808 and 1834 plans of the town. On the former, a wide road is shown with a building on the south side of the street between Church Street and LITTLE LANE. On the latter, a little more is depicted, including a new building on the eastern side of Little Lane and the row of cottages on the north side of Monks Dyke Road, a little further down the street, which are still there today. There was also a bridge across the Monks' Dyke just to the west of this terrace by that date, which led into a large close. William Brown's 1844 sketch of the town (made from the spire of St James's Church) and his finished Panorama of 1847–56 both offer further details, showing a road that was only partially developed, with fields and agricultural activity on both sides for much of its length, along with a scattering of buildings. From 1848, the road here was crossed by the railway (its course south of Monks Dyke Road is now preserved by a footpath leading through to

WOOD LANE and then STEWTON LANE), and Brown's Panorma shows a number of houses and other buildings beyond this crossing, including a windmill.

The latter was also present on Brown's 1844 sketch and it belonged to the brickyard of John Edwards, which was located between the railway line and that section of Monks Dyke Road which runs southwards from the modern TRINITY LANE junction before turning to continue eastwards once again—the windmill was possibly used to pump water out of brick pits here. The Edwards family also ran the Charles Street brickworks with John Dunstan Naull for a time, and John Edwards was listed as brick and tile maker on Monks Dyke from 1835. In 1851, he was living on JAMES STREET as a master bricklayer, and his widow and their family were residing on EVE STREET in 1861. John Edwards' daughter married Simeon Boss, a member of a Jewish family who lived in Louth in the 1840s and 1850s (see further James Street), and his son, Jonathan Edwards, was something of a notorious character in the town. In 1850, he was somehow involved in a fight between his brother-in-law, Simeon Boss, and William Sugden (see James Street for details), and he appeared before the court on other occasions too. In January 1848, for example, he was seventeen years old and appeared with three other teenagers on a charge of assaulting Thomas Hatcliffe of Asterby in Withcall parish—they were accused of attacking him and stealing a purse containing £3 14s (equivalent to around £290 today), although they were acquitted of this charge later the same month. In December 1852, Jonathan Edwards was in front of the court again, although this time as a supposed victim. He charged George King, a porter, with assaulting him—Edwards was apparently repeatedly 'intruding his presence' upon Ann Evison, a 'nymph-au-pave' (prostitute) who kept a brothel in the Gatherums, despite her making it clear that this was 'contrary to her wishes'. She saw George King pass by and requested his help to 'remove the intruder from the house', which he did by taking Jonathan Edwards by the collar and turfing him out into the street. The complaint by Edwards was dismissed by S. Trought, Cornelius Parker and J. B. Sharpley, who ordered Edwards to pay costs.

Other businesses on Monks Dyke Road in the mid-nineteenth century include farms and nurseries, which are visible from the Panorama (one of which was used by Valentine Fell, poulterer of Louth, for fattening 4,000 geese ready for the London Christmas market in

1849), and also a railway signals manufacturer. The latter was run by a Mr Ward 'in a building at Monk's Dyke-side'. In October 1851, it was reported that an explosion destroyed the building and burnt Mr Ward and one other, but no lives lost. This was apparently the fourth explosion in two years resulting from the making of railway signals in Louth, the first of which had resulted in a significant loss of life (see EASTGATE). After the explosion, 'young urchins' apparently purloined a number of the explosive signals from Ward's premises and 'amused themselves by throwing them at the dwelling houses of the peaceable inhabitants, causing a fearful explosion to their great alarm'! In addition to the above, there were two cabinet makers and joiners (William Edwards and William Goddard) and a wheelwright (William Beaumont) listed on Monks Dyke Road in 1835, and subsequent nineteenth-century directories listed a number of other trades here including cowkeepers, tailors, joiners, carters, horse dealers and market gardeners. The market gardening business belonged to the Mitchell family and was listed at Monks' Dyke Head in 1856 and 41 Monks Dyke Road in 1889 and 1896. By 1905, the Mitchell market garden on Monks Dyke was no longer listed, but one belonging to John Housam was, and in 1909 this appears to have been in turn replaced by two market gardens, run respectively by Peter Arliss and John Tyson. Both of these businesses were still active after World War One, when William Robinson & Sons' market gardening business (see NEWMARKET and Little Lane) was also listed on this road.

The major development in the first half of the twentieth century on Monks Dyke Road was the construction of a new 11–14 school, Monks' Dyke School, which was initially designed to have a capacity of 400 students. Discussions regarding this project began in 1924 and the proposal was initially controversial in the town, with some local worthies—especially Alderman Blaze—opposing it as waste of money, a position supported by letters in the local press (Louth ratepayers had to provide £7,000 of the £16–17,000 cost of the new school). Nonetheless, a three acre site—owned by William Robinson & Sons, see above—was chosen on Monks Dyke Road for the school and construction went ahead with a modern, open-air building design that offered a marked contrast with the older schools in the town—one letter writer in 1927 complained that the proposed buildings were palatial and that it was more like a seaside pavilion than a school! The school opened in 1929, with 295 students aged 11–14 drawn from the WESTGATE, Enginegate (BROADBANK), KIDGATE, EASTFIELD and Newmarket schools. Monks' Dyke School originally had separate entrances for boys and girls, and separate playgrounds too. For reasons of cost, the fourth part of main quadrangle was not finally completed until 1939, by which time the school had expanded to 583 pupils. This expansion was partly a result of senior pupils from the surrounding village schools being transferred to this site, and the senior pupils from the St Michael's School on Church Street were similarly relocated to Monks' Dyke School in 1939. From 1929, Monks' Dyke School used the Technical School on James Street as an annexe, in order to meet demand for places, and further pressure was placed on the school in 1947, when the leaving age was raised from 14 to 15. This added 110 pupils to the school's roll; by 1953, 654 pupils were educated here, with temporary classrooms being used to accommodate some of them. This overcrowding was eventually dealt with through the opening of a new secondary school for Louth in 1956: High Holme Road Secondary School, now Cordeaux School (see NORTH HOLME ROAD). In 1974, part of the Monks' Dyke School grounds were used for new primary school buildings, to be used by the pupils of St Michael's Church School on Church Street, with the old school on that road being demolished five years later.

Monks Dyke Road saw a considerable amount of development from the mid-twentieth century onwards. By the early 1950s, new properties had been constructed on the opposite side of the road to where Edwards' brickyard once was, and by the mid-1950s properties had been constructed along Monks Dyke Road in the area around its junction with the new ST BERNARDS AVENUE. Further new housing was developed on the road into the later twentieth century, including the properties of ALMOND CRESCENT and MILLGOOD CLOSE, which were built in the 1970s. The late twentieth century also saw considerable new building on the Monks' Dyke School site (renamed Monks' Dyke Technology College in the 1990s) and the development of the land opposite this into a supermarket car park. In the early twenty-first century, the eastern end of Monks Dyke Road was extended and a new housing estate was developed there, for which the new section of Monks Dyke Road acted as a spine.

Early inhabitants of Monks Dyke Road included Joseph Morley, the railway gatekeeper on this road in 1849, who was accused of stealing a silk handkerchief from the pack of James Marchant, hawker and lodging-house keeper (see QUEEN STREET); he was apparently very drunk at the time and the case was eventually dismissed. In 1851, Joseph Morley was killed by a railway engine whilst walking up the line from the railway station back to his gatehouse—his back and his leg were broken when the engine ran over him and he died fifteen minutes later, declaring that he had never heard the engine coming. Two other residents were Mark Hatcliffe, a hawker (travelling salesman), and John Diall, a tinner and brazier (maker of tin and brass articles), who were charged in 1848 with stealing some trousers and a blue frock coat from a house on the Riverhead, crimes of which they both were discharged due to a lack of evidence. Thomas Bratley, a tile maker, was similarly an inhabitant of this road—he was fined 2s 6d for making a disturbance at two in the morning at Monks' Dyke Head in February 1851—as was Mary Ann Goulding, who was charged in 1853 with neglecting the maintenance of 'two of her bastard children' (she was ordered to pay towards their maintenance or be sent to the House of Correction). Monks Dyke Road was also home to John Goodall or Goodhall, a carpet weaver who was born about 1807 and lived on Monks Dyke Road in 1851 with his wife Ann and his son George, who was also a carpet weaver. In August 1854, John Goodhall, carpet weaver of 'Monk's dyke-side', was charged with 'attempting to commit an indecent assault upon a child', named Maria Corden (aged 12), and also with 'an attempt of a like nature' upon another child of the same age. Maria Corden was the daughter of Thomas Corden, nail maker, whose household was listed immediately before the assailant's in the 1851 census, under MOUNT PLEASANT. The Mayor of Louth apparently 'strongly reprimanded the prisoner'; however, 'although he had pursued the child to enable him to carry out his abominable designs upon her', because Goodhall had not actually achieved these, the Mayor did not 'feel warranted in committing' him to prison. Instead, Goodhall was fined 5s and costs on a charge of having been drunk (equivalent to around £18 today).

MOUNT OLIVET

Mount Olivet (or Mount Olivet Road) runs north-west from HIGH HOLME ROAD and ultimately takes its name from Mount Olivet, or the Mount of Olives, in the Holy Land—this is one of three peaks of a mountain ridge that lies east of Jerusalem's Old City, the slopes of which were once covered in olive groves. It is mentioned a number of times in the New Testament and was the site of Jesus' Ascension into Heaven, according to Acts 1: 9–12.

Mount Olivet is not depicted on Brown's sketch of the town from 1844, nor on his final Panorama (last updated in 1856), although both the sketch and the 1824 OS map do show a four-sailed post windmill near to the northern end of modern Mount Olivet—its painted-out form can be discerned on the Panorama too and it would have stood in the grounds of Louth County Hospital, near to the phlebotomy centre (it is shown as accessible via a track from GRIMSBY ROAD on the 1824 map). In 1871, Mount Olivet appears in the census as the site of six households, the inhabitants of which included a bricklayer (John Dann) and a joiner (Charles B. Clark). In 1872, it was also the listed address for two businesses, John Dann's bricklaying and building business and a lodging-house run by Eliza Pearson. However, no businesses were listed here in subsequent directories and the street thereafter appears to have been entirely residential. The 1889 OS map depicts the road and marks the row of four terraced houses on its west side as Mount Olivet. These were presumably the houses that were numbered 1–4 Mount Olivet in the 1871 census, with the other two properties on this road given the address Mount Olivet Road.

MOUNT PLEASANT

See LITTLE LANE & MOUNT PLEASANT

MOUNT PLEASANT AVENUE

A small-scale council housing project of the inter-war years, constructed running south from MOUNT PLEASANT. The houses here were provided with hot water, bathrooms and electricity.

NEW LANE ROAD

New Lane Road ran from Hollowgate Head on the GRIMSBY ROAD through to South Elkington, across the old North Field of the town. It was blocked up by Enclosure Commisioners in 1805, but its route is still traceable on aerial photographs. The name of the road might suggest a fairly recent origin. However, given that it actually ran by the large South Elkington–Louth Anglo-Saxon cremation cemetery on the hill at Acthorpe Top, it is possible that this road may have been, in origin, a track or footway of some antiquity.

NEW STREET

New Street runs from the CORNMARKET through to EASTGATE. New Street is not present on Armstrong's 1778 plan of Louth, although it is marked on the 1808 plan, and the road would seem to have been created sometime around 1790. New Street runs through the site of the former Old King's Head inn. This closed down in 1788 and was apparently purchased by William Dunn, who demolished part of the inn and cut the new road through to Eastgate—this new road took up the width of a single medieval burgage plot on both Cornmarket and Eastgate, with the kink halfway along the road marking the point where the two plots met and resulting from their slightly different alignments.

The Old King's Head is mentioned in 1755 in connection with the Louth Races of that year—also mentioned were the New King's Head on MERCER ROW, the Blue Stone Inn on UPGATE and the Fleece Inn in the MARKET PLACE—and it similarly appears in Christian Frederick Esberger's journal for 1764, where he mentions meeting with a Mr Brumley at the Old King's Head on April 11 to buy two rings from him. After the creation of New Street, the building that ran north from 5 Cornmarket and formed the western side of New Street was incorporated into the Crown and Sceptre Inn and became its frontage. This was the remaining, undemolished part of the Old King's Head, and the inn here became known as the Crown and Woolpack or the Woolpack during the first half of the nineteenth century. The Crown and Woolpack had its own brewery complex, which extended behind numbers 5–11 Cornmarket, with street access onto Eastgate. The Crown and Woolpack inn appears to have functioned until the 1860s, from which point the site acted as the premises and brewery of the Birkett family, who were wine, spirit, ale and porter merchants. On the 1889 OS map the property was marked as the Woolpack Brewery, and the business was subsequently taken over by Richard Dawson, who ran it in the 1890s and 1900s, although in the 1930s the property became the

Crown and Woolpack once again and remained a public house into the late twentieth century.

In addition to the Crown and Woolpack, this new, late eighteenth-century street was also home to the town's Dispensary from 1803, which was designed to afford medical aid to the poor. In 1872, the Louth Dispensary was said to be helping around 1,000 patients annually, with Dr Dymock as the physician and F. S. Tate, Esq., as the surgeon; the Committee of the Dispensary were responsible for the campaign to build the new hospital and dispensary on CROWTREE LANE (opened 1873). A little later, the Louth Antiquarian and Naturalists' Society, which was founded 1884, had use of two rooms on New Street as a small museum from 1894, although these proved too small for the growing collection and the present museum on BROADBANK was opened in 1910. The Inland Revenue office was likewise located on New Street from at least 1872 through to the early twentieth century, at number 5, and a 'refreshment house' called the Temperance Hotel was based in number 7 from the late nineteenth century through into the early twentieth, run first by Charles Elsom and later by George Wright. A number of other commercial businesses and tradesmen also operated from New Street during the nineteenth and earlier twentieth centuries, including a watchmaker, a shoemaker, a grocer, a butcher, a hairdresser, a publisher and stationer, an estate agent, a brush maker, and several attorneys and solicitors (for example, Christopher Byron of Broadbank House was based here in the early nineteenth century, and James Wood operated from this street in the second half of the nineteenth century). The street continues to be home to a number of small shops at its northern end in the early twenty-first century, including a seafood shop and a sweet shop, and the late twentieth-century New Market Hall also has an entrance from New Street—this new shopping area was built on land previously occupied by the Woolpack Brewery and the Masons Arms Hotel yard.

NEWBRIDGE HILL

Newbridge Hill (or New Bridge Hill) runs north-west and then north from RAMSGATE through to a junction with KEDDINGTON ROAD and the modern NORTH HOLME ROAD (formerly with HIGH HOLME ROAD). Newbridge Hill was apparently considered part of Keddington Road at time of enclosure (1805), and in the nineteenth

189

century the houses on LEAKE'S ROW was numbered as part of Newbridge Hill on the censuses. The name Newbridge Hill probably derives from the Ramsgate bridge over the Lud, which is relatively close to the southern end of the road and was called the New Bridge in the eighteenth century (for example, in the mid-eighteenth-century the proposed canal that would have terminated at Ramsgate was described as a canal 'from Tetney Haven to the New Bridge in Louth').

In the first half of the nineteenth century, Newbridge Hill primarily saw activity on its western side at the northern end of the road, with William Brown's 1844 sketch depicting a market garden and house where Newbridge Hill met Holmes Lane (High Holme Road) and a row of houses a little further to the south, with the road being otherwise dominated by fields at that time. However, by the time of Brown's finished Panorama—which was first exhibited in 1847 and last updated in 1856—Newbridge Hill had seen some significant changes. The most important of these was the arrival of the railway and its associated buildings to the east of the road, replacing the fields that once had been there. There were also now buildings at the southern end of the road, by the Ramsgate junction, and the terrace of houses present in 1844 appears to have been significantly extended. The latter houses are marked as Sharpley's Row on the 1889 OS map and were demolished in 1951, when the new Lin Pac factory—which manufactured corrugated cardboard for packing—was built on this site (a canning factory facing onto CHARLES STREET was also demolished to make way for this). The 1889 map also shows the nursery at the north end of Newbridge Hill still to have been functioning then—it had closed by 1906, however—and depicts a large new building on the eastern side of the road, marked as a malthouse. This was built by James Thorpe in around 1870, and was later owned by Gilstrap, Earp & Co. and then Associated British Maltsters (ABM) from 1929, although the latter were still trading under the Gilstrap name in Louth in 1937. The malthouse here was destroyed in 1940 by German incendiary bombs, and after the war a new malt kiln (the present structure) was built on the same site, in order to qualify for war compensation. Work began in 1949 on what was then the biggest malt kiln in Europe and it took two years to complete—the building was still the fourth largest malt kiln in Europe in the 1970s, supplying breweries both in Britain and abroad.

The late twentieth and early twenty-first centuries saw further changes on this road. ABM was taken over by Dalgety's in 1982 and Paul's Malt became the owners of the Newbridge Hill malt kiln in 1987, although it shut down in the 1990s after permission was refused to expand the site in 1989. Attempts were made to demolish the building in 2004, but it continues to dominate this part of Louth. In 2003, the Lin Pac factory on the west side of the road was successfully demolished to make way for a large residential housing development, begun in 2006 (see further BOLLE ROAD), which has transformed this side of the street. Finally, after the closure of the railway in 1980, the area it had previously occupied was developed, with a car dealership at the north end of the street (now a Co-op supermarket) and Louth Station Estate—a small industrial and commercial estate—just to the south of this by the end of the 1980s.

Inhabitants of Newbridge Hill in 1861 included Henry Boothby junior, a boot and shoe seller whose place of business was at 27 Market Place but who lived in Holmes Cottage on Newbridge Hill (roughly opposite the entrance to the Louth Station Estate, where a new pair of houses stand) from at least 1856 through into the 1880s. He had retired from this trade by 1871 and in 1881 he was listed as a newspaper correspondent; his son, George Boothby, was listed as a fancy poultry dealer here in 1872. Another inhabitant in 1861 was Francis Arnott, at 5 Newbridge Hill, joint proprietor of Fairbank and Arnott's steam saw mills, timber merchants and cabinet makers. This business was listed on Newbridge Hill in 1861, but is absent from the 1868 directory, although a Samuel Archdeacon Smith is listed as a miller on Newbridge Hill in that year and an Edward Bannister is listed as a corn miller on Newbridge Hill in 1872 (his house was at 2 BURNT HILL LANE). Also in 1861, a Francis Bond was listed as the proprietor of an 'asphalte, black varnish and naphtha works' on Newbridge Hill, and a journeyman distiller of this was living at 7 Newbridge Hill at the time of the 1861 census (he was called Stephenson White). The proprietor of this business was Mrs Elizabeth Bond in 1868, and in 1872 it was in the hands of the executors of Francis Bond. There were also a number of other businesses and tradespeople listed on this road in the second half of the nineteenth century, including several shopkeepers (for example, Sandy France, 8 Newbridge Hill) and, in 1896, Samuel Bateman's private boys' school (number 4).

NEWMARKET

Newmarket runs east and then south-east from UPGATE through to KENWICK ROAD. The part of Newmarket leading up to the Cattle Market from Upgate was formerly called Quarry Hill, and all or part of the road may have been once known as Leckeburngate, a named recorded in 1317 and sometimes considered to be the original name for Newmarket.

The early name Quarry Hill for part of this road refers to the presence here of the Quarry, or Quarrell, which is now used for the town's Cattle Market. This is located on the south side of the western end of Newmarket and was a major feature of the town during the medieval period and after, despite being separated from it by fields until the early nineteenth century. For example, in the 1430s William Guage and William Day were fined 2d each for playing tennis and other 'unlawful games' in the Quarry, and in the sixteenth and seventeenth centuries the Quarry was the site of the Butts, where a yearly archery pageant took place (see also BOWLING GREEN LANE for other pastimes in this area of Louth). The Quarry was also the occasional scene of duels, as in 1631 when John Legard killed Richard Bolls here, after they quarrelled over an old debt and Bolls called Legard a liar and a coward. A friend of Richard Bolls, named Jackson, prevented the fight being broken up by a smith that lived near the Quarry, who had rushed over with his staff to part the two when he saw their swords being drawn, and it was also Jackson who persuaded Bolls to continue fighting Legard after he had already been hurt. The Corporation of Louth subsequently made a number of payments relating to the duel, including one of 4d paid 'at the death of m^r Richard Bolles' to a labourer 'for covering of a noysome pitt in the quarry'.

The Quarry also provided the stone for Louth Park Abbey and in later centuries the quarried chalk from here was burnt to make agricultural lime. In 1628, for example, it was declared that 'none shall digg anye stones in the quarrill to be burned into lime' without permission and without paying for what they dig, and chalk was still being quarried and processed from the south-west corner of the Quarry into the twentieth century. Indeed, two lime works were marked in the south-western part of the Quarry on OS maps from 1889 through until the mid-1950s, one being labelled as the 'Julian Bower Lime Works' and the other simply as 'Lime Works', and both probably existed from at least the early nineteenth century. So, in 1828–9, Issac Crow and John Gillott were both listed as lime burners at 'Quarry Hill', and in 1841 Samuel Appleby and Isaac Crow were both listed as lime burners at 'Quarry', the former being based at the Julian Bower Lime Works with Charles Mumby in the mid-nineteenth century. In the 1950s, there was infilling and levelling of the southern part of the Quarry, where the lime works had been based, in order to extend access and parking in this area.

Perhaps the Quarry is best known, however, as the site of a regular livestock market. Edward VI's charter of 1551 granted to the Warden and the Six Assistants the right to 'have, hold and enjoy, within the said void piece of land, called the Quarry, one market of oxen, sheep and swine... to be kept on Wednesday in every week forever'. The use of the Quarry for this new beast market appears to have been short-lived, however, for the Warden and the Six Assistants successfully petitioned in 1605 for permission to move it from the Quarry to the Beast Market (CORNMARKET) in the centre of Louth. In 1785, the 'Sheep and Pig Markett' was moved again, to the 'New Markett Place in Upgate', and it was eventually moved back to the Quarry in 1802 (specifically, to 'some place in the Quarrell to be set out by the Corporation for that purpose'), though whether the cattle market returned to the Quarry before or after the sheep and pig market moved there is not entirely clear. In 1817, it was resolved that 'a Market for the sale of fat and lean cattle be holden in the Quarry in Louth on Friday the 18th day of April Instant and on every Friday fortnight afterwards.' The above shift of the regular beast markets from the centre of town out to the Quarry, where Edward VI had originally established them in 1551, may well explain the street-name Newmarket.

In the nineteenth century, Newmarket became more than simply the location of the Quarry and its associated activities. According to the 1808 plan of Louth, there were already a few buildings present on the road by that time. These included the Boar's Head Inn, which was first licensed in 1802. In 1828–9 and 1835, this establishment was listed on 'Quarry Hill' and was run by William Binkly, although by 1841 its location was instead given as 'Newmarkt' and it had a new landlord, William Broom Atkin. The Boar's Head Inn occasionally features in the mid-nineteenth century court reports. For example, in 1850 Richard Bell of Binbrook accused Benjamin Ashton of Louth of assaulting him in the

Boar's Head over a gambling dispute, and in 1851 one of the outbuildings of the Boar's Head was set on fire by William Scupham, who had lain down to sleep there having become intoxicated and accidentally set the straw on fire with his pipe. In addition to the inn, there were also residential properties on this road. A small number of properties can be seen on the 1808 and 1834 plans of the town and the 1839 map depicts a quantity of housing on both the south and the north side of Newmarket down to the junction with Long Lane (CHURCH STREET). This is confirmed by William Brown's 1844 sketch of this road, which shows that the long terrace between what is now ST MICHAEL'S ROAD and Church Street was already in place by that point, along with further housing beyond Church Street and also on the opposite side of the road. On Brown's finished Panorama of 1847–56, it is clear that there was housing all along the northern and eastern side of the street then, almost down to the junction with STEWTON LANE, with the opposite side of the road having seen further development since 1844 too. Indeed, in 1861 there were over 500 people living on Newmarket, and yet more buildings had been erected on this road by the late nineteenth century, including the new Sydenham Terrace, opposite the Newmarket–Church Street junction. By 1889, there were properties along most of both sides of Newmarket, with only a few gaps, and these were filled in during the course of the twentieth century. For example, TENNYSON ROAD was developed between Newmarket and LINDEN WALK in the inter-war years, and the SEYMOUR AVENUE housing estate was established off Newmarket in the late twentieth century.

This development of Newmarket as a significant residential street in the nineteenth century led to the establishment of two places of worship in this part of town. One was St Michael's Church on Church Street, which was built in 1862–3 and represented the Church of England's response to the population expansion in the Newmarket area. The other was on Newmarket itself and was a Wesleyan Methodist chapel, built in 1849. This was taken over by the Free Methodists in around 1857 and converted into a day school in 1858, which served 125 pupils a day in 1861, with a new chapel opened in 1868. The new chapel continued in use until 1974, whilst the Wesleyan Day School saw its senior pupils (older than 11) moved to other local schools in 1926 and the school closed completely in December 1828—the boys were sent to the

WESTGATE school and the girls were transferred to the Technical School on JAMES STREET. It was subsequently used as the Playgoers Theatre from 1948 through to 2002, when this moved to a new, purpose-built theatre on VICTORIA ROAD. Newmarket also saw its share of problems in the nineteenth century, as the population increased. There were, for example, occasional reports of drunkenness on the road here, as in 1847, when John Rhodes, a labour living on LEE STREET, was found drunk and incapable of looking after himself on Newmarket. Similarly, in 1849 Richard Jackson, a labourer, was charged with shouting and brawling on the road and assaulting Michael Medley, a bricklayer and owner of a brickyard off EDWARD STREET. Other crimes recorded on Newmarket in the period included a dispute between neighbours in 1852 that turned violent, with Martha Chiffins of Newmarket assaulting and threatening her neighbour Mary Melluish, 'putting her in bodily fear'—she was fined 20s and costs and ordered to find two sureties of £10 each to keep the peace for three months (equivalent to around £850 today). Finally, in 1849 a pig jobber (trader) called Josh Grantham—'an old and confirmed disorderly'—was charged by his wife with assaulting and beating her, 'which she stated to be his daily practice'. As a result he was fined 10s and costs (equivalent to around £40 today) and ordered to find sureties to keep the peace for six months.

In terms of trading activity in the nineteenth and early twentieth centuries, a wide range of businesses and trades were present on Newmarket, including joiners and cabinet makers, wheelwrights, rope makers, blacksmiths, stone masons, shopkeepers, poulterers, grocers and bakers, carpenters, butchers, dressmakers, market gardeners, and beer retailers. For example, in 1841 there were four beer retailers on Newmarket in addition to the landlord of the Boar's Head, namely John Gillot, Thomas Bee, Anthony Bradshaw and James Cribb, up from two on 'Quarry hill' in 1835 (John Gillott and James Milson); in 1856 and 1861, there were two beer houses once again, run by John Gillott and Robert Smith. Smith ran the White Horse, which is now usually treated as being on Kenwick Road, and Gillott ran the Brown Cow—or Newmarket Inn—on the corner of Newmarket and Church Street: assuming that Gillott had not moved his beerhouse, it would thus appear that the Brown Cow has its origins at least as far back as 1835 (certainly, Gillott ran it in 1851, when it already had the name The Brown Cow). In 1868 there were three beerhouses on Newmarket, belonging to John

Clark Barnard, presumably the John Clark who ran the Brown Cow in 1871 and 1872, John Speed and Henry Joseph Patrick. Also based on Newmarket in the 1860s and 1870s was John Hodgson, blacksmith and agricultural implement maker, whose works—known as the Perseverance Ironworks in the early 1870s—were apparently located between Upgate and Bowling Green Lane; John Hodgson & Son, engineers and iron founders, continued to function into the twentieth century, although the business was then listed on Upgate. Another notable business off Newmarket was the market garden of William Robinson, later William Robinson & Son. This long-lived business was listed as being on Upgate in, for example, the 1856 directory, but the nursery itself was actually located on land off Newmarket, around WATTS LANE and to the south of MOUNT PLEASANT, some of which was awarded to the family under the 1805 Enclosure Award. The nursery here persisted until the late twentieth century, when the large ROBINSON LANE housing estate was built on the former nursery land between Mount Pleasant and Watts Lane; however, Robinson's greengrocer's shop continues to operate from 125 EASTGATE.

In the twentieth and twenty-first centuries, a number of businesses have both opened and closed on Newmarket. For example, in the twentieth century several garages were opened on the road, including one on the corner of Watts Lane and another opposite St Michael's Road, both operating from the mid-twentieth century, with these being joined by a filling station on the corner of St Michael's Road in the late twentieth century. The filling station still remains, run by Esso, but the garage opposite this is now a carpet warehouse (Ashtons of Louth), whilst that on the corner of Watts Lane has been demolished and the site is presently unused. Another new development on Newmarket has been the demolition of the nineteenth century houses that were once just to the north of the latter garage and their eventual replacement by the new Newmarket Medical Practice building, which opened in 2001 (the practice had previously been based on BRIDGE STREET). Finally, it is worth noting that the former Bridge House Kindergarten, at the southern end of Newmarket, was set up by Miss Welton in 1966 and was at that time the only pre-school in the town.

NICHOL HILL

Nichol Hill runs north from EASTGATE through to a junction with CHEQUERGATE and NORTHGATE. It was first mentioned in 1443 and may have been a relatively late addition to Louth's medieval street-plan, linking Eastgate with its back access routes. The name itself appears to preserve the Anglo-Norman name of Lincoln and it has been suggested it may indicate that this area of Eastgate was where merchants from Lincoln established themselves in Louth, just as they apparently settled in Lincoln Lane and Stonebow Lane in Boston. Arthur Owen has suggested that a Roman-era fortification was originally located to the east of the road, with Nichol Hill following the line of its western wall; there is, however, no real evidence to support this hypothesis.

Louth Methodist Church, currently the only Methodist establishment still in use in town, is located on the east side of Nichol Hill. The church site was secured in 1805 and at its maximum extent, after 1835, the Methodist church here could seat 1,600 worshippers, although the number of pews was reduced in favour of greater comfort in 1854. The church was refashioned in 1977, at a cost of £110,000, removing the Victorian box pews and galleries and adding a new entrance onto Nichol Hill (it had previously been entered from Eastgate). The Wesleyan Sunday School here, opened in 1912 as a replacement for the old schoolroom, was used as the Louth Red Cross Auxiliary Hospital during the First World War—it opened as this only three weeks after the declaration of war, in August 1914, and it closed at the end of March 1919, after admitting around 2,300 patients.

A number of businesses have been based on Nichol Hill in the nineteenth and early twentieth centuries. In 1828–9, there was a shopkeeper listed here named Thomas Smith, along with a tailor (Joseph Wilson), and in 1841 there was a shoemaker working from this street (Thomas Wilkinson). By the mid-1850s, the street was home to a shoemaker, a butcher, a cabinet maker and upholsterer, a music professor (organist), and a shopkeeper. In 1896, those listed on the street included a pianoforte tuner, Charles Joseph Archer (number 4); a shopkeeper, George Edward Colam (numbers 9 & 11); a builder, George Parsons (number 1); another shopkeeper, Joshua Smith (number 5); and Henry Emerson's fried fish shop (number 3). Emerson was still in business there in 1913 as a fried fish dealer and was listed as a fishmonger at this address in 1919. In the early twenty-first century, Nichol Hill lacks shops such as these, though it is home to the Louth and Horncastle Conservative Association and also Nichols Youth Project—the latter is based in the fine early nineteenth century building at 2 Nichol Hill.

NORMANDY CLOSE

Normandy Close runs off PARK AVENUE and was part of the estate of prefabricated homes built here in the mid-1940s. In the early twenty-first century, the properties on Park Avenue and Normandy Close—which were erected under the Temporary Housing Act of 1944 and designed to last ten years—were rebuilt as new brick bungalows. The land that these properties are built on was originally part of Louth's old East Field.

NORTH HOLME ROAD

North Holme Road was constructed across the fields north of Louth in the mid-twentieth century and extends from the junction of HIGH HOLME ROAD and NEWBRIDGE HILL through to GRIMSBY ROAD—it was described as a 'new road' in October 1960, 'intended to join Grimsby Road when it is completed'. By the time of the 1968 OS map, the eastern half of the road had been built, with the first elements of the FAIRFIELD INDUSTRIAL ESTATE present on the north side (an Egg Packing Station and a Travelling Crane are labelled), and a school and the beginnings of a new housing estate on the south side. With regard to the latter, only CHATSWORTH DRIVE and HAREWOOD CRESCENT had been developed by the time of the 1968 OS map, but by the mid-1970s the estate here had been nearly fully developed, as had North Holme Road itself, which by then linked through to Grimsby Road. Businesses marked on the 1974–6 OS map on the north side of North Holme Road included a Tyre Depot (currently Bush Tyres), an Agricultural Engineering Depot (currently Lincolnshire Motors Ltd, suppliers of agricultural and garden machinery), a clothing factory (a site now occupied by the B&Q do-it-yourself store), and a plastics factory (now home to Trotter's Traders, amongst others). On the south side, the road was entirely taken up by

Cordeaux High School and the housing estate, apart from at the junction with Grimsby Road, where The Lady of Shalott public house was built (also known as The Lord Tennyson). This opened in the 1960s and was finally closed and demolished in the early twentieth century; in 2012, the Wolds Care Centre, a care home for the elderly, was opened on this site.

A dominant feature at the southern end of North Holme Road is Cordeaux School. Opened to the public in 1956, this school was first known as High Holme Secondary School, before being renamed Cordeaux High School in the 1960s, later simply Cordeaux School. It took its new name from Captain Edward Cawdron Cordeaux, a distinguished Royal Navy officer and later High Sheriff of Lincolnshire who officially opened the school in October 1957. The school was initially established to alleviate overcrowding at Monks' Dyke Secondary School on MONKS DYKE ROAD and cost £100,000 to build (equivalent to over £2,000,000 today). In 2007, work began on Wolds College, built on the site of Cordeaux's former boarding house. Wolds College was established to provide vocational courses for 14–19 year olds and in 2012 its day-to-day running was taken over by Cordeaux School.

NORTHGATE

Northgate runs from CHEQUERGATE through to a junction with EASTGATE. Northgate is only one of the names used since the medieval period for this street, the others being Padehole and Finkle Street, both of which appear on the 1808 plan of the town. The road is first mentioned under the name Padehole ('toad-hollow') in 1317, with the name Northgate recorded first in 1450 and Finkle Street—'stinking street' or 'fart street', presumably a nick-name—in the modern period. Northgate, like Chequergate and the western half of KIDGATE, was probably originally a back access-way for properties that fronted onto one of the main streets of the town, in this case EASTGATE. The first reference to the street comes in a charter of Thomas de Luda, chapter clerk of Lincoln Cathedral, which was drawn up in 1317. He provided an endowment to pay for a daily mass to be said for the salvation of his own soul, and for the souls of his father, William, and his mother, Margaret, his brother, his benefactors, and all the faithful dead. The endowment included six messuages (usually defined as a dwelling house

199

with outbuildings and the site on which it stood), three of which were on Eastgate, including one said to be near Padehole, something which implies that Padehole (Northgate) already extended round to its junction with Eastgate at that point. Further evidence of Northgate's medieval origins is provided by finds of a late twelfth- or thirteenth-century buckle-plate and sherds of fourteenth- to fifteenth-century pottery here, and a few medieval property boundaries still exist on the south side of the road, to the east of VICKERS LANE. Quite how early Northgate was founded is, however, unclear—Arthur Owen has suggested that a Roman-era fortification was based to the south and west of Northgate, with the road following the line of its northern and eastern walls, which might suggest a very early origin. There is, however, no real evidence to support this hypothesis.

Despite its probable origin as a back access-way, Northgate or Padehole had developed into a street in its own right by the early modern period. In 1636, for example, three houses on Padehole were mentioned, which were based on the northern side of the street at its east end, opposite the eighteenth-century Poor House (see below). These houses were given by Robert Osney to Wright's Coal Charity in his will of that year, in order to provide, out of their rent, six pence of bread each week for six poor children in Louth, with the remainder to go to poor single men living in 'St Maries Church' (see BRIDGE STREET). This gift's income was, in the mid-eighteenth century, mainly devoted to the reduction of debts incurred in repairing these houses in Padehole; eventually, the Charity was united with Wright's Butter Charity and, in 1878, part of income from it was appropriated for the foundation of scholarships at the town's Grammar School. Another post-medieval use of Northgate was as the site of an elementary school. Dr Robert Mapletoft, Dean of Ely and a former pupil of Louth Grammar School, founded and endowed a Petit Free School in Padehole in 1677, to teach the local children reading, writing and arithmetic, thus preparing them for the Grammar School. The school was located on the west corner of what is now BROADBANK and Northgate and is marked there on the 1808 plan of the town. In 1790, Thomas Espin was elected the master of this school, and it continued in use until 1878, educating 60 children as a preparatory for Grammar School—Samuel Cresswell, the master at Northgate, was pensioned off in 1878, but he continued to utilise the Northgate premises as a private school until 1900. Subsequently, the site was used for the Parish Rooms and the modern flats of Northgate Court are now situated there.

If people were living and being educated on Northgate in the seventeenth and eighteenth centuries, this doesn't necessarily mean that it was an especially desirable or pleasant part of town then. The name Finkle Street probably belongs to this period, being first recorded in 1808, and its meaning—'stinking street', or 'fart street'—would certainly point in this direction. This road was also where Louth's eighteenth-century Poor House, or House of Industry, was established in 1734. Younger paupers were probably transferred here from the 'Jersey School' (in the House of Correction on EASTGATE) and the present buildings were erected in 1791. In 1837, a new 'Union Workhouse' was built at the top of Broadbank, and the old Poor House was subsequently used as a beer shop and tap room, before it was acquired by the Primitive Methodists who constructed a schoolroom here in 1873. Now used for flats, the building was last operated commercially by A. Dales & Sons, poulterers, whose name remains above the entranceway.

By the late eighteenth century, there appear to have been buildings all along the northern and eastern sides of Northgate, but no significant development on the south side or the west, to judge from Armstrong's plan of 1778. Whether this was indeed the case is, however, open to debate, as Armstrong's plan has a number of identifiable errors and is questionable in places. Espin's plan of 1808 is, in contrast, more carefully drawn and offers a more nuanced view of the street at the end of the eighteenth century and start of the nineteenth. He shows buildings along much of the northern side of the street, though not an unbroken run as Armstrong does, along with a handful of structures on the eastern side of that section of Northgate which links to Eastgate. On the south side, Espin shows a long stretch of gardens, but he also depicts a number of buildings here, not least the eighteenth-century Poor House, whilst on the western side of the street, down to Eastgate, Espin shows an almost unbroken line of buildings. A similar picture is provided by the 1834 plan of the town, which also shows further buildings constructed on the south side of the road, where the gardens once were, along with the development of CANNON STREET between Northgate and Eastgate. By the time of William Brown's Panorama, first shown in 1847 and last updated in 1856, the street appears to have been almost completely developed on all sides.

The trade directories from the first half of the nineteenth century support the view that Northgate was, by that point, a busy and well-developed street. In 1828–9, for example, businesses listed here included a baker and flour dealer (Edward Fields), a bricklayer (Banks Richardson), a joiner and builder (William Thurold Leak), a shoemaker (Robert Harris), a maltster (John Musgrave), a smith (John Kirk), a maltster and brewer (Thomas Bogg), and a tannery (that of Fridlington & Kemp, who were also fellmongers—a dealer in hides or skins who might also prepare skins for tanning). With regard to brewers and maltsters, Thomas Bogg retired due to ill health in 1835 (he died the same year) and he is listed then as possessing an ale and porter brewery, a malt kiln, a drying kiln, and a public house—The Lord Nelson—on Northgate, with the business here having apparently functioned for over 50 years by 1835. A family member, Edward Bogg, appears to have initially taken over the running of the site in 1835, but quite who bought the business after its sale in 1835 is not clear. Subsequently, Fuller & Co. were listed as maltsters, brewers and porter merchants on Northgate in 1841 and 1842, Henry Lucas was listed as brewer there in 1842, and Hall & Robinson were listed as brewers on the street in 1849, whilst John Hallam appears to have operated as a maltster on Northgate from at least 1841. A three-storey malthouse and hay or corn stacks belonging to Hallam are visible at the site of the current Co-operative supermarket, to the north of Northgate, on both William Brown's 1844 sketch of the town and his final Panorama. Hallam was described from 1841 as a maltster and in 1851 as a maltster, an ironmonger and a farmer of 56 acres, employing three men—his beerhouse faced onto Northgate and was known as the Malt Shovel (now the Miller's Daughter). Whether Hallam was the first to have a malthouse on this particular site is unknown, but it is possible that one or more of the earlier Northgate maltsters and brewers had been based here previously, and if it was Bogg, then the Malt Shovel could have been a renamed Lord Nelson. Hallam's business was subsequently run by his widow and, from the 1880s, by his daughter and her husband, Esther and William Barton—the inn here was re-fronted in 1905 (hence the date stone) and Esther Barton is last listed as a beer retailer here in 1919.

Other beerhouses on Northgate included the Volunteer Arms, at 11 Northgate, apparently named from Louth Volunteers. In 1871, this establishment was run by Ann Smithson Clark, previously a butcher on

NEW STREET, and it continued to operate here through until 1968. This building was subsequently demolished to make way for the modern flats of Northgate Court. Another drinking establishment was the Pack Horse Tap, at the rear of the Pack Horse Inn (now the site of Louth Library; see Eastgate for the Pack Horse), which was run by John Perkins in 1889, and yet another was the King's Arms, 57 Northgate, run by William King in the 1870s and 1880s—he had previously been the publican at the Temperance Hotel and the Woodman on Eastgate, in 1871 and 1861 respectively. The site of the King's Arms became the Linpac Club in the twentieth century and is now a private residence, standing at the eastern end of the road.

Northgate was also home to two chapels in the nineteenth and earlier twentieth centuries. One of these was a Baptist chapel on the site of Cannon Street House. This was built at the western end of the road in 1800 as the Northgate chapel of the General Baptists and originally had a small burial ground in front of it. After the construction of Cannon Street, the chapel—now accessed from the new street—was rebuilt in 1827 and further altered in 1840, with the current facade said to date from 1851. The chapel stayed in use until 1919, when the Baptists transferred to the Eastgate Baptist Chapel on the corner of Eastgate and RAMSGATE (Eastgate Union Church), and the Cannon Street chapel was subsequently sold to the Pentecostalists. From 1938, Cannon Street House functioned as the offices of Louth Rural District Council, although it has recently regained a religious role as the home of the Louth Christian Fellowship. The other chapel was built by 1820 to the west of the Poor House, where Louth Library now stands, and belonged to the Primitive Methodists. A more substantial chapel was constructed here in 1836 and the chapel was rebuilt again in 1850—the previous chapel sometimes had been too full to admit all the prospective worshippers, so the new structure was designed to allow 800 to be seated, at a cost of £1,500 (equivalent to around £175,000 today). The Primitive Methodist chapel finally closed in 1954 and became Pickford's warehouse; it was demolished in 1976 when the roof fell in.

Another significant nineteenth-century building on Northgate is the British Legion Hall. This was erected in 1863 as the Church of England Free Evening School, which was supported by voluntary subscriptions. Operating first on LEE STREET (from 1856) for the benefit of those adults and youths who had been taken too early from school and so needed tuition in reading, writing and arithmetic, the success of this venture led to around £1,000 being spent on erecting a new building for the school on Northgate in 1863. In 1868, around 90 adults attended the classes here, along with 140 youths, and they all had access to a 400 volume library and reading rooms. In 1869, around 300 scholars of the Free Evening School and their wives attended the annual tea party of the school. However, by 1872 numbers had dropped to around 50 adults and 100 youths, and the school closed in the 1880s. The building was subsequently used as a drill hall and to show films (in around 1910), and it became the British Legion Headquarters from 1946.

The twentieth and twenty-first centuries saw significant changes to Northgate, most notably a substantial amount of demolition and rebuilding on both sides of the road, especially the south. On the north side, the site of the Volunteer Arms and the Free School is now occupied by the late twentieth-century Northgate Court, the area to the north of the road where once was Hallam's malthouse was redeveloped as the Co-operative supermarket (initially branded as Leo's) in the late 1980s, and a new residential court—Kings Mews—has been developed at the eastern end of the road in the early twenty-first century. On the south side, the terraced housing and properties that once stood between Cannon Street and Vickers Lane have been replaced entirely by late twentieth-century properties, the late twentieth-century Louth Library occupies the land on which the nineteenth-century Pack Horse Tap and the Primitive Methodist chapel were situated, and the site of the terraced housing on the west side of Northgate, north of its junction with Eastgate, is now a car park. The latter car park, opposite the British Legion Headquarters, once held ten cottages and the last town crier of Louth, John Norton Blythe, lived in one of these in the early twentieth century. Louth had employed a town crier since at least 1662, when a man named Fenicke was engaged in this role—in 1748, the town crier was paid 6d to cry 'not to sell or shave on Sundays'; in 1754, Thomas Bradley, the town crier, was paid 6d to cry against 'foot Ball & other unlawfull Games'; and in 1783, Thomas Naull was paid 6d to cry down the 'playing of Skittles and going to the River Head'.

With regard to the inhabitants of Northgate in the nineteenth century, several came to notice of the local courts. One was a woman named Sarah Burton, who was described in 1879 as 'a well-known brothel-keeper, living in Northgate'. She is presumably the same Sarah

Burton who previously kept a brothel in the GATHERUMS in 1850 and who kept a 'more than questionable establishment' at an unspecified location in Louth in 1865. Another was Samuel Walker, a shoemaker. In 1850, when he was aged 16, he was charged by his sister, Ann, with acting violently towards her and his whole family, putting her in bodily fear due to his threats. For example, 'on Sunday last, because some cabbage had not been boiled to his satisfaction, he took up a knife, pursued and threatened to stab her.' Walker was ordered to find sureties to keep peace for one month. Later the same year, he absconded from the service of his master, Mr Furnish, a shoemaker (presumably William Furnish of Chequergate, a shoemaker with two apprentices in 1851); the action against him was withdrawn on his promising to return. Finally, 7 Northgate was, from the 1850s through to the 1870s, home to what would appear to have been a Jewish family. The head of the household was Jacob Cohen, who was born in Prussia and appears to have married the widow of Herman Boss, a 'well-known Jew' from Berlin who lived on Vickers Lane in the 1840s and 1850s—see Vickers Lane and JAMES STREET. Cohen and his wife, Augusta (who was also born in Prussia), lived at number 7 in 1861, along with several children and a German servant, Jette Lesser, and they ran a watchmaking and jewellery business from here for a number of years. The first mention of the family in Louth comes in 1857, when Cohen, described as a jeweller of Northgate, informed the police that he had been offered a stolen silver hunting horn 'with a promptitude which does him honour'. In 1870, Augusta Cohen was described as a widow with four children who was carrying on the jewellery and watchmaking business: she was robbed in that year by a Polish lodger, 'a countryman of hers', named Louis Waller, and another man named Phillips. They stole £200 of jewellery and watches (equivalent to around £15,000 today), including a brooch containing a photo of her late husband. A detective tracked the thieves down to German hotel in Soho, London, where they were arrested.

OAK CLOSE

Oak Close runs south-west from SYCAMORE DRIVE, which is the spine of a late twentieth-century housing estate to the south of WOOD LANE. Each road in this estate is named after a different type of tree.

OLD MILL PARK

The street-name Old Mill Park commemorates the water mill that once operated on the corner of this road and RAMSGATE, off which Old Mill Park runs. The watermill in question mainly dates from the mid- and later nineteenth century, although it includes a date-stone of 1716, and it was finally shut down in 1981, when the mill was sold for residential development. The last miller here was Bryan Hall, who was also the last independent miller in Lincolnshire. Under him, the mill derived its power from the river Lud but was supplemented by a diesel engine, and it produced animal feeds and Three Crowns branded flour. The houses of Old Mill Park were built in the late twentieth century on what had previously been undeveloped land, with at least three of them erected in 1995.

ORCHARD CLOSE

Orchard Close runs south-east from KEDDINGTON ROAD. It is a late twentieth-century residential road that was built on the site of a former orchard, which was marked on OS maps of the area from 1906 onwards. At the southern end of Orchard Close is a large pond that was once a pit associated with the brick yard off RAMSGATE.

ORME LANE

The entrance to Orme Lane is located on the south side of EASTGATE, opposite the Orme Almshouses, which were built in 1885 and named after their benefactor, the Rev. Frederick Orme. The road is missing from the early maps and plans of the town but is present on the 1889 OS map. The road at that time appears to have extended only into the area to the south of Eastgate before it curved west, rather than running straight all the way through to MONKS DYKE ROAD, as it does now. In 1889, this area was the site of a number of buildings and a disused brickyard, which had once been the brickworks of James Hunter Ryley (see Eastgate and CHEQUERGATE).

By the time that the 1906 OS map was surveyed, Orme Lane had been extended through to Monks Dyke Road, with the land of the former brick yard on the west of the road and what appears to be a market garden with a greenhouse to its east—the latter was shown in 1889 as a well-developed orchard with a greenhouse that was accessed via a bridge over the Monks' Dyke, and this bridge was being used by Orme Lane in 1906. With regard to the brickyard, this still stood largely empty in 1906, although an Iron Foundry is marked in this area near the southern end of Leake's Court (ALBION PLACE). Little had changed by the time of the 1932 OS map, but in 1947 F. G. Wright's bus company, established in 1925, had built a large new depot on Orme Lane. This local company was sold to the Lincolnshire Road Car Company in 1950 and a bus depot still stands on Orme Lane. In the late twentieth century, a garage was constructed on the east side of Orme Lane, and this area is now home to both a garage (Ron Larder) and Dreamland beds and mattresses. On the western side of the road, the area to the south and west of the bus depot was made into a car park and a servicing area for the new supermarket that faced onto Eastgate (currently Morrisons).

PADDOCK, THE

The Paddock is a modern road that runs south from CROWTREE LANE. The road runs along the western side of the former Louth & District Hospital (now part of King Edward VI Grammar School) and serves a small number of large residential properties that were built before 2003.

PARK AVENUE

Park Avenue was built in the mid-1940s on land that had been part of Louth's old open East Field through until the Enclosure Act of 1801 (both the road and the houses here are shown on the 1951 OS map of the town). In the early twenty-first century, the prefabricated homes on Park Avenue—which were erected under the Temporary Housing Act of 1944 and designed to last ten years—were rebuilt as new, brick properties by Linx Homes. From 1958, Louth United Football Club had a ground on Park Avenue—their original home having been on HIGH HOLME ROAD—and from 2007 the ground here has been used by Louth Town FC.

PARK ROW

Park Row runs south-east from EASTFIELD ROAD and is depicted on
both William Brown's sketch of 1844 and his finished Panorama of
1847–56, although nothing is marked in this location on the 1824 OS
map. In 1889 the houses here were labelled Park Buildings, with the
name Park Row only appearing on OS maps from the mid-twentieth
century—the land that the road and these houses were built on was part
of Louth Park in the nineteenth and earlier twentieth centuries, and
traces of medieval ridge and furrow have been observed in this area from
aerial photographs. In 1911, inhabitants of these houses included Lucy
Wakelin (of private means); Hannah Harrison (of private means);
Charles Tomlinson (retired printer's compositor); William Black (retired
groom and gardener); James Appleby (retired gas works engineer); and
Charles Norton (miller's carter).

PARSONS HALT

Parsons Halt runs west from STATION APPROACH and is part of a
late twentieth-century residential housing development built to the north
of RAMSGATE. The original road to the railway station has been
removed and Parsons Halt—constructed across the northern end of that
road—now offers access to the station. The railway line running south
from Louth railway station once ran over the eastern part of Parsons
Halt; it was opened in 1848 and closed in 1970.

PASTURE DRIVE

Pasture Drive runs south-east from the southern end of HAWKER
DRIVE, which in turn runs south from STEWTON LANE. This area
was fields up until the late twentieth century, when the housing estate
here was built—Hawker Drive and HAVELOK CLOSE were built first,
with Pasture Drive developed in the 1980s. These fields were already
enclosed at the start of the nineteenth century, but they had once been
part of the old South Field of the town—medieval ridge and furrow
from this has been observed on aerial photographs of this area. At the
end of the 1990s, the 'Weavers Tryst' housing estate was built to the east

of Pasture Drive, with the new GRAYE DRIVE connecting to the south-eastern end of Pasture Drive.

PAWNSHOP PASSAGE

Pawnshop Passage runs from MERCER ROW through to KIDGATE. The name Pawnshop Passage is of relatively recent origin, deriving from the former presence of a pawnshop on this footway; it was earlier known as Hurton's Passage or, most usually, Hurton's Yard (as on the 1889 OS map, also spelled Horton's Yard). In the late eighteenth century, the Golden Ball public house was based here—it is mentioned in 1782 and was last licensed in 1793. More recently, the early nineteenth-century warehouse and adjoining buildings at the southern end of the passageway have been operated as a drinking establishment, formerly known as Scarfe's Wine Bar and Kai's Bar and currently the Joseph Morton pub, part of the J. D. Wetherspoon chain. Immediately to the west of the Joseph Morton, facing onto Kidgate, is an open area that apparently used to be known as Mawer's Square, presumably due to the usage of this end of Hurton's Yard by Mawer Brothers, builders, contractors, carpenters and monumental masons, into the late twentieth century. It was here, according to C. S. Carter, that all the fights of the 1840s between the Grammar School boys, 'the Tigers', and the boys of Roger's school at The Priory, 'the Bull Dogs', took place. On the opposite side of Mawer's Square were warehouses, since demolished, that are said to have served as the barracks for both French prisoners during the Napoleonic War and 'the Yeomanry' (see further Kidgate on Mawer Brothers and the barracks).

In 1869, the properties on the eastern side of Hurton's Yard were offered for sale. That at the north end, 22 Mercer Row, was described as having recently been in the occupation of Mr R. S. Robinson, tailor and outfitter. Immediately behind this, in Hurton's Yard itself, was a shop with granaries over it, occupied by Mr Green and Mr W. Robinson, and behind this there were two more shops with a tailor's workshop over them and a warehouse adjoining, which were occupied by Mr Sargeant, Mr R. S. Robinson's Assignees, and Mr W. Robinson. Further to the south still were three more shops or warehouses, occupied by the last two named above along with a Mr Macdonald and a Mr Handley. The nineteenth- and twentieth-century trade directories offer details of the kinds of trades taking place in such shops and workshops. For example, in 1861 and 1868 pawnbrokers Sudbury and Burton were listed in Hurton's Yard, and in 1872 John Sudbury, pawnbroker, was listed as operating on his own here. In the same year, Hurton's Yard was also the place of business of Thomas Cuthbert Green, tinner and brazier (a maker of tin and brass articles, also here in 1861 and 1868), and Samuel Handley, nail maker. These were presumably the Mr Green and Mr Handley mentioned on the eastern side of Hurton's Yard in 1869. Richard Lionel Lucas junior, solicitor, was also based on Hurton's Yard in 1872 (he lived at 10 UPGATE), as was John Wheeler, nail maker, who lived at 51 Kidgate, whilst Thomas Cole had run an eating house in Hurton's Yard in the 1850s and 1860s.

In the 1880s and after, Hurton's Yard continued to be the location for a pawnbroker: John Sudbury was still listed here in 1885, at numbers 5 & 7; an Edwin Richardson, pawnbroker, was listed at number 5 from 1889 until 1905; and the Millard Brothers' pawnshop was listed in Hurton's Yard in 1909 (location unstated, but clearly not number 5, as that was then occupied by William Pridgeon, boot maker). There continued to be a pawnshop in Hurton's Yard until the Second World War, and the new name for the passageway—Pawnshop Passage— derived from this. Harriet Green also continued her late husband's business at number 8 through until at least 1913, and Hurton's Yard was still the base for both a solicitor (then William Haddon Owen) and a nail maker (John Wheeler) in the 1880s. In the early twentieth century, Hurton's Yard was additionally the home of Hodgson's bicycle manufacturing business, which described itself as the maker of the 'the "Luda" cycle', and the southern end was used as a builder's yard by Mawer Brothers into the late twentieth century. This same area also saw significant alterations in this period, with the demolition of a number of buildings and the construction of others in the latter part of the twentieth century, including the standalone building currently occupied by Café Rico.

PIPPIN CLOSE

Pippin Close runs south-east from ROBINSON LANE and is part of a late twentieth-century housing estate built to the south of MOUNT PLEASANT. This estate was constructed in the mid-1990s on land that had formerly been used by the Robinson family for its market garden and nursery, and all the roads that run off Robinson Lane are named after varieties of apple.

PLEASANT PLACE

Pleasant Place runs west from RAMSGATE and is depicted on the 1889 OS map of this area, when it was already well-established. In the 1885 and 1889 directories, 1a Pleasant Place was listed as the address of Henry Swingler, a painter, and number 6 was home to Edwin Strawson, a coach builder—Strawson had lived here since at least 1871. By 1891, 39 people lived on this road, including a school mistress (Charlotte Neale), a bricklayer (John M. Wilson), and an upholsterer (William Vickers). In the twentieth century, new buildings were constructed on the south side of the road, notably the Lincoln & Lindsey Blind Society building.

PRIORY CLOSE

Priory Close runs north-east from PRIORY ROAD on land between EASTGATE and MONKS DYKE ROAD. This was an open area with a large pit in 1889, which was the former brickworks of Bellamy & Co. (see Eastgate). By 1906, an iron foundry had been established at what is now the eastern end of Priory Close and it was still marked here on the 1956 OS map; MONKS AVENUE may have provided access to this. There was also a large, unidentified building on the western side of the site that was accessed by a track running south from Eastgate, near to the junction with Priory Road. By the late 1960s, the iron foundry and the other building had gone and this area was a Builders Merchant's Yard and Public Works Contractor's Depot, with the latter accessed via Monks Avenue. The houses of PRIORY CLOSE were constructed on this land in the late twentieth century, with at least two of them built in 1980.

PRIORY ROAD

Priory Road, which runs from EASTGATE through to MONKS DYKE ROAD, was originally called Union Court. Terraced housing is depicted here on Bayley's 1834 plan of the town, the 1839 map of Louth, and

William Brown's 1844 sketch made from the spire of St James's Church, although the road at that point didn't yet run through to Monks Dyke Road.

In the mid-nineteenth century, Union Court lay in the midst of two brickworks and a ropery. The ropery appears to have lain immediately to the west of Union Court—this was Elisha Ryall's ropery, which is visible on William Brown's finished Panorama of 1847–56 ('Ryall's Ropery' is shown painted on the side of a building here). The brickworks were those of Nicholas Pearson Bellamy, located immediately to the east of Union Court, and James Hunter Ryley, located to the west of Ryall's ropery, in the area of ORME LANE; the Bellamy brickworks, which adjoined Union Court, were probably run previously by Edward Arliss, who was listed as a brick maker on Union Court in 1828–9 and 1835 (see further Eastgate and PRIORY CLOSE on the brickyard here and its later history). The industrial character of this area is partly reflected in the occupations of the mid-nineteenth-century inhabitants of this street, with six brick makers or brick labourers listed on Union Court in 1851 (John Heath, John Irragan, George Thoresay, Joseph Hainton, John Ashton, Edward Ashton). Also living on the street then were two hawkers, fourteen labourers or agricultural labourers, a waterman or boatman, three paupers, an oil cake manufacturer and an oil miller, a carpet weaver, two shoemakers and a laundress. In 1861, around 120 people were living on Union Court, including a brickyard boy (Alfred Stork Ingoldmells), a bricklayer (William Slight) and two ropemakers (Henry Haywood and William Dales), Union Court is also said to have been a one of the principal locations in Louth for brothels in the early 1840s, alongside the GATHERUMS and SPRING GARDENS, and in July 1843 an unnamed 'lady of the pavé' (prostitute) who lived on Union Court was involved in a fight in Louth's MARKET PLACE.

By 1889, Union Court had been renamed Priory Road and extended through to Monks Dyke Road. In the twentieth century, further houses were built on the west side of the street, towards Monks Dyke Road, and the terrace on the east side of Priory Road was replaced by new semi-detached properties. In the late twentieth century, the land to the east of the road was redeveloped as Priory Close.

QUARRY, THE

See NEWMARKET.

QUARRY ROAD

Quarry Road, sometimes called South Quarry Road or Quarry Lane, runs south-west from LINDEN WALK and led to Rock Cottage and the Julian Bower Lime Works in the Quarry in late nineteenth century (see NEWMARKET on the Quarry and the lime works). Quarry Road is marked on the 1839 map of Louth and on both William Brown's preliminary sketch of 1844 and his finished Panorama of 1847–56, with buildings depicted only at its western end then. By the late nineteenth century, Quarry Terrace had been established halfway along this lane and in 1881 the inhabitants of the road included William Emmerson, a toll collector and milk seller; Charles Thompson, a tailor; David Lewis, a grocer's porter; George Thacker, a labourer; and Joseph Onn, a carpenter. The Lewis and Onn families were still there in the early twentieth century, living at 3 and 4 Quarry Terrace. In 1911, William Strawson, a confectioner and fruiterer who had shops on ASWELL STREET and in the MARKET PLACE, lived in Rock Cottage (he had previously lived at 30 Aswell Street), although by 1919 it had become the home of John Wyman, a market gardener.

QUARRYSIDE

Quarryside runs west from Upgate and is a late twentieth-century housing estate. At least one of the houses here was constructed in the late 1980s and the estate as a whole was built by the end of the 1980s within the 'Old Chalk Pit' off Upgate (as it was labelled on OS maps from 1889 through to the 1950s). This pit can be seen on both William Brown's preliminary sketch of 1844 and his final Panorama of 1847–56, and it was probably used for lime burning in the 1830s and 1840s by Thomas Haywood and William Colam (see Upgate). It was subsequently used by David Field, lime burner of Upgate, in the 1890s.

QUEEN STREET

Queen Street runs from the MARKET PLACE through to CHURCH
STREET and was called Walkergate or Fullers' Road until it was
renamed in 1887, the year of Queen Victoria's Golden Jubilee. The street
was already in existence by 1235–53, when a house and land is said to
have extended from Fullers' Road to the Aswell spring. Similarly, a
messuage on Walkergate—usually defined as a dwelling house with
outbuildings and land—is mentioned in 1311 and 1317, this being the
property of Thomas de Luda, chapter clerk of Lincoln Cathedral.
Whether the road ran all the way down to Maiden Row (modern Church
Street) in the medieval period is, however, uncertain, and the eastern
sections of Queen Street are usually thought to have been on the
periphery of the medieval town.

The fact that this road was called Walkergate/Fullers' Road in the
thirteenth and fourteenth centuries strongly suggests that Louth's cloth-
finishing industry was based here in the medieval period—fullers or
walkers were cloth-processors who stamped on cloth in pure water to
felt it and give it a smooth finish, and their presence on the road bearing
their name is confirmed by, for example, the Manor Court Roll for 1443,
which refers to 'Robert Curteys, Walker' and 'Robert Curteys of
Walkergate'. Walkergate also appears to have been home to dye-works
associated with cloth-production in this period—the house and land
mentioned on Fullers' Road in 1235–53 belonged to one Gilbert the dyer
and, in 1431, a Robert ffynche was reported to the Manor Court for
washing newly dyed black cloths in the Aswell spring. The latter ran
along the southern end of the medieval properties on the south side of
Walkergate and the fullers of this area would have similarly used the
waters of the Aswell spring in their trade (see the GATHERUMS &
SPRINGSIDE on the Aswell spring).

With regard to Louth's cloth industry, it is worth remembering that
Louth was actually one of the most important textile centres in both
Lincolnshire and eastern England in the thirteenth and fourteenth
centuries, producing, like Lincoln and Beverley, a distinctive fine cloth
that was mentioned by name in customs accounts of that period—for
example, in 1307 a substantial cargo of 'Louth say' (a cloth of fine
texture) was loaded in Hull for Gerard Nerle of Florence on the galley of
Andali de Nigro. Louth's distinctive cloth continued to be exported well

into the fourteenth century, and the cloth-processing industry in Louth still provided employment for thirteen walkers or fullers in the late fourteenth century, according to the 1379 poll tax list. Indeed, the cloth industry in the town is thought to have remained in reasonable health through the fifteenth century and into the sixteenth, with the early sixteenth-century Churchwardens' Accounts referring to sixteen weavers and ten fullers, along with others associated with the trade. By the end of the sixteenth century, cloth processing appears to have been a declining area of local employment, however. Nonetheless, it did continue. There was at least one fulling mill, which mechanised the fulling process, in Louth in the late sixteenth century—this belonged to John Bradley and is mentioned in his will of 1590—and there was a fulling mill working the Aswell spring, to the south of Walkergate, in the early nineteenth century (see Church Street for the mill, which fronted onto that road).

Dyers and fullers were not the only people using the waters of the Aswell spring in the medieval period and after. In 1449, the Aswell spring was said to provide the people of Louth with 'clean water for making their beer', and in 1835 there were three brewers based on Walkergate: John Hickling, Lucas Cheetham & Co., and Richard Luck. Richard Luck was also listed as a hop merchant on Walkergate in that year and the Luck family continued to run a brewery here into the 1870s in the area of the Queen Street car park. In 1881 Henry Luck was living at 34 Walkergate and was described as a 'brewer's agent', whilst James Dickenson lived at The Tap in Luck's Yard and is listed as a general assistant to a brewer's agent and keeper of The Tap, which was presumably a beerhouse. This was known as 'Luck's Tap' in 1891, though the person living there then was a butcher (William Wells Rose), and Luck's beerhouse has been identified with the Pig & Whistle, which was in Luck's Yard and is recorded in 1901 on Queen Street. This establishment apparently had a skittle alley behind it and was where the Parish Church Choir had its supper; it is said to have closed in 1909.

Needless to say, the Pig & Whistle was not the only drinking establishment on Walkergate/Queen Street in the nineteenth century. There was, for example, the Brown Horse at the eastern end of the street, at number 77. This building still bears traces of a painted sign on its side from its time as a public house, and the beerhouse here was run by James Harrison from at least 1841 and continued to operate into the mid-twentieth century. In 1855, William Moncaster and Martha Arliss of

KILN YARD were charged with stealing a fowl from James Harrison, although they were eventually discharged as Harrison refused, for some reason, to identify the creature. In 1851, Harrison's beerhouse was reported to have been where the prostitute Fanny Jepson met William Scupham, who claimed to have been robbed by her after they visited a beerhouse on Maiden Row and two brothels together. Another drinking establishment on Walkergate was the Rising Sun, at the western end of the street (number 9). This is first recorded in 1782 and was given a new frontage in 1897, when it was operated by Soulby Sons & Winch; it maintained its name for many years, but has recently seen a number of changes and rebirths (it is currently 'Bar Ritz'). In 1857, a bricklayer named John Elston stole a German silver teaspoon and a saltspoon from the Rising Sun; the missing items were found on him by the police, who he attempted to bribe with a sovereign to remain silent about their discovery. He was ultimately sentenced to two months in Louth House of Correction. The Rising Sun itself also ran into trouble in 1843, when the landlord was reprimanded for 'allowing prostitutes to congregate and drink the maddening alcohol'.

In addition to these, there were also a number of more short-lived beerhouses present on Walkergate. One of these was the Marrowbone and Cleaver, run by a man named Walker in the 1830s. In March 1839, Walker's house was raided by the police, who had been informed that it was being run as a brothel—when inside they found 14 or 15 prostitutes, who were dancing to two fiddles along with a number of 'bad characters'. The prostitutes were all said to be 14 to 18 years of age, although at least one was younger than this, as a prostitute who had been dancing at Walker's was interviewed by the magistrates and she was said to be 'under 14' and 'exceedingly small of her age'. This girl, named Elizabeth Stone, was given a 'fatherly lecture' by the magistrate, Samuel Trought, Esq., before being sent back to the House of Correction, where she had been committed for a month as a prostitute; Walker was fined £5 and costs, equivalent to around £350 today. The Marrowbone and Cleaver had closed down by 1850, when it was being used as a lodging-house by one James Marchant. It was the scene, in that year, of a three hour fight between two families of lodgers there and some of the local residents, and at its height involved around twenty people and implements ranging from mallets and kettles to saws, knives and hammers. The families subsequently retreated into the lodging-house and engaged in a battle with the local police force to prevent them from entering and arresting them, a battle they eventually lost.

There were also other breweries on Walkergate/Queen Street besides that of the Luck family. One of these was the Old Phoenix brewery, which was run by Robert Andrews from at least 1849 through until the early 1870s (he was still listed here in 1871 but appears to have died in early 1872), and Christopher Hill Parker in the 1870s and mid-1880s. Andrews lived at 43 Walkergate and Parker lived at 43–45 Walkergate in 1881, so the brewery was presumably in this area, on the north side of the road and slightly to the east of the Queen Street car park. In 1861, Andrews was listed as a brewer, maltster and farmer of 51 acres, employing nine men. Although it isn't specified anywhere, it seems likely that there was a beerhouse attached to the Old Phoenix brewery, as there was at the Luck's brewery, as Parker was listed as a 'retired publican' in 1891 (he then lived at 11 NEWMARKET). Another major brewery was East & Co.'s Maiden Row brewery, discussed at more length under Church Street. William East's malt kilns were located behind Walkergate, off Kiln Yard, with the main brewery buildings occupied a site fronting onto Walkergate and then running south along Maiden Row (Church Street). This business was acquired by Thomas Montague Winch in 1895–6, and the building on the corner of Queen Street and Church Street still bears the name T M Winch & Co on its side. By 1898, the brewery was trading as Soulby, Sons & Winch and the brewery was known as the Queen Street Brewery in 1907, although brewing ceased on the site in the early twentieth century and the buildings were subsequently used only for storage and distribution. From the mid-1920s, the buildings became print works—they were used by Allinson & Wilcox, printers and bookbinders, now Allinson Print Ltd, until 2004, when the company moved onto the FAIRFIELD INDUSTRIAL ESTATE. By 1913, all four brewery companies still operating in Louth were based on Queen Street, including the Wellow Brewery Co., which occupied the premises on the south-western corner of BURNT HILL LANE and Queen Street (see Burnt Hill Lane on this company).

A significant range of other businesses were, of course, based on Walkergate/Queen Street in the nineteenth and twentieth centuries, and the road was fully developed along both sides by the time of the 1808 plan of Louth. For example, in 1835 this street was home to Miss Jane

Brown's private school, an attorney (Richard Paddison), three bakers, three brewers, two bricklayers/builders (including Michael Medley—see EDWARD STREET), two butchers, a joiner, an earthenware dealer, a grocer, a beer retailer (Thomas Crowston), a hairdresser, a maltster, a plumber and glazier, a porter merchant (Overton & East), a seed merchant (Richard Luck), a straw hat maker, a surgeon, two tailors, two clock makers, a wheelwright, and a veterinary surgeon. The latter was Thomas Darby, who was listed on both Burnt Hill Lane and Walkergate in the first half of the nineteenth century and occupied the premises on the eastern corner of both these streets (now Louth Family Dental Practice)—the Darby family operated a veterinary practice here from at least the 1820s and continued at this location as a dog and cat specialist into the twentieth century. The mid-nineteenth century also saw the creation of an Association Methodist, or Warrenite, chapel on Walkergate. Established in 1837, the chapel was located on the north side of the street, to the west of Burnt Hill Lane, and initially had seating for 300, which was increased to 500 with a gallery in 1845. The building was sold shortly afterwards, in 1848, to the General Baptists, and it subsequently functioned as the gymnasium, reading room, and smoke room of the Louth and District Athletic Club, founded 1862, after which it became the Liberal Club; it is currently the Masonic Hall. In the late 1840s, the yard behind the Warrenite chapel was notorious as a 'den of prostitutes'—see Burnt Hill Lane.

In 1909, there were a similarly large number of businesses and tradespeople based on Queen Street, including a steam miller (James Pocklington of the Victoria mills, who was still there in 1937), three general shopkeepers, two bakers, two fishmongers (including Joseph Morely, number 19, who also had a fried fish shop on Burnt Hill Lane), two grocers, five butchers, two beer retailers (Joseph Dannatt, number 34a—presumably the Pig & Whistle—and Elias Wood at number 77, the Brown Horse), a plumber, three blacksmiths, a cycle maker (John Charles Grundy at number 18), a carpenter, two boot makers, a tobacconist (numbers 3–5), a painter, a builder (George Henry Vickers, number 34), and a marine store dealer, Clarke & Son, in the Victoria buildings. The name 'Victoria buildings' seems to refer to the large Victorian warehouse on the north side of Queen Street, which bears the date 1869. This once belonged to John Walmsley, who also owned a notoriously smelly bone-crushing mill on Holmes Lane (HIGH

HOLME ROAD). He was listed on Walkergate as a 'wholesale haberdasher and marine store dealer' (a dealer in scrap materials) in 1861 and a 'general merchant' in 1885. He purchased and subsequently demolished the former House of Correction on EASTGATE in 1872, using some of the materials—including the old prison clock—to extend and improve his warehouse on the north side of QUEEN STREET: the prison clock is still affixed high up on the front of the warehouse and had apparently once also adorned the old Town Hall in the Market Place, which was demolished in 1815. John Walmsley died in 1885 and his widow, Elizabeth, was running his business from the 'Victoria buildings' in 1889; by 1905, the business was being operated by Clarke & Co. and was described then as 'late John Walmsley'. The directory for 1909 also mentions the Louth Motor Garage Company, which was founded in 1908 and was the first motor garage in Louth. The Louth Motor Garage Co. was listed on QUEEN STREET PLACE in 1909 and the manager then was Thomas Linton Wilson, who lived at 90 UPGATE in 1911. In 1913, Wilson was still the manager but the garage was then listed on both Queen Street Place and Queen Street, and in 1914 the business was bought by George Harniess, who is given as the proprietor in the 1919 directory. The garage was originally a dealer for Ford and Overland, but from 1924–1984 it had the Morris dealership, later British Leyland and Austin Rover. In the late twentieth century, Harniess's garage was a Skoda dealer and the business remained at the Queen Street site until the early twenty-first century, when it moved out to the Fairfield Industrial Estate.

In the later twentieth and early twenty-first centuries, Queen Street continued to be home to a number of businesses, but it also witnessed some significant changes. For example, the south side of the street to the east of Queen Street Place saw major remodelling, as a consequence of both the establishment of the mid-twentieth-century clinic (Kidgate Surgery) here and the creation of the Queen Street car park in the 1970s. Similarly, the properties on the north side at the far eastern end of the road (including the Gelsthorp tannery, which was sometimes listed on Walkergate—see Church Street) were demolished in the twentieth century to make way for a car park and Louth Bus Station. Nonetheless, Queen Street still retains a significant number of interesting, pre-twentieth-century buildings, including the former Warrenite chapel and Walmsley's Victorian warehouse, and the medieval layout of

Walkergate/Fullers' Road is still traceable in part, especially on the north side of the road to the west of Burnt Hill Lane.

QUEEN STREET PLACE

Queen Street Place runs south from QUEEN STREET to connect with WALKERGATE PLACE. The name Queen Street replaced that of Walkergate in 1887; as such, the street-name Queen Street Place is unlikely to date from before this. The road itself is shown on the 1889 OS map of the town, although it is not named on it, and the first directory to list the street is that of 1896: in that year, a blacksmith named Joseph East was based on Queen Street Place, as he was in 1905 too. In 1909, the Louth Motor Garage Company (founded in 1908) was listed on Queen Street Place, the manager of this being one Thomas Linton Wilson, who lived at 90 UPGATE in 1911. In 1914 the business was bought by George Harniess and Harniess's garage operated from here until the early twenty-first century. The property subsequently has been a bed shop and bath shop; it currently stands empty (see further Queen Street on Harniess's garage). Also present on Queen Street Place in 1909 was a coal dealer named William Wood, who was there in 1913 too, when a blacksmith named Alfred Willoughby was also listed, although only the latter was still operating from Queen Street Place after the First World War.

QUEENSWAY

Queensway runs west from ST BERNARDS AVENUE through to WALLIS ROAD and is part of the large, post-World War Two St Bernards Avenue council housing scheme, this element of it having been laid out after the time that the 1956 OS map was surveyed. The land it stands on was originally part of Louth's old open South Field.

RAMSGATE

Ramsgate (or Ramsgate Road) runs north from EASTGATE to NEWBRIDGE HILL and then east and north-east through to the RIVERHEAD. Sir Charles Bolle supposedly hid under the bridge across the Lud on Ramsgate during the Civil War in order to escape his pursuers, who apparently galloped on over it—the incident is said to have occurred in 1643, when there was a skirmish at Louth between the Royalist and Parliamentary forces, although Bolle is not actually listed as a commander in the records of that skirmish. In the eighteenth century, the Ramsgate bridge was called the New Bridge, implying that it had been then recently constructed. For example, the proposed canal that terminated at Ramsgate was described as a canal 'from Tetney Haven to the New Bridge in Louth' in 1757. Similarly, in 1717 reference is made to a Mr George Ballow paying two fat hens in rent for a close 'at New Bridge'. The road running east to the Riverhead was probably originally constructed as part of the canal development—in September 1769, the Commissioners decided to build a new road to the Mallard Ings/Riverhead on the north side of river, and appointed Dr Clarke, Mr Wrigglesworth and Richard Wharfe to superintend the work. Under the Louth Turnpike Act of 1770, Ramsgate was made into a turnpike between the town and the new Riverhead, although no charge was made for the use of this section of road.

The 1808 plan of the town only shows a small portion of Ramsgate, with the House of Correction depicted on the eastern corner of its junction with Eastgate (see further under that road) and then some buildings on the western side of the road between the Ramsgate bridge and JAMES STREET. By 1834, this area had seen further building and there was also a long terrace of houses on the opposite side of the road, north of the bridge—the 1839 map shows the terrace on the eastern side extending all the way through to the junction with Newbridge Hill, and it is also visible on William Brown's 1844 sketch and his final Panorama of 1847–56. By the late nineteenth century, the part of Ramsgate to the south of the Lud had also seen significant development. ALEXANDRA ROAD and PLEASANT PLACE had been developed here, running east and west of the road respectively; the old House of Correction and the Ramsgate Sessions House—built by John Hunter Ryley in 1850—had been replaced by the Orme Almshouses (see Eastgate); Sunday School buildings associated with the 1864 Eastgate Baptist Chapel had been built facing onto Ramsgate, now Eastgate Union Church Hall; and there was housing to the south of the river, on the west side of the road.

At the junction with Newbridge Hill, the major development in the mid-nineteenth century was the establishment of the railway station. A short road leading north-west to the station was built from the

Ramsgate–Newbridge Hill junction, and the railway line running southwards crossed Ramsgate a little to the east. The road to the station is now gone and a new block of buildings named Pullman Terrace—dated 1989—stands where its entranceway once was, but the railway station itself survives. This is a mock-Tudor Gothic building that was opened in 1848, with the foundation stone having been laid on 8 July 1847 by Miss Charlotte Pye ('Claribel'). There was a regular passenger service to Grimsby from March 1848 and the line to Boston was completed in September 1848, which allowed onwards travel to Peterborough and London. A branch line to Bardney was added in 1876, for connections to Lincoln, and one to Mablethorpe in 1877. The station closed to passenger traffic in October 1970, although a single track remained in place northwards to Grimsby until 1980 to serve the needs of ABM on Newbridge Hill; the branch lines to Bardney and Mablethorpe had shut to passengers in 1951 and 1960, respectively. Another significant, related development at the Ramsgate–Newbridge Hill junction was the construction of the Wellington Hotel. This was apparently first listed in 1850 and its construction is probably to be associated with the opening of railway here. In 1861 it was described as a 'commercial hotel' and the landlord, Francis Bond, was also listed as a brewer (see also Newbridge Hill on Bond). In 1939, a platoon of the Northumberland Fusiliers, led by Captain Lord Hugh Percy, the Duke of Northumberland, was stationed in the Wellington before being sent on active service. The Wellington closed in 2005 and has subsequently been converted into residential dwellings.

The road eastwards from Newbridge Hill was less developed in the mid-nineteenth century and has continued to be so, with the River Lud flowing along its southern side. Notable buildings and sites along here include the water mill on the southern side of the road, accessed by a bridge over the river (which now leads to OLD MILL PARK). The present watermill mainly dates from the mid- and later nineteenth century, although it includes a date-stone of 1716. In 1889, the mill was a flour mill called the River Head Roller Mills and it was subsequently known as the Crown Mills, operated by Bryan Hall from the early twentieth century (Bryan Hall is first listed here in 1909). The mill derived its power from the river Lud, supplemented by a diesel engine, and it produced animal feeds and Three Crowns branded flour. The last miller here was a later Bryan Hall, who joined the family business in

1946; one April, he apparently managed to convince a local newspaper that the mill would be expanding into the production of woad, as a joke. Bryan Hall retired in 1981 and sold the site for residential development.

Another interesting building is the twin-towered, mock-Tudor building on the opposite side of Ramsgate to the mill. This was originally designed as a roller skating rink in the Edwardian period and was subsequently the Louth Motor Body Works of F. M. Thompson in 1920s, fitting the bodywork and coachwork of cars and buses. This business employed fifty people in the 1920s and in 1926 they built ten double-decker buses for Birmingham Corporation—it is said that the entire workforce had to climb aboard the buses in order to lower them sufficiently on their springs so that they could get out of the building. In 1935, the rink was used for a children's tea party to celebrate the Jubilee of that year, and the old roller rink has more recently been used to keep hens in, to store peas and grain, and by Hi-Lite Signs. There was also a nineteenth-century brickyard off this section of Ramsgate, accessed via a track to the north-east of the roller rink. The brick-pit here is set well back from the road and is now filled with water—it was run by Henry Chapman in 1835, when its address was given as Ramsgate, and it was probably his in 1828–9 too (his brick-making business was listed at the Fish Shambles, on Eastgate, in that year, but this must have been his shop as the brickworks cannot have been there). By 1841, the brickyard on Ramsgate was run by both Henry Chapman and Thomas Simons, although the address was now given as 'River head'. The brickyard was subsequently operated by Cartwright and William Cheffins in the later nineteenth century (as in 1872).

The twentieth century saw significant changes along Ramsgate. The railway and the entrance to the railway station both disappeared, as noted above, and in their place the STATION APPROACH residential estate was developed in the late twentieth century. There was also an increased quantity of housing developed off Ramsgate between Newbridge Hill and the Riverhead, adding to that small amount established there by the end of the nineteenth century. Most dramatic, however, were the changes on Ramsgate between Eastgate and Newbridge Hill that occurred as a result of the 1920 Louth Flood—the buildings on the corner of Ramsgate and James Street were, for example, demolished as a result of this and rebuilt in the inter-war years as council housing on an entirely new alignment. Ramsgate also suffered damage from a German raid on the town in 1941, with several houses destroyed and a number of deaths, including that of Peter Arliss at 60 Ramsgate, aged two.

With regard to the mid-nineteenth-century newspapers, Ramsgate makes a number of appearances in their pages. In 1854, for example, reference was made to a brothel or 'house of ill fame' on Ramsgate. This 'common bawdy house' was run by one William Forman and his wife Catherine, and they were charged in that year with having beaten and robbed William Horton—a somewhat notable patron of the local brothels, see SPRING GARDENS and the GATHERUMS—of £17 10s, equivalent to around £1,250 today. Forman apparently took Horton from the Marquis of Granby tavern on Eastgate to his brothel on Ramsgate and then brought a certain Mrs Cotchiefer to him (who lived on what is now ALBION PLACE). The newspaper report stated that 'what took place there is not fit for publication', but the end result was that Horton was 'very much beaten' and robbed. Ramsgate was mentioned again in 1866, when a correspondent of the *Hull Packet* noted that the watermen of the town were accustomed to filling their water carts from Ramsgate Bridge, but were having difficulties due to the quantity of 'filth' accumulating in the river, which checked the action of their pumps. Finally, in 1855 Ramsgate was, like many streets in Louth, troubled by beggars—one, who had been 'deprived of his tongue and one of his eyes', was sentenced to 21 days in the House of Correction for 'begging and intimidating the inhabitants of Ramsgate'.

RIVERHEAD ROAD & RIVERHEAD

Riverhead Road runs from RAMSGATE through to EASTFIELD ROAD, with Riverhead (or Riverhead Terrace) running north-east from this on the north bank of the canal. For reasons of cost, the Louth canal, which was completed in 1770, terminated somewhat short of the contemporary town and a new industrial village and docklands consequently grew up in this area, known as the Riverhead. Not only were shipyards and warehouses built here, but there were also granaries, coalyards, breweries, a woodyard, a soapery, and a leather factory, and by 1790 a greater weight of fish was being landed daily at the Riverhead than at Grimsby. By 1842, the Riverhead was second only to EASTGATE in Louth in terms of the number of commercial and industrial properties operating. However, the canal declined significantly in the nineteenth century, especially after the arrival of the railway (see Ramsgate). The last boat building yard had closed down before 1900 and only two coal merchants were still by the canal in 1913, with most then located in the railway yard. The Riverhead area remained a centre of fertiliser production in the early–mid twentieth century, but the canal finally closed for navigation in 1924, after sustaining serious damage in the 1920 Louth Flood.

Significant buildings on Riverhead Road and Riverhead Terrace include the two warehouses that stand either side of the end of the canal. These are thought to have been built in the late eighteenth century, perhaps around the time that the canal was opened. The northern warehouse was owned by Stephen Gray in the 1820s and was used for the storage of grain for export and, later, foreign wheat in the nineteenth century. The southern warehouse was occupied by Sharpley and Lawrence in the 1820s and was similarly used for storing grain—since the closure of the canal, this warehouse had been used by an electrical contractor, Seymour & Castle, and it has now been transformed into a large single dwelling. Another early warehouse still standing on Riverhead Road is the large, four-storey building on the opposite side of the road, near to the junction with Eastfield Road. This was built in 1818 on the site of a tree nursery, not 1881 as the figures on it currently read: it was used as a grain store by Theodore West & Co. and has now been converted into flats. Another warehouse owned by Theodore West & Co. lay opposite the canal but has been demolished and replaced by the apartments of Forlander Place, named after the sloop Annie Forlander.

There were also two notable inns on Riverhead Road. One of these was the Ship Inn, first recorded in 1782 and still operating in the early twentieth century, with its landlord being one William Cartwright in 1822. This inn was set a little back from Riverhead Road, between the old Louth Swimming Pool and the Woolpack (see below on both of these). In 1833, it was run by William Jackson and had its own brewery—in the November of that year, the brewer, named James Bullivant, apparently found himself 'rather cold' and is said to have 'most impudently laid himself down upon the cover of the brewing copper, which gave way'. He was so badly injured that, 'after lingering in the most excruciating torment till the next day', he died. In 1852, the landlord of the Ship Inn, then John Meanwell, was in trouble with the courts, having apparently cut the ropes of a stack belonging to his neighbour, John Naylor. The other inn was the Woolpack, which may have been built around 1772 and still continues in business today (the 1813 date on the front is that of a change of ownership, when it was bought by Stephen Gray). The Woolpack appears a number of times in the mid-nineteenth-century court reports. In 1855, Eliza Clark was the proprietor and charged John Wilson of Brackenborough with attempting to force entrance to the inn at one in the morning, breaking thirteen panes of glass when he was refused admittance. In 1854, the ostler, or stableman, of the Woolpack Tavern—'an old offender, whose bloated appearance afforded a miserable example of the deplorable effects of a continued course of intemperance'—was charged with assaulting William Buck and throwing him down the passage of the inn. And, in 1848, the landlord of the Woolpack, a former coachman called William Day, was charged with assaulting John Markham, the driver of the Louth–Lincoln coach, in the Old Rein Deer Inn in MERCER ROW.

As well as inns, there was a Wesleyan Methodist chapel somewhere at the Riverhead. The exact location of this building is unclear: it was in existence by 1825 and was removed, brick-by-brick, to Theddlethorpe in 1854. The building that was so removed must have been the 'new Wesleyan chapel at the River Head' that was begun in 1848 and completed in February 1849; this was 'a commodious edifice', which presumably replaced an earlier building that had served as a chapel since the early nineteenth century. The Holy Trinity Parochial School was another interesting building, constructed on the corner of Riverhead Road and Eastfield Road in 1865 (see further Eastfield Road). It ceased to be used as a school in 1979, when the Infants moved to Eastfield Infants' School, off LACEY GARDENS. Subsequently, it was used by Lincoln Technology College from the 1980s and was demolished in 2007 to make way for flats. Finally, Louth Swimming Pool was opened on Riverhead Road in 1974 by Dr Mary Archer, on land that had been the site of a farm in 1828. This closed in the early twenty-first century, after the construction of the Meridian Leisure Centre on WOOD LANE.

Riverhead, or Riverhead Terrace, was not explicitly depicted on the 1805 Enclosure Award map, the 1824 OS map of the Riverhead, or Padley's 1828 plan of the area, although a section of road was marked on the latter. It is, however, certainly present on the 1889 OS map, as are the Riverhead Cottages which stand around halfway down the road; the terraced housing immediately to east of Woolpack is more recent in date and built on what had been a coal yard in 1828, whilst that just to the south-west of Riverhead Cottages dates from the late twentieth century. The early twenty-first century has seen further development of the road via an extension of it to the north-east, known as the Waterside development, with STANLEY CLOSE built running off this new part of Riverhead. At the back of the Riverhead Cottages was Leather Mill Lane, also known as Eelmire Road and The Moorings. The road was named after the Dog Mill, a leather mill that stood to the north of the canal on the former course of the Lud, and the cottages here are marked on the 1889 OS map; like Riverhead Terrace, this area has seen new building in the latter part of the twentieth century. The 1889 OS map also shows a 'Chemical Manure Works' on the northern side of the canal, to the north-east of Leather Mill Lane. William Nell and Thomas Elkington Smith had manufactured artificial manure on the north bank of the canal from 1876 and T. E. Smith carried on the business alone from 1882; the Smiths continued to manufacture artificial manure here through until at least 1945, and the 'Chemical Manure Works' were still marked on the 1956 OS map.

With regard to the canal itself, this makes a number of appearances in the mid-nineteenth-century newspapers. For example, the sloops on the canal were sometimes the scene of crimes, as in 1847, when George Holmes was charged by Thomas Dickinson of the Louth sloop 'Zephyr' with stealing a pair of boots from the Zephyr whilst it lay at the Riverhead. Similarly, in 1857, a silver watch and £2 9s in gold and silver was stolen by a riverman from the cabin of the sloop 'Perseverance' at the Riverhead. The canal was also occasionally the scene of suicides. For example, on Christmas Day 1852, John Hall of Little Cawthorpe drowned himself near to the Riverhead, having become 'much depressed in mind' after his wife had deserted him twelve months earlier.

ROBINSON LANE

Robinson Lane is the spine of a late twentieth-century housing estate built to the south of MOUNT PLEASANT. It was built in the mid-1990s on land that had formerly been used by the Robinson family for its market garden and nursery, with the houses here sold as new builds until 1997. This land was enclosed from the old open fields of Louth after the 1801 Enclosure Act.

ROSEMARY LANE

Rosemary Lane extends from the western end of the CORNMARKET through to EASTGATE, running alongside the former site of the Corn Exchange and the Theatre (see MARKET PLACE & CORNMARKET on these). Although it currently runs straight between the two roads, in 1889 the lane had a dog-leg in it at the rear of the Corn Exchange, running briefly east before continuing north to Eastgate.

In 1851, Rosemary Lane was home to Jane Laking, a widow; Susannah Dickenson, another widow who lived there with her five children, aged from four to eighteen (she herself was only twenty-nine!); and a tailor named Charles T. Pidd. In 1847, Jane Laking took in a lodger named Frances Eardley, who she accused of stealing a pinafore, a flannel petticoat and a spoon—Eardley was discharged due to a lack of evidence. In 1861, only Odling Parker, a plasterer, was living on Rosemary Lane with his family, with the other two houses then standing empty, and in 1871 numbers 1 and 2 Rosemary Lane were being used as a lodging-house by Rosanna Thomas. This lodging-house was still operating in 1881, when it was run by John Thomas and was home to six lodgers, including Edward Smith, an umbrella maker. A 'monthly nurse'—that is, a nurse who attended women in the first weeks after childbirth—named Elizabeth Atkin lived at 3 Rosemary Lane in 1881.

At least one of the houses on Rosemary Lane was used as a brothel in the 1850s, as in 1854 a Mary Fletcher was described as 'late the keeper of a notorious house of ill-fame, in Rosemary-lane'—she was charged in that year with absconding and leaving two of her children chargeable to the parish of Louth, for which crime she was sent to prison for one month as a rogue and a vagabond. Rosemary Lane would also appear to have been the occasional scene of drunkenness, as in 1850 when Joseph Grantham, a pig jobber (trader), was charged with being drunk and causing an obstruction in Rosemary Lane, for which he was fined 20s.

RUSSET DRIVE

Russet Drive runs south and west from ROBINSON LANE and is part of a late twentieth-century housing estate built to the south of MOUNT PLEASANT. This estate was constructed in the mid-1990s on land that had formerly been used by the Robinson family for its market garden and nursery, and all the roads that run off Robinson Lane are named after varieties of apple.

SANDRINGHAM DRIVE

Sandringham Drive runs south from ARUNDEL DRIVE and is part of a large housing estate built to the south of NORTH HOLME ROAD in the 1960s and 1970s. The road is absent from the 1968 OS map but it had been laid out and largely developed by the time that the 1974–6 map was surveyed. The land that it is built on was originally part of Louth's old open North Field.

SCHOOLHOUSE LANE

Schoolhouse Lane runs from GOSPELGATE through to WESTGATE and was formerly known as Gulpyn Lane. The name Schoolhouse Lane derives from the fact that Louth Grammar School was located on this road from at least the late 1550s. This road was potentially also where the school was located in the medieval period, given that the earlier name, Gulpyn Lane (first recorded in the fifteenth century), may derive from the dialect word 'gulp' or 'gulpin', which was used in Lincolnshire and elsewhere for a child.

The first record of a school in Louth comes from 1276, when a Simon de Luda was named as the Master of Louth School. In 1433, the Manor Court Roll refers to a Thomas Rydlay, Master of the Grammar School of Louth, who was sued by William Smyth for not paying for eighteen yards of linen cloth, and in 1475–6 Nicholas Gysburgh was the Master of the Grammar School, when he paid £1 in rent for the house that he occupied. In the fifteenth century, the Trinity Gild appear to have maintained the school (with it being said in the mid-sixteenth century that 'a grammar Scole hath been contynuallie kept in Louth... with the revenues of the Guylde or fraternytie of the holie Trynytie in louthe'), although it was probably not alone—the Master of Louth Grammar School lived in a house rented from St Mary's Gild in 1475–6, and in 1535 the salary of the Master, John Goodall, was partly funded by St Mary's Gild, the Corpus Christi Gild and St Peter's Gild. In 1551, the school was refounded by King Edward VI in the recently-closed St Mary's Church, or Chapel, off BRIDGE STREET, but it was soon

229

found to be too cold and inhospitable for teaching and the school was moved to (or back to) Schoolhouse Lane in 1557–8.

Aside from, potentially, the Grammar School, the pre-Reformation Gulpyn Lane (Schoolhouse Lane) was also home to a barn and a Bedehouse, or almshouse. The barn on Gulpyn Lane was mentioned in 1528–9, when it was used by the Gild of the Holy Trinity for repairing and storing the pageants (either wheeled or on poles) that were carried in procession on Corpus Christi Day. The Bedehouse belonged to St Mary's Gild and was first mentioned as being on Gulpyn Lane in 1474–5, when it had a chamber above it that was let for 3s 4d each year. 'Our Lady's Beidhouse' was originally intended to provide for six men or women, but it housed only women by 1617, with the men presumably being lodged elsewhere (poor men were lodged in the old leper hospital on SPITAL HILL and the former St Mary's Church, off Bridge Street, in the sixteenth and seventeenth centuries). The school, when it moved to this road from St Mary's Church in 1557–8, occupied the two rooms above the Bedehouse that had previously been utilised as lodgings for priests. The school probably catered for around twenty boys at this time and the building it was based in was thatched and timber-framed—for example, in 1754 William Chant was paid 6d for 'Stopping the Thatch Blowing off from the School'. There was also a 'greate windowe in the ende of the schoole', which was mended in 1626. By 1766, the Grammar School and Bedehouse was so ruinous and out of repair that it needed to be taken down and rebuilt, at a total cost of £334 1s 8d, with the only surviving remnant of the Tudor school being the statue of Edward VI— this was originally put up above Grammar School entrance by Peter Bradley in 1647, as a subtle gesture of royalist defiance to the new Commonwealth government. The new school of 1766 was that attended by Tennyson, and it had twelve apartments for Bedeswomen on the ground floor (the Trinity Bedehouse, in the CORNMARKET, was united with Our Lady's Bedehouse and both established in the new building). The current school buildings and separate Bedehouses were the product of a subsequent rebuilding in 1868–9: designed by local architect James Fowler, the mid-nineteenth-century school was intended to be large enough for 150 boys and the whole project cost around £2,540. The buildings here were used by the Boys' Grammar School until 1933, when it moved to its new EDWARD STREET buildings, and the Victorian school hall was subsequently used by the Girls' Grammar School.

In the early nineteenth century, the western side of the road was entirely taken up by Westgate House and its gardens, and the wall that ran along this side of the street, festooned by wild weeds, was famously said by Tennyson to be one of his only favourable memories of the Grammar School. The first bank in Louth, called the North Lincolnshire Bank, was run from Westgate House by Charles Wigelsworth from 1775–99, with the entrance to his banking department being on Schoolhouse Lane (now bricked up).

SEYMOUR AVENUE

Seymour Avenue runs south-west from NEWMARKET and is the main road of the Seymour Avenue housing estate that was constructed in the late twentieth century to the south of TENNYSON ROAD, between Newmarket and LINDEN WALK. Seymour Avenue was the first part of this estate to be constructed, beginning in the 1970s, on land that was once part of the old open South Field of Louth.

SHERWOOD CLOSE

Sherwood Close is a short road that runs north-east from NEWMARKET and runs to the end of GRESLEY ROAD (the two roads are separated by bollards). The land that the road was built on was once part of Louth's old open South Field, but by 1889 the land immediately to the north of Sherwood Close was marked as a Rope Walk, where long strands of material were laid before being twisted into rope. This was still marked here on the 1906 and 1932 OS maps, but was not present on later maps. By the late 1960s, there had been significant industrial development in this area of town, with a number of large buildings (including a plastics factory) constructed off Newmarket here. By the late twentieth century, some of these had been removed and a road and yard in the area of the modern Sherwood Close ended in a large factory—this has since been demolished and replaced by the new properties of Gresley Road, which was developed around the same time as Sherwood Close.

SIDINGS, THE

The Sidings runs west and then north-west from STATION
APPROACH and is part of a late twentieth-century residential housing
development built to the north of RAMSGATE. The north-western end
of the road stops just to the east of the sidings that once lay next to the
malthouse on NEWBRIDGE HILL, and The Sidings cuts across the
line of the former road from Ramsgate to the railway station.

SOMERSBY COURT

Somersby Court runs north from GOSPELGATE. It was built in the
1990s on land that once formed the gardens of Westgate House. In the
aftermath of the merger of the Boys' and Girls' Grammar Schools in
1965, this area was used for temporary buildings for the new King
Edward VI Grammar School—these were most recently used as exam
halls before their demolition.

SOMERSBY WAY

Somersby Way runs northwards from MONKS DYKE ROAD and is
part of an early twenty-first-century housing estate developed off an
eastern extension of the latter road. The land that it is built on was
originally part of Louth's old open East Field, before this was enclosed
under the Enclosure Act of 1801, and medieval ridge and furrow has
been observed from this area on aerial photographs.

SOUTH STREET

South Street runs from HORNCASTLE ROAD through to
NEWMARKET and is shown on the 1808 plan of the town, when it
was almost entirely undeveloped and called Tinker Lane. It still had this
name in 1834 and 1839, when some development had begun on the
south side of the road, including the laying out of SPITAL HILL. In
1841, Tinker Lane was mentioned as the business location for a
bricklayer named William Colam (see LEE STREET and Spital Hill), but
the name South Street was being used in newspaper reports in the mid-
1840s. By the time of William Brown's 1844 sketch of the town, the

north side of the road had also been significantly developed, and in 1861 South Street was home to 95 people. Inhabitants of the street in that year included a master shoemaker, employing ten men and two boys (Albert Dodson, number 25); a landed proprietor (Elizabeth Young, number 6); a grocer (George Strawson, number 15); a dressmaker (Sarah Kennington, number 11); and a cattle dealer (Thomas Horton, number 2).

In the mid-nineteenth century, South Street was mentioned a number of times in the court reports. For example, in 1846 John Shepherd and James Wilson, labourers from Stone in Staffordshire, were charged with begging in South Street and were both sent to the House of Correction for one month, and Sarah Webden of Stockton-on-Tees was similarly charged with begging here in 1851 (she was sent to prison for two weeks). In 1847, Eliza Davis of South Street and her neighbour, Lucy Preston, both appeared before the court as a result of a dispute between them and an alleged assault—the newspaper reporter suggested that this was 'one of those cases... in which the application of a good fire engine would be more appropriate than an application to a magistrate for a summons', noting that the language used in court was 'disgusting and disgraceful to womankind'. In the twentieth century, the remaining undeveloped parts of South Street, on the south side at the western end of the road, saw residential properties constructed upon them. The mid-nineteenth-century Elm Tree House also saw changes, being converted into The Beeches residential care home.

SOUTH TERRACE

South Terrace is located at the southern end of CHURCH STREET, at the junction with NEWMARKET, and runs north-east from these roads. The terrace of houses here would appear to be depicted on William Brown's sketch made from the spire of St James's Church in 1844. In 1889, the houses on the north side were marked 'South Terrace', with a nursery garden (including greenhouses) marked on the southern side of the road. The road then extended north-eastwards as a track to the orchards that once lay on the site of the ROBINSON LANE housing estate: nurseries and orchards continued to operate off this track into the later twentieth century, although the southern side of South Terrace itself had seen residential housing erected by that time. In

1891, 49 people were living on South Terrace, including a night watchman on the railway (Joseph Simon), several gardeners (for example, Bennett Graves, at number 5, and James Parker), agricultural labourers (such as Joseph Ingamells at number 9), shoemakers (John Taylor, number 12, and William Taylor, number 7), a dressmaker (Mary Ann East, number 8), and a wheelwright (William Broadbent, number 3).

SOUTHFIELD DRIVE

Southfield Drive runs south from TUDOR DRIVE and both are part of the SEYMOUR AVENUE housing estate, which was constructed off NEWMARKET in the late twentieth century. Southfield Drive is built on land that was once part of the old open South Field of Louth, although a more immediate predecessor was J. North & Son's market garden off LINDEN WALK. This market garden was first recorded in the mid-nineteenth century and still appeared on OS maps into the mid-twentieth century—the houses on the western side of Southfield Drive are constructed on its former grounds.

SOUTHLANDS AVENUE

Southlands Avenue runs east from KENWICK ROAD. The road was built on land that was originally part of Louth's old open South Field and it was constructed in the mid-twentieth century. It is depicted on the 1951 OS map of the area and is marked as 'Southlands Lane' on the 1967–8 and 1989 OS maps.

SPAW LANE

Spaw Lane is marked on the 1808 plan of the town and currently runs south-west from BROADBANK through to the south-eastern end of GRAY'S ROAD. Its present name is presumably a corruption of Spa Lane, the name usually applied to this road in the nineteenth century (as in the censuses, on maps and in the newspapers). The street-name Spa Lane, and its occasional nineteenth-century variant 'Bath Road', refers to the presence of a spa spring and a bath house at the south-western end of this road in the nineteenth century. Writing in 1852, William Brown noted that water, 'apparently of a chalybeate nature' (that is, containing salts of iron), flowed from 'the spa spring' here, which '40 years ago, before the Woodhall spa... was much frequented by the inhabitants of the town and the neighbouring villages'. At the time Brown was writing, a bath house had been recently erected on 'Spa-lane', making use of the spa spring: 'the baths consist of cold, tepid, vapour, shower, and warm, containing 60 to 70 tons of water of the finest quality'. The bath house is marked on the 1889 OS map on the western side of the junction between Gray's Road and Spa Lane, next to the river. On Brown's Panorama (last updated 1856), the buildings depicted in this area then included one with a tall chimney and a small waterwheel next to the river, at the end of Spa Lane. Quite what this was is not entirely clear from the painting, but it may well be that the buildings, chimney and waterwheel that Brown painted here were associated with the new bath house. The original proprietor of the baths was a man named John Harrison, and it may be relevant that he was listed both as the proprietor of 'Louth Baths' and as a machinist in the 1860s.

John Harrison was still the proprietor of the Louth Baths in 1872, which were variously listed as being on Spa Lane, Spaw Lane, Bath Road (apparently an alternative name for Spaw Lane), Enginegate (the earlier name for Broadbank) and Gray's Road in the nineteenth and early twentieth centuries. However, by 1885 the baths had passed to John Joseph Harrison, his son, who was also the engineer and manager of the Louth Waterworks Company. John Joseph Harrison was similarly listed as the proprietor in 1889, but in 1896 and 1909 Henry Pooles Thacker (a former railway engine driver) was the operator of the baths. The Louth Baths appear to have closed sometime between 1909 and 1913, as they were not listed in the latter directory.

SPIRE VIEW ROAD

Spire View Road runs north-west from WOOD LANE and is the main road of a new housing development that was constructed here in the late twentieth century, with at least two of the properties on Spire View Road being built in 1980. The land it is built upon was once part of Louth's old open South Field and was partly occupied by allotment gardens in the mid- to late twentieth century. In the same period, a new playing field and playground was established between WATTS LANE and Spire

View Road, on former allotment land that had once stood to the east of the Louth–Bardney branch line.

SPITAL HILL

Spital Hill, sometimes Spittle Hill or Spittal Hill, is currently the name of a road running south from SOUTH STREET, although it appears to have been originally the name of the high ground located to the south of South Street and the west of modern UPGATE (the section of Upgate that runs south from its junction with South Street and NEWMARKET was probably called 'Spittle hill laine' in the early seventeenth century—see further LONDON ROAD). The name Spital Hill derives from the fact that this area was the site of a leper hospital in the later medieval period. The leper hospital was first mentioned in 1314, when John Dalderby, Bishop of Lincoln, granted an indulgence to those who supported its inmates, and the Manor Court Roll mentions the 'domus leprosorum', leper house, that was situated upon 'Spytylhyll' in 1488. The hospital was probably also known as 'Bethlehem' or 'Bedlam', with a proctor of Bedelem named John Condon mentioned in the Court Roll for 1453. The hospital appears to have survived into the sixteenth century as 'Spittlehouse' or 'Spittilhows', with this being given to the Grammar School by the merchant John Bradley in 1556–7. The former leper house was being used as a poor house in 1572, with its proctor said to be Raffe Robson in 1575. The Spittlehouse was subsequently rebuilt in 1594 and seems to have been in use for much of next century, with the ringing of its bell being mentioned as late as 1685. In addition to a leper hospital, Spital Hill would also appear to have been the site of the town's gallows: first mentioned in 1274–5, the Court Roll for 1447 says that 'Galotre Wange' was near to the 'Spytill'.

The modern road called Spital Hill was laid out in the early nineteenth century—it is absent from the 1808 plan of the town, which shows South Street almost entirely undeveloped, but is present on the 1834 plan and the 1839 map of Louth. The houses built here were primarily cheap cottages designed to house labourers. In 1841, 187 people were living on Spital Hill, including a very large number of labourers (for example, Charles Grist, George Parker and George Wheatley), bricklayers (for example, John Ludley), a school mistress (Rebecca Beecham), and a number of paupers (such as Mary Borman and Susan Frankish). The vast majority of these people were born in Lincolnshire, with only three born in Ireland and one in Scotland. In 1851, the population was more varied and had a noticeable Irish element within it. For example, one resident was Mary Greenfield, a pauper and charwoman—she was born in Wales; her daughter, Ellen (aged nine), was born in Ireland; and her son, William (aged seven), was born in Upper Canada! Similarly, both Thomas Burke, a labourer in an oil mill, and his wife, Sarah, were born in Ireland, although their children were all born in Louth. This diversification of the population of Spital Hill accelerated rapidly during the 1850s, and by 1861 over a third of those living at Spital Hill were recorded as having been born in Ireland. The cottages on Spital Hill continued to be inhabited into the twentieth century, but were demolished by the mid-twentieth century; the area to the west of the road subsequently remained empty until the late twentieth century.

Spital Hill seems to have been primarily a residential area in the nineteenth and early twentieth centuries, with only a few businesses listed there then. In the 1820s, Misses Mawer and Goodhall ran a young ladies' boarding school at Spital Hill Cottage, charging £18 per year for the standard English education. In 1835, Edward West's bricklaying business was listed on 'Spittle Hill', as was that of Haywood & Colam— the latter had been previously listed on LEE STREET. In 1841, a cabinet maker and joiner named George Emerson was listed on 'Spittal hill' alongside Edward West, whilst Colam was listed on Tinker Lane, or South Street, in that year—he was, however, probably still operating out of Spital Hill, given that he was listed on there in 1842 and 'Colam's Yard' was off Spital Hill in 1889. In the early 1860s, the only business actually listed on Spital Hill appears to have been a shop run by Thomas Winter.

Needless to say, the inhabitants of Spital Hill in the mid-nineteenth century did make a number of appearances before the courts. For example, in 1856 Thomas Kenny, an Irish labourer of Spital Hill, was charged with being drunk and causing an obstruction in ASWELL STREET. In 1858, Mary Ann Hammond of Spital Hill, a child of only seven years, was charged with stealing money from the till of Mr Johnson's confectionary shop on EASTGATE, having crept into the shop unobserved. It was claimed that her parents, William and Elizabeth Hammond, were both 'notorious vagrants and bad characters' who trained their children to beg and steal, and when Mary Ann was searched she was found to have on her a pair of jet bracelets which she had earlier stolen from Mr Wilman's toy shop on Eastgate. The magistrate declined to send the child to prison and instead adjourned the case to consider what course he should pursue with regard to the parents. Finally, in 1855 three Irish labourers living on Spital Hill—John Burke, Edward Burke and Michael Burke—were charged by 'a fellow countryman', John Donally, with 'murthering him entirely', by splitting his head in pieces with a shovel in Spital Hill. The dispute apparently occurred as a result of something that Donally had said concerning Edward Burke's daughter, and the magistrates eventually fined Burke 2s 6d for the deed, on the basis that Donally had not, in fact, been entirely murdered as he claimed. Such brawls and disputes between neighbours occur repeatedly in this period on Spital Hill—in 1848, Ann Rhodes and John Rhodes, neighbours on Spital Hill, appeared before the court, with the court reporter recommending the use of 'a good fire engine' on the two to cool them down; in 1851, Eliza Simons of Spital Hill was charged with assaulting Mary Ann Freeston, also of Spital Hill (the language used between the two was apparently 'disgusting' and 'most degrading to the female sex); and in 1852, a rag-gatherer named Thomas Williams of Spital Hill was charged with violently assaulting Eliza Simons (he was fined 10s).

SPOUT YARD

Spout Yard is marked on the 1889 OS map of Louth as the passageway that runs northwards from NORTHGATE to a bridge over the Lud and SPAW LANE, with the yard itself lying to the west of this passageway (a site currently occupied by the Spout Yard Community Park).

There is evidence for a degree of early, occasional activity in this part of Louth, with an Early Bronze Age (c. 2200–1500 BC) flint scraper— used in the preparation of skins, wood and bone—found at Spout Yard in 2000. The lack of wear on this item suggests that it was not deposited by the nearby river and it may thus reflect at least occasional Bronze Age activity in the town. More significantly, there is also evidence for medieval activity here. A fourteenth- and/or fifteenth-century pit lined with wickerwork was excavated at Spout Yard in 2000, with straw and hay found deposited above this lining and a fill lying over this containing late medieval pottery, animal bone, and hammerscale from iron-working. In addition, two wooden stakes from a presumed associated superstructure were found adjacent to the pit. Quite what the function of this set-up was is unclear, however, and the environmental evidence preserved at this site indicates that this area of Louth was not a significant settlement or industrial zone in the medieval period, but was rather primarily a woodland habitat.

Activity appears to have ceased in the Spout Yard area in the post-medieval period and only resumed in the eighteenth century. This apparently took the form of attempts to raise the ground level here via the dumping of soils and other materials, presumably to avoid flooding from the Lud, and the building of some structures, with a number of buildings visible at Spout Yard on Espin's 1808 plan of the town. In the nineteenth century, the yard itself appears to have functioned as a tannery, processing skins and hides into leather. The 1841 directory mentions a tannery based at Spout Yard belonging to Laurence Milson & Co., and the tannery here was depicted on William Brown's 1844 sketch and his final Panorama of 1847–56, when it is said to have been operated by William Horn. In 1852, William Storr & Co. were listed as tanners in Spout Yard (they had been listed as on 'Northgate' in 1849), and in 1856 the tanyard at 'Spout yd, Northgt' was run by Storr, Welch and Gelsthorp, with William Storr continuing to work as a tanner and fellmonger (a dealer in skins and hides) at Spout Yard into the 1870s and 1880s. The tannery in Spout Yard was still marked on the 1906 OS map of the area and was damaged during the 1920 Louth Flood.

The tannery was not the only business operating from Spout Yard in the nineteenth and early twentieth centuries. In 1835 and 1841, John Howlett was listed as a tailor in Spout Yard, in 1856 a cart owner (William Harrison) was listed there, and in 1872 a coach builder—Jared Gray—was listed on Spout Yard. Jared Gray was also listed as a coach builder in the 1868 directory and his profession was given as a coach maker in the 1851 and 1861 censuses. His 1872 coach works presumably became the Northgate Carriage Works that is marked on the west side of Spout Yard, just north of Northgate, on the 1889 OS map—certainly, Jared Gray's works were also listed at 5 Northgate in 1872, which stands on the western corner of Spout Yard and Northgate, and in 1885, 1889 and 1896 this was the location for James Wright Richardson's coach building business. This enterprise was still operating in the early twentieth century as J. W. Richardson & Son, of 5 Northgate and Enginegate (BROADBANK): in 1913, it advertised itself as 'designers & builders of up-to-date carriages of every description, as exhibited at the Royal shows; rubber tyres & motor work a speciality.' The works and offices were then at 5 Northgate, with showrooms on Enginegate and Chequergate.

Spout Yard was also home to a small number of people. In 1861, thirty-two people lived here, including a seamstress (Ann Horby, number 10), a tanner (Charles Riggall, number 8), a leather dresser (George Haworth, number 7), a currier (James Evans, number 2—a currier dressed, finished and coloured leather), a coach maker (James Marshall, also number 2), and a carter (George Sharp, number 6). In 1857, Spout Yard was home to Mary Ann Dauby, a prostitute who kept 'a house of ill-fame', or brothel, here. In that year, she appears to have narrowly avoided having her throat slit with a razor on ASWELL STREET by her lover, John Risdale, a painter recently discharged from the 42nd Highlanders, after refusing to continue to 'support him with the proceeds of her miserable and degraded calling'. Risdale was sent to prison for six months, although he could have walked free if he had provided sufficient sureties. Another interesting resident of Spout Yard was Morris Louis Boss, who lived at 1 Spout Yard from at least 1881 through to his death in 1913—born in Prussia around 1835, he was probably a member of the Jewish Boss family who were present in the town during the mid-nineteenth century (see JAMES STREET).

After the Louth Flood of 1920, Spout Yard itself appears to have been cleared and levelled and no buildings are shown here on the 1932 OS map. It was subsequently surfaced with concrete and tarmac and used as a depot. In the early twenty-first century, the yard was redeveloped into the Spout Yard Community Park, opened in 2007, with an associated residential development.

SPRING GARDENS

Spring Gardens runs south from QUEEN STREET and was already established by 1841, when 109 people were living there; it is named from the Aswell Spring that once ran at its southern end (see the GATHERUMS & SPRINGSIDE). Residents in 1841 included William Dales, a labourer; John Wright, a joiner; Thomas Fanthorpe, an agricultural labourer; George Hanson, a pauper; and Bryan Rice, a hawker and, it would appear, a lodging-house keeper, given that he had fourteen people living there in 1841, including seven agricultural labourers. In 1851, 115 people were living in Spring Gardens, with several of the residents keeping lodging-houses then too—for example, Robert Wilerton (or Wilterton) was listed as a coal porter but also had six lodgers living with him in that year, and Deborah Wilkinson was explicitly listed as a lodging-house keeper, with one of her lodgers being a cattle drover named William Howard, from Buckinghamshire. Other inhabitants of the street in 1851 included Hannah Barnes, a dressmaker; Ann Cummins, a hawker; Thirza Reed, a pauper; and John Narey, an agricultural labourer. John Narey, who was born in Ireland, was presumably a relative of Patrick Nary, an Irish labourer, who lived in Spring Gardens in 1850. His son, James, was killed in that year, aged only three, after running out of Spring Gardens and between the wheels of waggon travelling along Queen Street, which passed over his head, 'bespattering the brains in a most awful manner'.

In the mid-nineteenth century, Spring Gardens was one of the more infamous areas of Louth. For example, in 1847 it was home to a 'notorious brothel' run by a woman named Chapman—a railway labourer from Louth, named John May, was charged in that year with stealing 2s 6d from a prostitute he had spent the night with here, called Mary Wilkinson. Similarly, in 1849 a woman named Ellen Reece, better known as Nell Reece, was described as the 'keeper of a notorious brothel in Spring Gardens' and was said to have been assaulted by Henry Dales, also of Spring Gardens. The court reporter noted that it 'appeared that Ellen, who is anything but "Ellen the fair," had on the night in question indulged in copious libations and became rather quarrelsome', which led to Dales committing the assault—she eventually withdrew the complaint and paid the costs. A brothel in Spring Gardens is mentioned in 1850 too, when a certain William Horton, a wool-buyer from Swinhope (near Binbrook), was brought up before the local court. He had gotten drunk after concluding his business in the town and had then 'sallied out in search of adventure among certain houses of questionable character'— being told he was 'too uproarious' to be allowed to enter a brothel in Spring Gardens, he burst through the door and 'valorously commenced an indiscriminate attack upon all the females he found therein, knocking them down right and left', causing broken noses and black eyes, until the police managed to restrain him and remove him to the Police Station (see also RAMSGATE and the Gatherums on Horton).

Yet another brothel in Spring Gardens is referenced in 1852. This 'house of ill-fame' was kept by Harriet North, and one of her girls, a member of 'the frail sisterhood' (that is, a prostitute) named Susanna Briggs, was charged in that year with 'secreting the birth of a male child', which she had 'placed in an ash-bin at the back of North's house' after it was born—it was found there two days later, covered with ashes. North's brothel was mentioned again in 1854, when four men were charged with assaulting Harriet North: in the end, only one of the men—William Huby—was fined, a mere 1s plus costs, and the others were discharged. The brothels and prostitutes of Spring Gardens also caused problems in the surrounding area. For example, a prostitute named Sarah Sanderson, who was living in Robert Wilterton's lodging-house in Spring Gardens in 1849, appeared several times before the court for being drunk, causing disturbances and behaving in an indecent manner in ASWELL STREET and Walkergate (Queen Street). Similarly, in 1850 Edward Blyth, an agricultural labourer from Keddington, exited one of the brothels based in Spring Gardens drunk and then proceeded to amuse himself by breaking windows in the surrounding neighbourhood—he was fined 5s and costs.

Few businesses other than lodging-houses and brothels appear to have operated from Spring Gardens in the nineteenth century, although there are exceptions. For example, a fishmonger named Robert Day had his business here in 1841, and John Rice was listed as a marine store dealer (a dealer in scrap materials) in Spring Gardens in the late nineteenth and early twentieth centuries, with a shop and house at number 1.

ST BERNARDS AVENUE

St Bernards Avenue (sometimes St Bernard's Avenue) runs from WOOD LANE through to EASTFIELD ROAD and is the spine of an ambitious, post-World War Two council housing scheme. The northern end of the road had been laid out and partially developed by the time that the 1951 OS map was surveyed, and the 1956 OS map shows the road fully developed down to MONKS DYKE ROAD, with elements of the estate to the south of that road then in the process of being built. In addition to residential properties, various recreational areas were established on the estate and a new Methodist chapel was opened here in 1960, on the corner of the LINK and VIRGINIA DRIVE—this closed in 1977, due to falling membership and a difficulty in providing ministers.

ST BERNARDS CLOSE

St Bernards Close runs north-east from ST BERNARDS AVENUE and is part of the large, post-World War Two St Bernards Avenue council housing scheme. It appears to have been laid out by the time that the 1951 OS map was surveyed and was shown as developed on the 1956 map. The land it stands on was originally part of Louth's old open East Field.

ST JAMES VIEW

St James View runs south-east and then east from MERIDIAN VIEW and is part of a late twentieth-century housing estate running west from UPGATE. The houses here were constructed in the 1990s on land that was once part of Louth's old open South Field—medieval ridge and furrow has been identified in this area from aerial photographs.

ST MARY'S LANE

St Mary's Lane was formerly known as Paradise Lane, although the name St Mary's Lane was current in the first half of the nineteenth century (it appears, for example, on the 1839 map of Louth). The lane was in existence at the time of the 1801 Enclosure Act and joined up with HIGH HOLME ROAD and KEDDINGTON ROAD to form a route across the north of the parish, with the old North Field of the town on its northern side.

In 1839, St Mary's Lane was almost entirely undeveloped, with only a small number of exceptions. At the eastern end of the road were both St Mary's Burying Ground and St Mary's Lime Works. The former had been extended up to St Mary's Lane in 1827 but was primarily accessed from BRIDGE STREET, whilst the latter belonged to George Tatam and was usually assigned to GRIMSBY ROAD (under which entry it is discussed at greater length), although it was located on the northern side of St Mary's Lane. At the western end of the road were The Cedars and, immediately opposite this along a track leading northwards from St Mary's Lane, a nursery. The nursery is marked on the 1839 map and visible on William Brown's 1844 sketch and his final Panorama (first exhibited in 1847 and last updated in 1856), both of which show not only nursery gardens here, but also a number of buildings and a windmill. The Cedars was a large house occupying extensive grounds to the south of St Mary's Lane and still stands today: it was built in 1830 by Henry Pye, a local solicitor and businessman who later became Mayor of Louth and county treasurer.

Treated as being on WESTGATE by the early censuses, The Cedars was the birthplace of Pye's daughter, Charlotte (who wrote, under the name 'Claribel', ballads that were popular in both England and America), and the Pye family lived here in a significant degree of luxury: in 1841, they had eight servants, and in 1861 their staff included a coachman, a housekeeper, two housemaids, a nurse and a cook. Charlotte Pye married Charles Cary Barnard in 1854 and they moved into The Firs on Westgate before moving to London in 1857. In 1868, Henry Pye was declared bankrupt and fled the country to Belgium—he not only owed large sums of money on mortgages and to his servants and family, but he was also discovered to have embezzled a significant amount of money from county funds. The *Louth Advertiser* at the end of July noted that his liabilities probably amounted to £100,000 (equivalent to around £7,000,000 today) and that he had appropriated several 'thousands of pounds of trust-money... to his own use'. It was further noted that 'for a great number of years he has lived in splendid style as a county man, and kept a large establishment at the expense of his relatives and servants', owing two of his servants £1,300 (now around £91,000) and Charlotte around £30,000 (now around £2,100,000). The scandal ruined Charlotte and her husband socially and they too left for the Continent; they returned to England for a holiday in early 1869, when Charlotte became ill and died near Dover, aged 38. The Cedars was subsequently owned by Joseph Bennett in 1871, a merchant said to employ 100 men and 30 boys, who lived there with a more modest total of three servants—a cook, a housemaid and a nursemaid.

In 1871, there were only three residential properties other The Cedars on St Mary's Lane, one occupied by a labourer named William

Fatchett, another by a lime burner named John Keightley, and the last by a labourer named Charles Oakes, and the area appears to have been generally quiet in the mid-nineteenth century. One exception was in 1852, when Jesse Wilson, aged about seventeen, was charged with using 'disgracefully obscene and brutal language to Sarah Osbourne and others, and lifting up her dress in a most obscene manner in St. Mary's-lane'. He was fined 20s and costs, and two others—John Hayle and Alfred Stevenson—were charged with using brutal language to the same party of young ladies at the same time and place (they were fined 1s and costs). In 1881 and 1891, St Mary's Lane was still largely undeveloped, with only three and four households listed there, respectively, but the 1889 OS map shows some changes from the time of Brown's Panorama, notably the large Highfield that had been built on the north side and a couple of properties on the south side opposite it. In 1891, Highfield was occupied by Joseph Morton, ironmonger, iron founder and Justice of the Peace (see WALKERGATE PLACE), who lived there with his wife and three servants; he had been listed at 1 St Mary's Lane in 1881 with his family and servants, which was presumably the same property, and on EASTGATE in 1871. In 1901, the situation appears to have been unchanged, with four houses listed on the road (one unoccupied), but the 1906 OS map shows Westnor and St Mary's Lodge to have been built here. By the mid-twentieth century, the road had seen significant development on both sides, including the interesting 1930s Modernist house at the western end of St Mary's Lane, number 72, built for Bert Hallam, the owner of the Playhouse Cinema (CANNON STREET). By the mid-1970s, ST MARY'S PARK had been developed to the north of St Mary's Lane, partially on land that had belonged to Highfield.

ST MARY'S PARK

St Mary's Park is a late twentieth-century housing development located to the north of ST MARY'S LANE, partially on land that had once belonged to a large, late nineteenth-century house named Highfield. Some of the houses here were built in 1971 and the estate is shown as nearly complete on the 1976 OS map.

ST MICHAEL'S ROAD

St Michael's Road runs between NEWMARKET and CHURCH STREET. The road is visible on William Brown's Panorama (first exhibited in 1847) with a handful of properties facing onto it, and it was originally known as the 'new cut', before being renamed St Michael's Road in 1864 (after the new St Michael's Church, recently completed in Church Street). The Sunday and Day Schools associated with St Michael's Church were initially run in an old carpenter's shop on St Michael's Road (number 4) and began in December 1864. By 1874, the number of children at the school had become too large for this site, however, and it was decided that a new school had to be built on Church Street, which opened in January 1876.

In 1871, St Michael's Road was home to 68 people, including a blacksmith (Frank Armitage), a bricklayer (Frederick Colam), a groom (Thomas Stephenson), a miller (John Fytche) and a brewer's foreman (William Holtby). On the 1889 OS map, the western part of the road was lined with properties on both sides, with the eastern part having only a small number of houses on it; by 1906, however, the northern side of the eastern part of the road had been fully developed too. The filling station at the Newmarket end of the street was built on the site of houses facing onto Newmarket in the late twentieth century.

STAINESWAY

See ELM DRIVE.

STANLEY CLOSE

Stanley Close is a new housing development built off RIVERHEAD TERRACE in the early twenty-first century. The houses here were sold as new builds in 2008 and 2009 and the road crosses the former, pre-canal course of the River Lud.

STATION APPROACH

Station Approach runs north from RAMSGATE and is the main spine of a late twentieth-century residential housing development built here.

Part of the street occupies land where the railway line travelling south from Louth once ran—this was opened in 1848 and closed in 1970—and the old railway station lies to the west of the northern part of the road.

STEWTON GARDENS

See WOOD LANE.

STEWTON LANE

Stewton Lane (or Stewton Road) runs from NEWMARKET through to Stewton village and was originally called Brog Lane, as it was at the time of the 1805 Enclosure Award—'brog' here probably derives from 'brook' and refers to the stream that flows alongside much of the road down to Stewton. Stewton Lane was apparently blocked in Stewton in 1770, as it bypassed the toll-bar of the Louth Turnpike to Saltfleet and Withern. The road also saw some alteration at its western end, in this case as a result of the construction of the branch line to Bardney, which was completed in 1876: the bend in the road and change in alignment just before Stewton Lane meets Newmarket is not apparent on William Brown's Panorama of 1847–56 or the Enclosure map of 1805, and so was presumably created after the construction of the branch line, which ran just to the north of the road here until its closure in 1956.

The 1889 OS map shows a small number of properties based on Stewton Lane—these were primarily located on the south side of the road before its junction with WOOD LANE, with Stewton House then on the north side of the road between Wood Lane and the railway line to Boston (which opened in 1848) and a handful of properties finally situated to the east of the Boston line. The 1906 and 1932 maps show few changes in this area, aside from what appears to be a new orchard depicted on the south side of the road, west of the railway line, joining the one that is shown to the east of the railway line and on the north side of the road from 1889. The 1951 and 1956 maps similarly show little further development on the road, but by the time of the 1967–8 map there had been significant changes. There were now houses on land formerly belonging to Stewton House near to the junction with Wood Lane (for example, 16 and 18 Stewton Lane, which stand on the corner of Stewton Lane and Wood Lane) and also either side of the railway line to Boston, which closed in 1970. In addition, new housing had been built on the south side of the road, opposite Stewton House. In the late twentieth century, Stewton Lane continued to develop, with the HAWKER DRIVE estate constructed to the south of the road, further new housing on both sides of the road, and ALEXANDRA DRIVE, GRESLEY ROAD and the New Linx Housing Trust offices constructed on the northern side of Stewton Lane between Newmarket and Wood Lane.

Stewton House is visible on both William Brown's final Panorama and his preliminary sketch of 1844, with Brown marking it as the property of Dr Banks on the sketch. This was John Tatam Banks, who took his degree at Edinburgh in 1827 and whose medical practice was based on UPGATE from at least 1835. He was living on Upgate in 1841, but by 1842 his practice was listed both on Upgate and at Stewton House, where he continued to live into the 1850s (Stewton House had previously been occupied, according to the 1828–9 directory, by Matthew Henry Lister, esq., later of Burwell Park, who was still there in 1831 when he appears to have committed his wife, Arabella, to a private asylum in Yorkshire). In 1851, Dr Banks of Stewton House was elected as Warden of Louth for the fifth time and the census return for Stewton House describes him as a Justice of the Peace and physician, attended by six servants. In May 1853, he was appeared in court accused of the attempted rape of Emma Lockwood of Tetford, aged sixteen years, in his consulting rooms—then on EASTGATE—after she had gone to him for medical advice. Dr Banks declined to make any defence or statement to the Louth magistrates and the court passed the case to the next sessions, with bail set at £1,000. Banks was acquitted and continued to be active in subsequent years as a doctor; however, he clearly tired of Louth after this, and in November 1853 he sold by auction all of the furnishings of Stewton House, his carriage, his gardening equipment, his wines and his library, and in 1854 he was based at Hougham Lodge, near Dover (Kent). Stewton House was subsequently owned by William Byron, Esq., listed here into the 1870s and described as a retired farmer in 1861. It is now a nursing home.

In 1851, twenty-two people were living on Stewton Road, as it was then called, including ten at Stewton House. Aside from the residents of the latter house, the inhabitants of the road included a gardener (John

Hudson), a railway gate keeper (William Heathcote), and two agricultural labourers (William Daf and John Evison). By 1881, the population had increased to eighty-two, including a gardener (Joseph Carter, number 1), a roper (Jonathon Singleton, number 3), a music seller (William Rose, number 1a) and a significant number of labourers and agricultural labourers (for example, James Baxter, a gardener's labourer at number 7, and William Dales, an agricultural labourer at number 24). In the early twentieth century, a wooden bungalow near to the railway line on Stewton Lane was home to Bertram Horace Kirby and his wife, Minnie Eleanor Kirby. In July 1927, Kirby was charged with the murder of his wife, using a heavy axe to strike her in the back of the head whilst she was writing a letter. Kirby had apparently attempted to kill himself in the past, had a violent temper and was in financial difficulties; although he pleaded insanity, he was sentenced to death at the Lincolnshire Assizes and was hung at Lincoln on 4 January 1928.

STOCKWITH DRIVE

Stockwith Drive runs westwards from HARVEYS LANE, and is part of an early twenty-first-century housing estate developed off an eastern extension of MONKS DYKE ROAD. The land that it is built on was originally part of Louth's old open East Field, before this was enclosed under the Enclosure Act of 1801, and medieval ridge and furrow has been observed from this area on aerial photographs.

STUTTE CLOSE

Stutte Close is part of the 'Weavers Tryst' housing estate that was begun in the late 1990s and runs east from BLANCHARD ROAD. The estate is built on land that was originally part of Louth's medieval open South Field, although most of the area had been enclosed prior to the 1801 Enclosure Act. The roads within it appear to be named after local worthies of the sixteenth and seventeenth centuries—a Roger Stutte was Warden of Louth in 1586, 1593 and 1599.

SUDBURY PLACE

Sudbury Place extends north from MERIDIAN VIEW and is part of a late twentieth-century housing estate running west from UPGATE. The houses here were constructed in the 1990s on land that was once part of Louth's old open South Field, and medieval ridge and furrow has been identified in this area from aerial photographs. The street-name presumably refers to one of the two medieval Vicars of Louth named Sudbury: either John Sudbury who held the post in 1450 or Thomas Sudbury who held it in the reign of Henry VII. The latter died in 1504 and was buried in St James's Church; the chest, or hutch, that he presented to the church shortly before his death still survives today and is known as the Sudbury Hutch.

SWALLOW DRIVE

Swallow Drive runs north-west from KEDDINGTON ROAD and was laid out with DOVE CLOSE in the late twentieth century, with both roads being shown on the 1990 OS map of this area. In the 1990s, Swallow Drive was extended to join the new FULMAR DRIVE, with HAWKSMEDE WAY and MARTIN CLOSE both belonging to this expansion of the road.

SYCAMORE DRIVE

Sycamore Drive runs south-east from WOOD LANE and is the spine of a late twentieth-century housing estate; each road in this estate is named after a different type of tree.

TEMPLE TERRACE

Temple Terrace runs north-east from BROADBANK. The road is not marked on the 1839 map of Louth or on William Brown's Panorama of 1847–56, but it is present on the 1889 OS map, which shows three large houses on the northern side of Temple Terrace. Both the houses and the road appear to have been built on part of the grounds of Broad Bank House in 1853. The first of the houses was demolished by 1932 and new dwellings were subsequently built in its place, set back slightly from the

250

road, along with a new property to the west of these. In 1861, only one of the houses on Temple Terrace—number 3—was occupied, by Thomas Ranshaw, draper, his family and two servants. In 1881, however, all three of the large houses here were occupied—number 1 by Robert Ranshaw, the son of Thomas Ranshaw; number 2 by John Beckett Hurst; and number 3 by John Bowmar Eve.

TENNYSON ROAD

Tennyson Road is a small-scale council housing project running between NEWMARKET and LINDEN WALK. The road and its properties were constructed in the inter-war years and one letter writer to the *Louth Standard* in November 1929 criticised the new houses of Tennyson Road as being 'workmen's palaces'. The land that this road was built upon was originally part of Louth's old open South Field.

THAMES STREET

Thames Street runs north-east from RIVERHEAD ROAD and was in existence by the time of the 1805 Enclosure Award map, although it was only developed on its north side then, with open land to the south. The road was part of the Riverhead industrial village that grew up around the canal in the late eighteenth century, with Thames Street running along the southern side of the canal. There were once two bone crushing mills here, along with a mill on the south side of the road. The latter was powered by a water wheel that utilised the River Lud—after the construction of the canal, the river used to run openly along the southern edge of Thames Street, and it was still marked as open on the 1967–8 OS map. From April 1826, the Louth Gas Light Company's gas works were also located on Thames Street, at the eastern end after Baines' flour mill. In order to celebrate the opening of these gas works, which were built under an Act of Parliament obtained in 1825, Mr Charles Green made an ascent in his coal-gas filled Royal Coronation Balloon from William Hardy's coal-yard here. The site of the former gasworks became that of the Luda Meaties dog biscuit factory in the mid-twentieth century, which had previously been based on EVE STREET.

Also listed on Thames Street in the nineteenth century were the premises of Nell & Smith, cake, corn and guano (fertiliser) merchants, and manufacturers of British guano, sulphate of ammonia, and lime, as was Nell, Nell & Graves, oil millers and seed crushers, and Robert Norfolk & Sons, seed and bone crushers and manure merchants. Opposite the Gas Light Company, where Willow Court now is, was a printing works from 1909—the Norman Davy Printing Company Ltd, which printed high-class stationary. After World War One these premises became a glove factory, then later a restaurant before being converted into flats following a fire in the 1970s. There was also at least one beerhouse on Thames Street. From 1868 through to at least 1913, this was run by the Finney family as the Lock Tavern (number 9), and William Finney had taken over the Lock Tavern from William Clark. Clark was listed as a beer retailer on Thames Street in the 1861 directory and described as the keeper of the Lock Tavern, at 9 Thames Street, in the 1861 census; he had probably operated this beerhouse since at least 1841, when he was first listed as a beer retailer with a general 'River head' location. In 1856, he was charged with using deficient earthenware measures in his beerhouse; he pleaded ignorance of their deficiency and promised not to use them again, paying costs of 8s 6d. More recently, the Fulstow Brewery has moved into the former Louth Gas Light Company offices on Thames Street, with the Gas Lamp Lounge opening here as a new pub serving real draught ales in 2010.

In 1861, around seventy people were living on Thames Street. Residents then included a printer's assistant (Arthur Wickman, number 8), two foremen at a steam oilcake mill (Francis Virtue, number 7, and John Dawson, number 23), a master of a river vessel (George Cawkwell, number 16), a grocer (William Stamper, number 6), two millers at a steam bone and flour mill (Joseph Smith, number 20, and William Ingamells, number 17), and a coal, corn and manure merchant, Thomas Elkington Smith (number 11). In 1891, around forty people lived on Thames Street, including a miller's labourer and baker (Joseph Brown and Arthur Brown, number 22), a foreman at an oil mill (John Dyer, number 23), the manager of the gasworks (John Cook, number 20), a painter (William Bell, number 12), an assistant weedkiller (William Truffett, number 1), and William Finney, beerhouse keeper at the Lock Tavern (number 9). In the twentieth and twenty-first centuries, Thames Street has seen a number of changes, not least the closure of the canal for navigation in 1924, after it sustained serious damage in the 1920 Louth Flood. Other changes include the replacement of the twentieth-century milk depot at the northern corner of the junction with Riverhead Road by modern houses, the building and rebuilding of the Scout Hut erected to the east of this in late twentieth century, and the construction of Lucerne Court and modern properties on the south side of the road in the same period.

TRINITY LANE

Trinity Lane runs south-east from EASTGATE through to MONKS DYKE ROAD. William Brown noted that houses were being built in Trinity Lane in 1842 and he depicted the terrace on the east side of the road on his 1844 sketch, as well as on his final Panorama of 1847–56. On Brown's Panorama, Trinity Lane did not yet run through to Monks Dyke Road, and this was the case in 1889 too—in fact, the road only appears to have been extended southwards in the mid-twentieth century.

In 1851, 103 people lived on this road, many of whom were associated with the canal at the RIVERHEAD. Inhabitants then included Charles Clark, a builder employing five men and one boy; Elizabeth Wilkinson, a sailor's wife; James Bell, a sailor; Richard Woodliffe, an agricultural labourer; Mary Skin, a sailor's widow; Mary Ann Nicholson, a Wesleyan preacher's wife; Caroline Wright, a schoolmistress; Thomas Roberts, a sailor; James Thompson, a coach maker; Charlotte Potts, a laundress; and Mary Sudgen, another sailor's wife. By the end of the nineteenth century, the population of Trinity Lane had increased to 146 and there were still people here who were associated with the canal, despite the decline that this had seen in the intervening period, with four mariners and a retired sea captain listed on Trinity Lane in 1891—for example, John and Roderic Wilkinson, both mariners living at 1 Trinity Lane. Other trades noted in that year include several dressmakers, a number of people 'living on their own means' (for example, Susanna Hall at number 5, a widow who lived there with her four daughters, aged 18 to 25, and her nephew, aged 22), a gardener (Thomas Kirkby, number 15), and an engine shunter (George Challands, number 2).

In the mid-nineteenth century, a number of businesses and tradespeople were listed on Trinity Lane in the local directories. In 1856,

William Pearson, auctioneer, had his address given as Trinity Lane, as did John Nelthorpe, a surgeon. In 1861, Nelthorpe was still listed here (he was based at number 8), alongside two shopkeepers, Adam Dawson and William Ostler Taylor (numbers 10 and 3), and a bellhanger, Charles Lingard—there was briefly a blacksmith listed here too in 1868, named Moses Handley. However, by the early twentieth century, the only business listed on Trinity Lane was Elizabeth Potts' lodging-house (Clarence House).

TUDOR DRIVE

Tudor Drive connects at both ends with SEYMOUR AVENUE, which is in turn located off NEWMARKET. It is part of the Seymour Avenue housing estate that was constructed in the late twentieth century to the south of TENNYSON ROAD, between Newmarket and LINDEN WALK, and appears to have been developed in the 1980s. Tudor Drive is built on land that was once part of the old open South Field of Louth, although a more immediate predecessor was J. North & Son's market garden off Linden Walk, over which the western part of Tudor Drive is built. This market garden was first recorded in the mid-nineteenth century and still appeared on OS maps into the mid-twentieth century.

UNION STREET

Union Street runs south-east from HIGH HOLME ROAD through to CISTERNGATE. There is no trace of it on the 1808 plan of the town, but it appears to be present as a track on the 1834 plan and, more clearly, on the 1839 map of Louth, with the latter showing new properties present to the west of the road that weren't there on the slightly earlier plan. Union Street appears even more built up on William Brown's 1844 sketch of the town, made from the spire of St James's Church, and his final Panorama of 1847 (last updated in 1856). In 1852, a bet was made by Mr Lundie of the Anacreontic Society, which met at the Fleece Inn in the MARKET PLACE each Saturday, that the distance from the Union Workhouse to the Spout Bridge (see SPOUT YARD) was shorter by the new road adjoining Captain Adlard's house—that is, Union Street—and GRAY'S ROAD than it was by BROADBANK and SPAW LANE, a bet he subsequently lost.

Several businesses and tradespeople were listed on Union Street in the nineteenth century. For example, a bricklayer (Christopher Wilson) was listed here in 1856, and in 1872 the street was home to a gunsmith, a shoemaker, a tailor and two lodging-house keepers—the lodging-house keepers were Ann Mason and Elizabeth Whisker, the latter of whom went on to run a grocery store on BRIDGE STREET during the 1880s and 1890s. From at least 1861, there was also a grocer's shop on Union Street at number 40 and a beerhouse at number 42 (now number 5). The former was run by John Dales in the 1860s and 1870s, John Dales Hood from the 1880s, William and Betsy Crowforth in the 1900s, and William Dady and Elizabeth Rushworth before and after World War One, respectively. The beerhouse—known originally as The Hole in the Wall and later as The Cross Keys—was kept by Jane Drew in 1856, William Kirk in 1861 and Leonard Lincoln in 1868. It was probably also the beerhouse listed on Cisterngate that belonged to William Drew in 1852 (he was listed as a brewer on Cisterngate in 1849) and Sarah Drew in 1841 and 1842. The Cross Keys continued to have a number of different keepers in the latter half of the nineteenth century, including James Corragan in 1871, George Meanwell in the 1880s and early 1890s, George Wright Whitton in the 1890s, and Joseph William Richardson at the turn of the century. It was thereafter run by Peter Mark Pogson from the 1900s through until at least 1937, and it finally became an off-licence, with this description still painted on the wall here.

UPGATE

Upgate is one of the main medieval streets of Louth, running southwards from BRIDGE STREET and St James's Church. It was first mentioned in the Manor Court Roll for 1442 and it has been noted that a number of medieval property boundaries exist on both sides of Upgate. The present line of the street southwards may date from the eleventh century, when at least part of the central area of Louth was probably remodelled by Bishop Remigius—this remodelling laid out long burgage tenements (which can still be traced today to the south of MERCER ROW) and the medieval MARKET PLACE, and it is thought to have also shifted the main north–south route through Louth onto its present course along Upgate, with its original course through the town most likely running under the new tenements.

The main feature at the northern end of Upgate is, of course, St James's Church. Although it has been occasionally suggested that the original parish church of Louth was St Mary's Church, or Chapel, north of the Lud off Bridge Street, this seems unlikely (see Bridge Street). Instead, the parish church was probably always on the site of the current St James's Church, with this developing somehow from the documented, tenth-century shrine of St Herefrith, a local Anglo-Saxon saint buried in Louth, especially given that St James's Church appears to have been dedicated to both St James and St Herefrith in the medieval period and that the church here housed the 'come of ivery that was saynt Herefridis' in 1486 (his body had been stolen from Louth in 973 and reinterred at the newly refounded minster at Thorney, Cambridgeshire). The earliest surviving architectural evidence so far found within the present church dates from around 1170 and presumably represents a rebuilding of an earlier church, as the parish church is first mentioned in 1146. The church of St Herefrith-St James was rebuilt once again in the 1240s, and the south doorway and pillars in the nave of the current fifteenth-century church date from this rebuild.

The cemetery of St James's Church lay both to the north and to the south of the church and was the usual place of burial for the town through until around 1700, when St Mary's Burying Ground off Bridge Street began to be used as an additional site—St James's continued to be used alongside St Mary's until 1770, after which no more burials were permitted there. Excavations in 1995 at 10a Upgate, to the south of church, have revealed five medieval skeletons from the old cemetery sealing a pit containing a thirteenth-century jug, and other excavations in 1999 just to the north of the church—for a new toilet block drain—led to the recovery of twenty-three further burials and a large quantity of disarticulated human remains. The pottery associated with the latter burials dated from the twelfth century onwards and the graves started just 20 cm below the ground surface, with later graves overlying earlier ones and the bottom of the sequence, representing the oldest graves, not reached due to the nature of the works.

The churchyard and cemetery attached to the church of St Herefrith-St James are mentioned a number of times during the medieval period and after. For example, in 1441, Robert Boston, a parchment-maker, was accused of assaulting Agnes Stanes with a stick in the cemetery, and in 1443, Robert Curteys (a fuller, see QUEEN STREET)

256

was accused of assaulting Thomas Rede with a drawn sword in the cemetery. In 1348, William Prest of Somercotes was convicted before the bailiffs of the Bishop of Lincoln at Louth of having broken into the house of Richard de Cateby, for which crime he was sentenced to death. After he was cut down from the gallows (presumably those on SPITAL HILL), his body was carried to the church of St Herefrith and was laid in the churchyard there awaiting burial when suddenly it 'miraculously came to life again'! William Prest was subsequently given a full pardon by the king. In the 1530s, the churchyard was home to the Song School, held in a thatched building that may have been where Church House is now, on Upgate. This was first mentioned in 1534 and was absorbed into the sixteenth-century petty school on CHEQUERGATE sometime around 1558. The churchyard also appears in the mid-nineteenth-century court reports, with Mary Bray of Dublin, 'an itinerant prostitute', charged in 1847 'with being a common prostitute' and with 'behaving in an indecent manner in the churchyard'. She was sent to the House of Correction for ten days for this, although she appears to have stayed in Louth after her release, being subsequently based on BURNT HILL LANE.

Turning to Upgate itself during the medieval period, the earliest documentary reference to Upgate from 1442 refers to a case of violence on this street: John Gandeby was assaulted on Vpgate (Upgate) in July, 1442, at the time of St James's fair, by Thomas Holme, of Steuton (Stewton), and Thomas Whytehead, who ambushed Gandeby and beat him with two sticks, 'valued at 2d', 'to the affrighting of the people of the lord King coming to the market'. Upgate is mentioned again in 1447, when William Wylson, mylner (miller), of Upgate was charged with constantly, by night and by day, receiving into his house 'common players at the cheker and the penepryke'. He was fined 4d and ordered to keep his house free of such players in future, under a penalty of 20s (equivalent to around £600 today). There have also been archaeological excavations at the rear of the Greyhound Inn on Upgate which have recovered evidence relating to the development of this road in the medieval period. These excavations indicate that this area was only occupied from the twelfth century and that it lay on the edge of the medieval town, with arable fields and wooded areas being located close by. Finds made include a substantial quantity of twelfth- and thirteenth-century pottery, along with horse shoes and horse harness fittings, leading to the suggestion that the first buildings on this site were stables, perhaps associated with an inn. This site continued in use for a period but appears to have been largely abandoned after the mid-fourteenth century, perhaps because of the Black Death, and was only reoccupied in the eighteenth century.

With regard to the Greyhound Inn, this is first mentioned by name in the eighteenth century, in 1767, and was previously known as the White Hart from 1751–66. In 1833, the landlord of the Greyhound, Joseph Wilson, was 'removing a great coat belonging to one of his guests' when 'a loaded pistol, which was in one of the pockets, went off, and he received the contents in his body, from the effects of which he died almost immediately'. It was subsequently run by Diana Wilson through until at least 1856, with William Johnson subsequently taking over as the landlord by 1861. In the mid-nineteenth century, the Greyhound appeared a number of times in the local court reports. In May 1847, for example, Diana Wilson charged Thomas Hildred of Market Stainton with stealing a plated pint mug, worth 12s, from the inn—he was discharged for want of sufficient evidence—and in April 1849, Diana Wilson was charged with opening too early on Good Friday and was fined 1s and costs. One curious case came before the court in May 1858—Joseph Grantham, a pig jobber (trader), apparently took pity on William Smith of Derby, aged 30, and William White, 'better known by the soubriquet of "Buck White"', aged 40, a 'horse cad', when they complained of being hungry and of having no money. He is said to have bought them both dinner in a local eating-house and then paid for their drinks in the Greyhound Inn. However, when he had had too much liquor, the 'ungrateful vagabonds' robbed him of three pairs of stockings and £2 in money.

The Greyhound was but one of a large number of inns and drinking establishments present on Upgate. In 1564, for example, 'Ye Inne' was mentioned on Upgate—it has been suggested that this was on the site of the property to the south of Church House (Upgate House). Another early inn was the Blue Stone Inn, which was located on the southern corner of Upgate and Mercer Row. This was said to have once extended back all the way to KIDGATE and to have been the largest inn in the county, according to C. S. Carter and R. S. Bayley. The Blue Stone Inn is first mentioned explicitly in 1677, when an innkeeper called John Langley sold a tenement commonly known as the Blue Stone ('Blew Stone') to Dymoke Walpole for £150. The Blue Stone, or the Louth

Stone, is a 4.5 ton boulder that stood on corner of Mercer Row and Upgate (it is now located outside Louth Museum). It was first mentioned in the Court Roll for 1503, when William Stoddard received 'the piece of land lying in Louth at Louth Stone' from the Lord of the Manor, and in 1745 the Warden of Louth was paid 6d for 'Jews Examined' at the 'Blew stone'. How much earlier than 1677 there was an inn by the Blue Stone is unclear. A house 'at Louth stone' is mentioned in 1540, which is presumably the same property, and the Churchwardens' Accounts mention 'a hous leyng agayn Louth stone' in 1520. In 1610, the 'great howse at Lowth Stone' was occupied by Hew Warde, who paid 5d in rent for it, and 'Mr Walpoole's blew-stone House' was mentioned in 1651. The Blue Stone Inn was sold by John Walpole to an innkeeper called Robert Shaw in 1728, and was later run Benjamin Cook in the mid-eighteenth century and by Shaw's son, Nicholas, who died in 1789. In 1761, the inhabitants of Louth were invited by the Corporation to 'meet in the afternoon upon the Market-hill and there Drink the health of the King Queen and Royal Family and from thence adjourn to the Blue Stone in the said Town for the Remainder of the Evening.' In the late eighteenth century, the Blue Stone Inn had poor reputation— managed by the innkeeper's widow, it was described as 'mean, dirty and ill-managed', and in 1799 John Cragg referred to it as 'an old wore out building with a very unfit person to manage it'. In 1800, the house became a private dwelling (occupied by Captain Gace), and in 1802 the part of the old premises that was opposite the end of Gospelgate was renamed the Three Tuns, which continued the old Blue Stone license and can be seen on William Brown's Panorama of 1847–56. In 1822, part of the premises was bought by Benjamin Fotherby, a printer, who removed the Blue Stone to his yard five years later, and at the time of the Panorama the property on the corner of Upgate and Mercer Row belonged to Abraham Gouldsborough Marshall, a bookseller, stationer, bookbinder, printer and pawnbroker (Marshall had been here since at least 1841).

There is occasionally some confusion between the Blue Stone Inn and the Blue Stone Tavern, both of which were located on Upgate. The latter occupied the site opposite the Mercer Row and Upgate junction, on the west side of the road, and was first licensed in 1809 as Trafalgar Tavern, before changing its name to the Blue Stone Tavern in the same year. The Blue Stone Tavern continued into the twentieth century, when it became the Blue Stone Dining Rooms, as in 1927. This tavern made a number of appearances in the mid-nineteenth-century court reports. For example, in January 1853 the landlord of the Blue Stone Tavern, William Rickett, was fined 1s for allowing 'drunkenness and disorderly conduct in his house' after twelve o'clock at night on the 24 December 1852. William Rickett subsequently left the country for New Zealand in 1856, leaving his wife to run the Blue Stone Tavern; she soon after quit the town and sublet the premises to North Newton, who in turn found himself in trouble with the law. In September 1858, he was warned by the magistrates before having his licence re-granted, on the basis of a conviction 'for having his dram-shop full of prostitutes' and a report of a drunken row in his house. In March 1864, the landlord of the Blue Stone Tavern appeared again in the local press, this time in response to defamatory statements circulated by the landlord of the Royal Oak—the landlord of the Blue Stone apparently took a 'stout ash stick' and thrashed the landlord of the Royal Oak in the public street!

The Royal Oak was based a little further north on Upgate and on the opposite side of the street, on the south corner of what is now Royal Oak Court. Clearly visible on Brown's mid-nineteenth-century Panorama, the Royal Oak was first mentioned in 1782 and was still in business in 1937, when three carriers were based there. In 1847, the landlord of the Royal Oak, Robert Hewson, was charged with allowing a number of prostitutes to assemble in his house, for which he was fined 10s and 14s costs (equivalent to around £85 today). Even more scandalous were the events that occurred just a little further north on Upgate, at the Dog and Duck beerhouse. This was located opposite the chancel of St James's Church, between Chequergate and EASTGATE; newly built in 1832, its first landlord was Thomas Wakelin. In 1847, Joseph Johnson was the landlord and he was charged in that year with resisting and refusing to admit two police constables to his beerhouse. The policemen entered the Dog and Duck on the night of the 5 January and attempted to go upstairs, at which point Johnson grabbed Police Constable Ryall around the neck to prevent him doing so, calling out "here's the police"! Forcing their way upstairs, the constables encountered around twenty men and some prostitutes dancing, and the defendant's wife pulling other prostitutes into a bedroom. PC Ryall attempted to see into the bedroom to identify the prostitutes, but was refused entry. Joseph Johnson had apparently been charged with similar offences in the past, his beer house being one of 'notoriously bad character', and he was fined £2 plus costs on this occasion. By 1852, Johnson had been replaced by Benjamin Turner as the landlord of the Dog and Duck, but he seems to have been equally uncooperative with the police, being severely reprimanded by the magistrates on the 24 December 1852 for refusing to admit the police into his beerhouse and permitting drunkenness in the Dog and Duck. Other inns and beerhouses once on Upgate include the Plough at 104 Upgate, on the south-western corner of the Upgate–NEWMARKET crossroads (now The Travellers B&B); the Lion, which lay opposite the Plough on the eastern side of the road; and the Black Bull, which was located on the west side of the street at 22 Upgate—the latter was first recorded in 1782 and eventually closed in 1970.

Other interesting buildings on Upgate include the Mansion House, or Assembly Rooms, which was built by the Corporation in the mid-eighteenth century. The Corporation gave a Ball for Ladies here in 1761 to mark the coronation of George III, and there was another ball in the Mansion House in 1788 for the 100th anniversary of the Glorious Revolution; Madame Tussaud's Wax Figures were also exhibited here in 1825 for five weeks. The furniture, wine, plate and the like from the Mansion House were sold off by the new, elected Corporation in the 1830s, who wished to distance themselves from the profligacy of the old Corporation, and they eventually sold the Mansion House itself too, with the Louth Mechanics' Institute moving here in 1852. Classes were offered in chemistry, drawing, arithmetic and the like, along with lectures on a wide range of subjects and a library of 2,500 volumes. In 1953, The Louth Naturalists', Antiquarian & Literary Society inherited the Mansion House from the Mechanics' Institute and the town library apparently opened up here in 1954—it remained at this site until 1990, when it moved to NORTHGATE. Also of interest is Cromwell House, on the north side of the junction of Mercer Row and Upgate—now the Helal Indian restaurant and previously the Lincolnshire Gun Shop, this building is variously described as late medieval or sixteenth-century in date. It is claimed that Oliver Cromwell once slept here on his way to the Battle of Winceby (1643) and the building is marked as the Horse & Jockey on an early nineteenth-century engraving of Upgate, although this may be artistic license. Finally, it is worth noting that the Corporation moved Louth's pig and sheep market to the 'New Market Place in

Upgate' in 1785 ('the Market' was said to be near to St James's Church in 1800) and it remained on Upgate until 1802, when it was moved to the QUARRY—see further the MARKET PLACE & CORNMARKET and Newmarket on the location of the sheep, pig and cattle markets.

Although the northern portion of Upgate was well-developed before the nineteenth century, south of the junction with Kidgate there appears to have been relatively little activity in that period. So, Armstrong's plan of Louth from 1778 depicts buildings on both sides of Upgate up to Kidgate, but apparently nothing to the south of this. Similarly, whilst the 1808 plan of the town shows some buildings between the Kidgate and Newmarket junctions (primarily on the western side of the road), the southern part of Upgate was still largely undeveloped at that point. The situation appears to have been little different in 1834, the two major exceptions being the addition of St Mary's Catholic Church on the north-eastern corner of the junction between Upgate and Newmarket—this was built in 1833, enlarged in 1845 and restored in 1884, and by 1878 there was a school for 130 children here—and the Plough beerhouse on the south-western corner of the same junction (George Thompson was the proprietor here from at least 1835 through into the 1860s). By 1839, the eastern side of Upgate between Kidgate and Newmarket began to be built up and the road here is shown as fully developed on both sides on William Brown's sketch of 1844.

South of the Newmarket junction, there had been some further development by 1839 and this part of the road was beginning to be built up at its northern end by the time of the Brown's sketch and his final Panorama (first exhibited in 1847 and last updated in 1856). This section of Upgate was sometimes treated as part of LONDON ROAD and was probably known as 'Spittle hill laine' in the early seventeenth century—see further SPITAL HILL on the medieval gallows and leper hospital that were located on the hill on the western side of this part of modern Upgate (the various names for this section of road are discussed under London Road). There were also lime quarries on both sides of the road here in the nineteenth century and probably before, with the Quarry on the eastern side of Upgate certainly used for lime burning from at least the seventeenth century. The use of the Quarry by lime works continued into the twentieth century and the OS maps still marked 'Lime Works' here through into the 1950s (see further Newmarket on these lime works). With regard to the western quarry, it is worth noting that two lime burning businesses were listed on Upgate in 1835, belonging to William Hurst and 'Haywood and Colam', with Thomas Haywood also being listed on London Road in 1841 and both Thomas Haywood and William Colam on 'Spittal Hill' in 1842 (William Hurst was listed on ASWELL STREET in both 1841 and 1842). The nineteenth-century road named Spital Hill was located to the west of Upgate and ran from the pit on the western side of Upgate northwards to join SOUTH STREET, and it seems likely that at least some of the above lime burners were based in this pit, where QUARRYSIDE is now located. This pit was marked simply as 'Old Chalk Pit' from 1889 onwards, with no lime works labelled here (in contrast to the eastern side of Upgate), although David Field does appear to have been a lime burner here in the 1890s. In the twentieth century, there was renewed residential development on this section of Upgate, with a small amount of new housing constructed on the eastern side of the road in the mid-twentieth century and two new housing estates built running west from Upgate in the late twentieth century (Quarryside and MERIDIAN VIEW).

As one of the main streets in town, Upgate was home to a large number of businesses, some of which have already been discussed. In 1828–9, Upgate was the place of business of not only a number of inns and beerhouses, but also an attorney (Christopher Ingoldby), three shoemakers (Robert Barton, Joseph Ryley and George Thompson—the latter was the landlord of the Plough from at least 1835), two builders/bricklayers (William Hurst and Francis Markham), a butcher (Elias Fields), two cabinet makers and joiners (James Copeland and Richard Hewison), a carver and gilder (Innocent Tara), a confectioner (Frances Medley), a gardener (William Kidd), a grocer, tallow chandler and soap boiler (Hyde & Sons—see CHURCH CLOSE on this business, which eventually became C. G. Smith & Sons of 26 Upgate), a grocer and cheesemonger (William Wood), two gun makers (Michael Lill and Michael Porter), two hatters (John Bellamy and Thomas Harrison), a linen dealer and silk mercer (William Goodman), two machine makers (Richard Hewison and Richard Medley), a malt dealer (Thomas Harrison), a corn and wool merchant (John Dauber), a plumber and glazier (Pearson Bellamy), a surgeon (Samuel Trought), and a woolstapler or dealer (Walker Phillips).

At the end of the nineteenth century, there was an even larger range of businesses and tradespeople listed on Upgate. For example, there was a pianoforte dealer (Charles Joseph Archer, number 25), an insurance agent (Edward Barker, number 45), a watch maker (Harry Colbeck, number 27), three butchers (John Britten, number 23; John Moncaster, number 44; and John Day Wilson, number 34), two surgeons (Palemon Best, number 10, and Charles Bell, number 61), a mineral water manufacturer (Bellamy Brothers, at Bellamy's Yard, opposite the junction with Kidgate), two hairdressers (Benjamin Carratt, number 17, and William Wright, number 42), two lime burners (Thomas Clapham, number 95 & GRIMSBY ROAD, and David Field), a plumber (William Driffill, number 11), a draper and outfitter (Goodhand & Co., number 21), an iron founder (John Hodgson), two bakers (Alfred Hall, number 38, and Edwin Arthur Rose, number 68), two grocers (Edmund Hallifield, number 52, and Sizer & Son, numbers 33c & b), three saddlers (George Hempstock, number 54; James Mawer, number 6; and Sarah & Charles Surfleet, number 30, also an auctioneer), three greengrocers (William Robinson, number 20—see WATTS LANE and ROBINSON LANE; Samuel Whelband, number 58; and Ann Wilson, number 66), a shopkeeper (Albert Shaw, number 48), a soap maker (Charles Goodwin & Sons, number 26—see Church Close), a hosier or seller of hosiery (Henry Stanley, number 36), a tobacconist (William Norman Wheatcroft, number 33), and a shoemaker (John Wright, number 50).

Upgate also was the scene of a number of crimes and breaches of the peace. Some of these were committed in the inns and beerhouses of this street and have been discussed above; others took place on the street itself. In May 1847, for instance, a 16 year-old butcher named Edward Field stabbed John Jacklin of Gayton-le-Wold with his butcher's knife, 'dividing the muscle of the arm', after he was kicked twice in the rear by Jacklin whilst wheeling a barrow down Upgate. The magistrates admitted that there was 'much provocation', but said that they 'could never countenance a practice so repugnant to the feelings and character of an Englishman as the use of a knife', fining Field 20s plus 19s 6d costs. In March 1851, Catherine Chapman of Scarborough, a 'nymph of the pavé' or prostitute, was charged with begging on Upgate—she was described as being in 'a most deplorable state of disease and destitution', presumably to such a degree that she couldn't ply her normal trade. She was committed to prison for fourteen days; whether she was the same Chapman who at one time ran a brothel in SPRING GARDENS is unclear. Another beggar on Upgate was John Williams of St Giles,

London, who, after he was arrested, destroyed his clothing in the police station and had to appear in court completely naked, aside from a bed rug that the police had put around him: he was committed to the House of Correction for one month in March 1850. A final example of crimes committed on Upgate comes from November 1850, when Nathaniel Bratley (aged 13), William Bratley (aged 9) and Bill Bratley (aged 8) were all charged with stealing a plum loaf from the shop of William Hall, baker: all three were sent to the House of Correction for two months hard labour and a private whipping. The boys were apparently part of a 'gang of juvenile thieves' who were operating at the time in Louth.

VANESSA ROAD

Vanessa Road is a residential street running south-east from HORNCASTLE ROAD. Established by the late 1960s, the housing here was built on what had previously been agricultural land, originally belonging to Louth's old open South Field.

VICKERS LANE

Vickers Lane runs between EASTGATE and NORTHGATE and has been known by a number of names. On the 1808 and 1834 plans of the town it is marked as Holland Lane, it is Vickers' Lane on a theatre poster from 1815, and it appears as both Vicar's Lane and Post Office Lane in the 1828–9 directory, the latter due to the Post Office that stood on the western corner of its junction with Eastgate by 1822 (a site now occupied by Heron Foods). The Post Office here was run by Sarah Allison and is said to have remained in this position until the late nineteenth century, when it moved into the MARKET PLACE. The name Post Office Lane appears to have dropped out of use fairly rapidly, but the name Vicar's Lane (and variants thereof) continued to be used in subsequent decades: the road was Vicar's Lane in the 1835, 1841 and 1852 directories, Vicar Lane in the 1842 directory, Vicars Lane in the 1851 census, Vicker's Lane in the 1841 census and the 1849 directory, Vickers' Lane in 1856, and mainly Vickers Lane subsequent to this point.

Vickers Lane is depicted as fully developed along both sides on the 1808 plan of Louth and it is also marked on the less reliable Armstrong plan of 1778, although on the latter it appears undeveloped. How much earlier than this the road existed is unclear. Both Northgate and Eastgate are medieval streets and it has been suggested that Vickers Lane, along with BURNT HILL LANE, represents the approximate eastern extent of the late eleventh-century town. On the other hand, the road itself has been considered to be an eighteenth-century street by Naomi Field. In the nineteenth century, a number of businesses and tradespeople were based on this road. One was Miss Elizabeth Valentine Flower's seminary for young ladies, which was located here in the 1820s—it offered courses in English grammar, geography, drawing, writing, arithmetic, needlework and a number of other subjects, at a starting price of sixteen guineas per annum for boarders, with each lady expected to supply her own linen, cutlery and table! Also present on Post Office Lane/Vicar's Lane in the 1820s were two dressmakers (Mary Burgess and Elizabeth & Hannah Byrne), a wood turner (Devereaux Miller), a tailor (Elisha Howlett) and a German clock maker (Magnus Pfaff). In the 1830s and 1840s, a number of other traders were based here, including a dyer (William Ping in 1835, Ann Weldale in 1841 and Christiana Weldale in 1849), a straw bonnet maker (Ann Gelstrap or Gilstrap in 1835 and 1841), a tailor (John Fields, 1835, 1841 and 1852), a shopkeeper (William Atkinson, 1841) and a painter. The last of these was William Brown, who painted the Louth Panorama—he lived on Vickers Lane from at least 1837 until 1854 and was listed as reporter and artist in the 1851 census.

In the 1840s and 1850s, Vickers Lane was also home to a member of the Jewish Boss family of Louth (see also JAMES STREET). In 1848, it was reported that 'a Jew pedlar, named Fiesch Lipmann,' was charged with stealing a silver thimble from a house in WESTGATE, the thimble being last 'seen on a table in the kitchen when the Jew was in the house, and... missed immediately after his departure.' It was apparently found, along with a silver spoon that Lipmann had stolen from a house in ASWELL STREET, 'in the possession of a well-known Jew, named Boss, who lives in Vicar's-lane'. This was Herman Boss, who was listed here in the 1851 census. Herman Boss and his wife, Augusta, were both born in Berlin and he is first mentioned in Louth in a report from 1844. In that year, Herman Boss, a silversmith and jeweller who was formerly of Hull, was charged at the Mansion House in Louth with knowingly receiving stolen silver plate that belonged to the Rev. John King of Hull in December 1843. Boss stated that he had suspected it was stolen, especially as an attempt had been made to scratch out the marks, and so had demanded a receipt from the seller. However, he said that he would not have bought it if he had known for certain it was stolen and if the seller hadn't been dressed like a nobleman, and further noted that he had paid a fair price for it, something confirmed by another witness to the court. It was also observed that Boss had apparently lived in Hull for fourteen years and had never been brought before a court there. Herman Boss died in Louth in 1853 and his wife Augusta appears to have subsequently married Jacob Cohen (see Northgate).

At the end of the nineteenth century and in the early twentieth century, Vickers Lane continued to be the location for a number of shops and businesses. In 1889, Vickers Lane was home to two boot makers (John Ashton, number 17, and William Marriott, number 9), three shopkeepers (Thomas Carpenter, number 7; John Pomeroy, number 13; and James Lane, number 25), a pork butcher (Martha Swift, number 11), a brazier (William Swingler, number 21), a cabinet maker (James Naylor, number 4) and a firm of accountants (Vere & Kiddall, number 2). Just before the First World War, the street was the place of business of a pianoforte tuner (Harold Archer, number 9), an accountant and auditor (John Thomas Boldon, number 2), a pork butcher (Herbert Fytche, number 13), a boot repairer (Edgar Hewitt, number 17), a cycle agent (Edward Kemp), an umbrella maker (Lizzie Horby, number 7), a fishmonger (George Horner, number 11), a joiner (John Maxey) and a furniture dealer (Horsewood & Son). Many of these people appear to have been based in a row of small buildings on the western side of the street. These were presumably those buildings visible on the early plans of the street and on William Brown's Panorama of 1847–56: they are clearly shown, with divisions, on the 1889 OS map and they were still there in the 1970s. These buildings were, however, demolished in the late twentieth century.

With regard to the early inhabitants of the street, they pursued a number of trades. In 1841, 79 people lived on Vickers Lane, including Ann Weldale, a dyer (see above); Ann Atkin, a lodging-house keeper, with five lodgers (for example, William Clackton, an agricultural labourer); James Handley, a brick maker; Charles Blythe, a letter carrier or postman; John Hubbard, a cabinet maker; William Brown, a painter; Joseph Barnes, a butcher; Mildred Atkinson, a grocer (presumably the widow of William Atkinson, mentioned above, who appears to have died in 1840); John Fields, a tailor; Deveraux Miller, a painter, living with

William Miller, a wood turner; and Abraham Spivey, a carpet weaver. In 1851, some of the same people were still there—including Abraham Spivey, John Fields and William Brown—but there were new faces too amongst the 68 inhabitants of the street, not least John Sugden, a potter; Herman Boss, a jeweller (discussed above); and Albert Marris, a painter.

VICTORIA ROAD

Victoria Road (or Victoria Street) runs from the junction of BRACKENBOROUGH ROAD and KEDDINGTON ROAD through to RIVERHEAD ROAD and RAMSGATE. It was apparently cut in 1876, in order to relieve the pressure on and bypass the level-crossing on Keddington Road, with the railway company providing £500 towards the creation of this new road. In 1881, only four households were listed on 'Victoria Street', their heads being William Brewer, a solicitor's general clerk (number 1), who had two servants; Francis Whitworth, a retired farmer who lived at number 2 with his housekeeper; Charles A. Kirby, a civil engineer who maintained two servants (number 3); and Malachi Bice, headmaster at the Holy Trinity Parochial School on the corner of Riverhead Road and EASTFIELD ROAD (number 4).

In 1889, there were still only four properties here, located on the western side of the street, a little to the north of the junction with MAPLE CLOSE—they formed a short terrace that still stands today as numbers 39–45. To the north of these was a 'Rose Nursery'. This was run by Henry Norton, who grew roses commercially from at least 1881 through until the early twentieth century, his nursery fronting onto Keddington Road and then stretching down the western side of Victoria Road. By 1906, however, things had begun to change: Norton's rose nursery had gone, with properties built on its land (the Spar shop on the corner of Keddington Road currently occupies one of these new buildings), and new terraces of houses had been constructed on both sides of the road. By the mid-twentieth century, the road was developed along much of its length, with a Children's Home at its northern end and a Drill Hall at its southern end. The former was initially opened as St Margaret's Home for Girls by the Church of England in 1912; it closed in 1969, by which point it cared for both boys and girls, and it is now the Beaumont Hotel. The latter building was once a drill hall, district library and ambulance station; it was converted into the new Louth Playgoers'

Riverhead Theatre in 2002, at a cost of around £2 million. In the late twentieth century, Maple Close was built running north-east from Victoria Road, just to the south of the Beaumont Hotel.

VIRGINIA DRIVE

Virginia Drive is part of the large, post-World War Two ST BERNARDS AVENUE council housing scheme, this element of it being laid out after the time that the 1956 OS map was surveyed. A Methodist chapel was established on the corner of THE LINK and Virginia Drive in 1960; it closed in 1977, due to falling membership and a difficulty in providing ministers. The land it stands on was originally part of Louth's old open South Field.

WALKERGATE PLACE

Walkergate Place runs south from QUEEN STREET and preserves the pre-1887 name of that road (Walkergate). It is not marked on any of the early plans of the town or the 1839 map of Louth, but it was clearly in existence by 1856, when a Mr Robert Ward is listed as living on 'Walkergate place' (a former grazier, he was listed on Walkergate in the 1841 and 1851 censuses). In 1861, there were 24 people living in Walkergate Place, including Nathaniel Fysh, a Free Methodist Missionary; James Boswell, a basket maker; Charles Brown, a stone mason; and Sarah Fell Brown, a dressmaker. By 1891, the number of residents had increased to 51 and trades represented on the road then included a butcher (John Jackson Proctor, number 13), a platelayer or trackman with the Great Northern Railway (Charles Foster Blanchard, number 4), two tailors (Frank Everitt, number 5, and Edmund George Browning, number 10), and a blacksmith (Joseph East, number 12).

The directories list few businesses on Walkergate Place, the exceptions being John Proctor's butcher shop at 13 Walkergate Place, listed in 1885, and Joseph East's blacksmith business, listed in 1889. Walkergate Place was, however, also home to Joseph Morton's iron foundry, which still stands and was built here on the eastern side of the road in 1878. Morton's shop was at 72 EASTGATE and was founded in 1832; it remained open until the 1970s and Joseph Morton lived on ST MARY'S LANE from at least 1881. His works specialised in domestic ironmongery (firegrates, boilers, bedsteads, buckets and the like) and farm items (such as wire netting and troughs), and it was still functioning well into the twentieth century, being listed in 1937, unlike the larger Ashley iron foundry on CINDER LANE.

Walkergate Place appears to have been fully established by the time of the 1889 OS map, although there was some further development of the road after this, not least the houses at the southern end of the street (on its east side), which were built by 1906 on a previously open area. By the 1970s, some of the buildings on the eastern side of the road had been demolished to form a track leading eastwards from the southern end of Walkergate Place.

WALLIS ROAD

Wallis Road runs west and north-west from ST BERNARDS AVENUE and is part of the large, post-World War Two St Bernards Avenue council housing scheme, this element of it being laid out after the time that the 1956 OS map was surveyed. The land it stands on was originally part of Louth's old open South Field.

WATTS LANE

Watts Lane runs east from NEWMARKET. The land here was originally part of Louth's old open South Field but was enclosed under the Enclosure Act of 1801, with the land to the south of the road being awarded to William Robinson. In subsequent years, this part of town was home to the market garden of William Robinson, later William Robinson & Son—although listed under UPGATE (as in the 1856 directory), the nursery itself was actually located on land around Watts Lane and to the south of MOUNT PLEASANT, including on that awarded to the family at the start of the nineteenth century. The Robinson nursery persisted in this area until the late twentieth century, when the large ROBINSON LANE housing estate was built on the former nursery land between Mount Pleasant and Watts Lane.

Watts Lane appears to be shown on William Brown's 1844 sketch of the town and his final Panorama of 1847–56, and the 1889 OS map depicts a reasonable number of properties on the south side of this road, along with nursery gardens and orchards to both its north and south. In

1861, 40 people were living on Watts Lane, including John Rawson, a ropemaker (number 8; note, a ropewalk is marked on the 1889 map off Newmarket, to the south of Watts Lane); Samuel Sutton, a cowkeeper (number 11); and William Charles, a blacksmith (number 3). By 1891, there were 66 people listed on this road, along with a family who were away visiting, with the occupations of the inhabitants ranging from gardener (Francis Ingoldmells, number 13a) and market gardener (George Nicholson, number 10) through to ratcatcher (George Taylor, number 3) and laundress (Emily Riggall, number 2). There were also a number of tradespeople who had Watts Lane listed as their place of business in the late nineteenth century. For example, in the 1880s a carpenter, Thomas Gilbert; a wheelwright, Charles Janney; a shopkeeper, Thomas Locking; a coal dealer, Mark Curtis; a tailor, William Weatherhog; and a market gardener, George Nicholson, all were listed on Watts Lane in the directories. In contrast, in the 1910s only nurserymen and market gardeners were listed on the road.

In 1906, only the area to the north of Watts Lane appears to be marked on the OS map as the site of an orchard or market garden, although nurseries were labelled on both sides of the road in the mid-twentieth century. Perhaps the most significant change in the twentieth century was, however, the development of the area to the north of Watts Lane. MOUNT PLEASANT AVENUE was built here in the inter-war years, joining the eastern ends of both Watts Lane and Mount Pleasant, and residential properties were constructed to the west of this new road, on the north side of Watts Lane, by the late 1960s. At the western end of Watts Lane, a motor engineering works and a garage were marked in the 1960s and 1970s, which continued into the early twenty-first century— this site has since been cleared and has been considered as a potential location for a small supermarket. Finally, in the mid-1990s, the Robinson Lane housing estate was built on the north side of the road, between the garage and the pre-existing houses to the west of Mount Pleasant Avenue, although this estate was only joined to Watts Lane by a footway.

WELBECK WAY

Welbeck Way runs west from MILL LANE, off HIGH HOLME ROAD. The road is built on land that was once part of George Moody's High Holme Nursery, founded in 1830, and it is marked as such on the

1906 OS map (see High Holme Road on this business). This land appears to have continued to be used by a nursery into the mid-twentieth century, with the present road and houses constructed here in the early 1970s.

WELLINGTON STREET

Wellington Street is presumably named from the former Wellington Hotel that faced onto RAMSGATE, with the street running from JAMES STREET round past the rear entrance to the hotel and through to NEWBRIDGE HILL. The 1852 plan of the carpet factory and its grounds on James Street shows that Wellington Street was in existence by then with that name, although on the 1864 plan it is marked simply as 'New Road'.

In 1871, only six households were based on Wellington Road, namely those of William S. Burton, tailor; George Bywater, bricklayer; Frederick Wilkinson, carter; Robert Rasdall, cabinet maker; George Walker, merchant clerk; and Thomas Dobbs, brewer. Rasdall, Walker, Wilkinson and Bywater were all listed on Wellington Street in the 1872 directory, whilst Dobbs was listed as the brewer at the 'Ramsgate Brewery' in that year. In 1881, there were still only seven households listed, with trades represented then including an engine fitter, a tailor and three builders. The builders were George Bywater, at number 4; Charles Harrison, at number 1; and Samuel Harrison, at number 2a—the last two of these builders were presumably the Harrison Brothers who were listed in the directories as builders on Wellington Street in the 1880s and 1890s. By the time of the 1889 OS map, however, there had clearly been some significant development of the street, with at least twice the number of houses on both sides of Wellington Street north of James Street as there were households in 1881—indeed, in 1891 there were 83 people recorded as living on the street. In the twentieth-century, further development occurred on the road, with new houses built here and Louth Pentecostal Church (Louth Christian Fellowship) established on the eastern side of the road in the 1930s, where it remained into the early twenty-first century.

The area to the west of Wellington Street was a paddock where wool was hung on posts to dry in good weather after it had been washed in the river, a function that it still had in 1864. In the late nineteenth century, this area became a timber yard belonging to William Frederick Hoggard—the firm was still here in 1920, when tree trunks were washed out of Hoggard & Co.'s timber yard into Wellington Street and jammed between the houses there by the Louth Flood—and it remained a timber yard with a saw mill into the late twentieth century. There were two roads leading westwards from Wellington Street into this area in the mid-to late twentieth century, located halfway along the road and at its northern end—only the southern one is shown on the earlier OS maps, however, and this was an access way known as Factory Road in 1852. These two roads are now both known as Woodlands and houses were built in this area at the end of the twentieth century and in the first years of the twenty-first.

WESTGATE

Westgate is one of the earliest documented streets in Louth, currently running from the junction between LINCOLN ROAD and ST MARY'S LANE through to St James's Church—it is generally thought that the Louth had come to encompass the vast majority of modern Westgate within its bounds by the end of the medieval period, although the stages by which this was achieved are uncertain.

The earliest surviving reference to Westgate is contained in a charter of Thomas de Luda, chapter clerk of Lincoln Cathedral, which was drawn up in 1317. He provided an endowment to pay for a daily mass to be said for the salvation of his own soul, and for the souls of his father, William, and his mother, Margaret, his brother, his benefactors, and all the faithful dead. The endowment included six messuages (usually defined as a dwelling house with outbuildings and the site on which it stood), one of which was in Westgate between the land of Simon, son of William de Luda, on the west, and the land of the Bishop of Lincoln on the east. Westgate is also the site of one of the most interesting archaeological discoveries relating to the medieval town, namely a splendid tessellated pavement of the thirteenth century that was discovered during works at Westgate House in 1801. This pavement must have come from an impressive building and its presence suggests that Westgate was already the site of some of Louth's grander houses even before the street made its first appearance in the documentary record. Other indications of the early importance of Westgate within the town include the establishment of the Gildhall of St Mary's Gild on this road by 1425 and the fact that John Bradley, a wealthy local wool merchant who played a major role in the refoundation of the Grammar School in 1551, lived at 44 Westgate and owned numerous other properties here, including one where The Limes is currently sited. Subsequently, Westgate appears to have retained its medieval and early modern status as the home of some of the wealthier inhabitants of the town—modern Westgate dates in the main from the eighteenth century, when many of the houses here were either built or rebuilt, with the quality and size of these properties offering a stark contrast to the cheap terraced cottages being then constructed elsewhere in the town.

At the western end of Westgate are a former watermill and a bridge over the Lud, both of which appear to have their ultimate origins in the medieval period. Although the Westgate bridge was erected by the trustees of the Dexthorpe Turnpike in 1789–91, it was not the first bridge to be built here—there was a bridge in this location in 1634, called 'the hall milne bridg', and the Lincoln Road appears to have been known as 'Schepe brygge lane' in 1446, implying the presence of a bridge then too. With regard to the watermill, this lies just across the bridge on the northern side of the Lud. This mill, known as Thorpe Hall Mill or the Old Paper Mill, was earlier called the Hall Mill or Hall Mills, presumably in reference to the neighbouring Thorpe Hall (see Lincoln Road). The first reference to the Hall Mill dates from 1452–3, when certain land is described as being situated near 'le halmylne', and in 1454 William Selby was fined for removing one load of gravel from the 'halmyln dam' that had been collected by Master Alan Barton for the use of the Church of St James of Louth. By the sixteenth century, the Hall Mill appears to have been augmented, as the Grave's Compotus for 1565 refers to 'the hall mylles', with the plural form being due to the fact that there were then said to be two mills operating under a single roof. These two mills were under the control of the Bolle family of Thorpe Hall in the seventeenth century—in 1650, for example, Sir Charles Bolle renewed his lease of 'the hall mylles' for sixty years at the previous rent rate (he is said to have added six rooms to the buildings here), and in the late seventeenth century the property of the Bolle family included 'two water mills near adjoining to the onset of Thorpe Hall', which must be these. The name Hall Mills continued in use until at least 1775.

Although Thorpe Hall Mill was probably originally a corn mill, it seems to have been converted into a paper mill in the late eighteenth century, with the current buildings said to date from that century. In 1801, a Mr Swift was the 'conductor of Louth paper-mill' and it has been suggested that the mill here began to be used to produce paper from either 1789 or 1794–5. The business then was owned by Charles Wigelsworth, lawyer and banker of Westgate House (see below), and after his death his widow, Elizabeth, ran the business alongside John Swift, possibly her brother, with a Michael Porter also being involved from the 1820s. The paper mill functioned until 1842, and an attempt was made to let it as a paper mill in January 1843—there were, however, no takers, and so the equipment was taken out and the mill equipped as a corn mill, being re-advertised in April 1844 to millers and corn merchants. It subsequently continued to operate as a corn mill until around 1920, with one of the millers here being Timothy Wold Topham (see EASTGATE).

There are also a number of interesting properties to the east of the bridge. The Mansion, number 21, is usually thought to date from around 1600, with a subsequent remodelling in the late seventeenth or early eighteenth centuries—it was first mentioned in 1610, when 'Oulde Mrs Halton' lived there, and it was used to quarter officers of the Northumberland Hussars in 1940. Previously, in 1826, Lieutenant General John Henry Loft had owned it, and while he lived there a sentry used to pace to and fro before it (see KIDGATE). Further along the road is Westgate House, situated on the western corner of SCHOOLHOUSE LANE. The main part of this building is sometimes dated to the mid-eighteenth century, with the frontage and curving staircases apparently added at the turn of the nineteenth century. Charles Wigelsworth lived in Westgate House from 1775–99 and ran the first bank in Louth, the North Lincolnshire Bank, from here, which was entered from Schoolhouse Lane: the bank ultimately failed and Charles Wigelsworth is said to have died 'raving' and in debt. The former gardens of Westgate House, which can be seen on William Brown's Panorama of 1847–56, were used by the Grammar School for temporary buildings in the aftermath of the merger of the boys' and girls' grammars in the 1960s, these being later utilised as exam halls before being demolished to make way for the new houses of SOMERSBY COURT in the 1990s. Westgate House itself was also used by the school in the twentieth century, but the Grammar retreated from this and other Westgate sites in the later twentieth century to become mainly focussed on its EDWARD STREET and CROWTREE LANE site.

Another interesting property thought to be located in the vicinity of the junction with Schoolhouse Lane was the Gildhall of the Blessed Mary, which stood in Westgate and was first mentioned in 1425, as was noted above. This hall was owned by St Mary's Gild but it was used by other gilds too, such as those of the Holy Trinity and St Peter, whose use of it is referred to in 1476. The Gildhall was enlarged in 1501 and it was where the reeve of Louth was to be elected in 1536 (it was this that John Heneage was due in town to preside over when the Lincolnshire Rising began in that year). In 1517, St Mary's Gildhall was used to imprison John Baly, a priest of the Trinity Gild who had broken into the chest at the end of the high alter. Robert Moos, the churchwarden, and the three constables had caught the thief, who was held here before being committed to Lincoln, and legend apparently states that he was betrayed by an associate and that his ghost haunted St Mary's Churchyard (off BRIDGE STREET).

To the east of Schoolhouse Lane are The Limes and Lindsey House. The sites of both properties were owned by John Bradley in the sixteenth century (d. 1590), along with seven cottages on Westgate, a tenement on Westgate and 'a stable and yard called Bugden's garth', which went down to the river and was 'over the way' from The Limes. Bradley, a merchant of the staple of the Town of Calais, acquired the site of The Limes from Clement Lyndesey in around 1540; the current Limes is said to date from the late eighteenth century whilst the current Lindsey House is of early nineteenth-century date. Auguste Alphonse Pahud lived at Lindsey House with his wife, Annie, in the late nineteenth century—in 1902, after her death, he committed suicide here with the cord of his dressing gown and Hubbard's Hills was ultimately given to the town as part of his bequest. Lindsey House became the Girls' Grammar School from 1904 (it was previously housed on JAMES STREET) and a laboratory and a gym were added in 1906, with The Limes acquired as a boarding house two years later and the two buildings united by an assembly hall. There were only fourteen pupils in the Girls' Grammar when it first opened, but by 1914 the school catered for 120 girls, making it slightly larger than the Boys' Grammar! The Boys' and

Girls' Grammars were eventually amalgamated in 1965 and are now primarily based at the site off Edward Street and Crowtree Lane.

Another interesting building is the site of the former National School for boys on Westgate, a voluntary elementary school for the poor. Located on the north side of the street and still bearing a plaque identifying it as the 'National School', this was formed in 1811 and attached to the parish of St James, although the present building was probably not built until 1812. The school was popular, with annual subscriptions exceeding £150, and in 1855 it was attended by about 100 pupils, rising to 140 in 1861 and 180 by 1896. Following the Louth Flood of 1920, the school was temporarily housed in the Town Hall on Eastgate and then in the Northgate Baptist Chapel on CANNON STREET. The senior pupils from the school were moved to the new Monks' Dyke School on MONKS DYKE ROAD in 1929 and the remaining pupils were transferred to KIDGATE School in 1930. Similarly noteworthy is 45 Westgate. This site was owned by George Fitzwilliam, Alderman of St Mary's Gild, before *c.* 1540, when John Bradley and William Dughty had it. The current building dates from about 1700 and was occupied by John Francis Maximilian de Cerjat in 1759. Born in Switzerland, he was a local character who kept a pack of pointers and was a zealous sportsman, and whilst he was a naturalised British subject, he apparently had a limited grasp of English vocabulary. R. W. Goulding records that Mr Cerjat once sent a servant to market to buy a cow and the servant returned with both a cow and a calf, to which his master responded 'Take the cub away, I don't want the cub'!

Immediately to the east of the last building is Church Precincts, number 47, which is first mentioned in 1610, when William Marley, baker, lived there, with it being said then to have been 'once Seamar's, since Wm Doughtie's, and late Mr Bredleyes'—the present building is said to date from the mid-eighteenth century. Finally, to the east of this is the Vicarage, which was designed by the Louth architect C. J. Carter in 1832, replacing an earlier structure here. In 1807, the earlier 'vicarage house' was described as an 'old thatched building' that stood 'contiguous to the church-yard'. This building appears to have been constructed in 1724, as there is a record from that year of the vicarage house being rebuilt—the new building was described as constructed with 'frames of wood, double walled with earth, and thatched with straw', and it is said to have contained three rooms, four chambers, a brewhouse, and a little

277

stable, along with a garden or orchard 'containing near half an acre of ground'. In the late 1780s, Wolley Jolland, the vicar (d. 1831), dressed the garden with a thatched building called The Hermitage, which he decorated in a rustic style. The church yard adjoining the vicarage is specified to be 'about one acre' in extent in 1724 and surrounded by stone walls (see further UPGATE on the church yard).

As well as grand houses, Westgate was also home to a number of businesses and tradespeople beyond those already mentioned above. In 1828–9, it was the place of business of two attorneys (Thomas Bentley Phillips and William Wilson), a shoemaker (William Paddison), a joinery and building business (Robert Foster & Son), a druggist (Zachariah Ferrears), a fishmonger (James Harrison), a machine maker, iron founder and millwright (John Saunderson), two paper makers (John Swift, also a stationer and rag merchant, and Wigelsworth & Porter), a physician (Charles Marshall Clarke), a porter merchant (Edward Elger), a general shopkeeper (Charles Attiwell), a watch and clock maker (Edward Smith), a worsted spinner and manufacturer (Joseph Northend, or Northern), and a 'distributer of stamps' (Langley Gace). The situation was similar in 1835, although the iron founder then was William Grounsell—see IRISH HILL on the various iron founders and machine makers of Westgate, at least some of whom were based at the junction of these two roads—and there was now a brewer, Josiah Berkinshaw, listed on the road in addition to Edward Elger, porter and ale merchant. By the end of the nineteenth century, there were far fewer tradespeople and businesses on Westgate—those that were there then included Sarah Brown, a dressmaker; Charles Thomas Ennals, a surgeon (Thornton House); Annie Laking, another dressmaker (number 6); Fanny Lucas, a shopkeeper (number 23a); Arthur Wilson, a gardener (number 45); and Wilson & Son, solicitors. In addition to such businesses, there were also a number of inns and beerhouses established on Westgate. The most famous of these is the Wheatsheaf, at the eastern end of the road. Mentioned by Christian Frederick Esberger in 1764, who refers to it as 'the Sign of the Wheatsheaf', the building it occupies is usually dated to the seventeenth century. Notable landlords include Thomas Clapham, who was landlord from at least 1849 and also a lime burner (see GRIMSBY ROAD). Another inn on the street was the King of Prussia. This was listed in 1782 and last licensed in 1787; it is now The Firs, at the western end of Westgate, which was subsequently a private house—

lived in for a brief time by Charlotte Alington Pye Barnard, see ST MARY'S LANE—and is currently a care home.

With regard to the street itself and its inhabitants, it is depicted as nearly completely developed on Armstrong's plan of 1778. This is unlikely to be true, however, given that the more accurate and reliable plan made by Espin in 1808 indicates that there were significant stretches of Westgate without buildings in the early nineteenth century, for example on the south side between LOVE LANE and The Mansion. By the 1830s, such gaps were beginning to be filled in, to judge from the 1834 plan and the map of 1839, and the road appears to have been fairly well built up along both sides by the time of William Brown's sketch of 1844 and his final Panorama of 1847–56. Whilst some of the houses on Westgate were indeed grand houses of the type discussed earlier, others were considerably more modest. In the sixteenth century, for example, John Bradley was said to have owned seven cottages on Westgate and Arthur Gray owned two (Gray gave these to the Grammar School in his will). Indeed, in 1861 the inhabitants of the road included not only wealthy business owners and landed proprietors who kept servants, but also a lodging-house keeper (Elizabeth Welch, number 3); a groom and coachman (John Wildman, number 21; his wife, Annie, was a dressmaker); a shoemaker (Benjamin Wilkinson, number 13); a laundress (Charlotte Crowson, number 8); a bricklayer (Christopher Wilson, number 19); an agricultural labourer (Henry Milson, number 9); and a washerwoman (Mary Northend, number 41).

Some of the early, notable inhabitants of Westgate have already been mentioned above, but a few more deserve mention simply because of the rather odd rents that they paid for their properties on Westgate. In 1697, for instance, one John Jones paid 40s and 200 gherkins in rent for a house in Westgate, whilst in 1717 Thomas Garrott paid '200 of Sparrow Grass', or asparagus, at Whitsunday for two cottages and a piece of ground in Westgate, and Martyn Browne, Esq., paid a fat turkey, or two shillings, in rent for a 'pingle'—a small piece of enclosed land—there. Also of interest are the numerous appearances that Westgate made in the mid-nineteenth-century court reports. There were a significant number of beggars apprehended on this road, as might be expected given its status as one of the wealthier parts of town. For example, John Brown of Dublin, a seaman, was charged with begging on Westgate in February 1847 and only discharged after he promised to leave town. Similarly, an unnamed man, aged about 50, was arrested here in September 1852—he had no tongue or left eye and had in his possession a 'begging paper' which stated that 'he had been thus mutilated while a prisoner in Turkey'. He was arrested for causing alarm with his 'strange and vehement gesticulations' at the house of W. G. Allison, Esq., in Westgate, and was sent to the House of Correction for fourteen days. Westgate was also the occasional scene of thefts from the houses here, as in February 1848, when a 'Jew pedlar' named Fiesch Lipmann was accused of stealing a silver thimble from the house of T. F. Waite, Esq., solicitor (see further VICKERS LANE). The Thorpe Hall Mill on Westgate also finds a place in the reports of this period. In August 1849, when Mr Topham ran the corn mill here, Thomas Marwood of Tothill appears to have committed suicide in the mill stream, despite it only being twelve inches deep, after having been observed only a hour before exhibiting 'evident symptoms of insanity' in different parts of the town.

WESTGATE PLACE

Westgate Place runs north-west from WESTGATE and was originally called Harvey's Hill, Alley or Lane, although it already had the name Westgate Place by the time of the 1828–9 directory. The cottages here were originally built in the late eighteenth century and the York stone and cobble street surface of the passageway has been retained. Towards the bottom of Westgate Place is the house where Alfred Lord Tennyson lodged with his grandmother when he attended the Grammar School on SCHOOLHOUSE LANE from 1816–20.

Westgate Place appears to have been primarily a residential area, with few businesses or tradespeople based here, although there were exceptions. For example, in 1835 Elizabeth Pindar, a dressmaker, had Westgate Place listed as her place of business, as had Susannah Riggall, a straw hat maker, and in 1856 there was a private school run from Westgate Place by Miss Betsy Hand. In 1861, a laundress named Mary Elvin was based here, and in the 1870s and 1880s a joiner—William Bailey—was listed at 5 Westgate Place. In 1861, there were sixteen people living on Westgate Place, including Mary Elvin at number 4; Jane Gray, a daily governess, at number 1; John Lawson, a gentleman's groom, at number 7; and Joseph Whittam, a retired tailor, at number 8. In 1891, 1 Westgate Place was inhabited by Mary Flowers, the principal of a girls' school, who lived here with two assistant teachers and three boarders aged ten to fourteen—in 1901, the school was still in business, but it was then listed at 60 Westgate, with 1 Westgate Place being given as the residence of an organist and teacher of music, George Henry Porter. Other inhabitants of Westgate Place at the end of the nineteenth century include John Bell, a gardener (number 5); Joseph Wright, a caretaker (number 4); and Henry Dodman, a retired publican (number 2).

WILLOW DRIVE

See BRACKENBOROUGH ROAD.

WOBURN CLOSE

Woburn Close runs off CHATSWORTH DRIVE and is part of a large housing estate built to the south of NORTH HOLME ROAD in the 1960s and 1970s. The road is shown as laid out but without buildings on the 1968 OS map and it had been fully developed by the mid-1970s. The land it is built on was originally part of Louth's old open North Field.

WOOD LANE

Wood Lane currently runs from STEWTON LANE through to ST BERNARDS AVENUE, before turning eastwards at the junction with the latter and eventually becoming a track. In 1871, only two households were listed on Wood Lane: that of William Crow, a cottager of fourteen acres, and that of Joshua Marshall, a market gardener. There were still only two households listed here in 1881, when an agricultural labourer named Benjamin Jesney lived here alongside Joshua Marshall, and again in 1891, when Joshua Marshall was joined by Newton Anderson, an agricultural farm foreman. By 1901, however, there was another household present—Joshua Marshall, market gardener, was listed on Wood Lane in the census of that year alongside George Robinson, a farm labourer, and Frederick Sandford, a domestic gardener. This general lack of development along Wood Lane during the nineteenth century is confirmed by the directories, which list only the Marshalls' market gardening business on the road, and also the 1889 and 1906 OS maps. These maps show Wood Lane running over the railway line to Boston (which opened in 1848 and closed in 1970) and then through largely undeveloped fields until it branched off into two tracks, the southern one leading to Wood Lane Farm and the northern one to what appears to have been an orchard with a pump and buildings. The only real exception to this was just before the railway line, where a track led to the back of Stewton House (see Stewton Lane)—this is the modern STEWTON GARDENS and it had a number of buildings depicted on it in both 1889 and 1906, including the two houses that still stand at the Wood Lane end of this road.

The mid- to late twentieth century saw considerable changes along Wood Lane. By the 1960s, it had been joined to St Bernards Avenue and houses had been developed along much of its eastern side, with what is now St Bernard's School established on its current site—labelled as the Junior Training Centre and Saint Bernard's House on the 1960s and 1970s OS maps—and a nursery marked off Stewton Gardens. Wood Lane Farm had also apparently been recently demolished by the 1960s (it was still marked on the 1956 OS map) and the orchard and buildings formerly situated at the end of the northern track from Wood Lane were by then Wood Lane Dairies (now demolished too). Subsequently, the SPIRE VIEW ROAD and SYCAMORE DRIVE housing estates were established off Wood Lane in the late twentieth century, Stewton Gardens ceased to be home to a nursery and was instead developed for housing, and the Meridian Leisure Centre was constructed on part of the twentieth-century playing fields that lay to the west of the road (between the former railway line and the junction with St Bernards Avenue) in the early twenty-first century, opening to the public in 2010.

WOOD WAY

Wood Way runs south-east from ST BERNARDS AVENUE through to VIRGINIA DRIVE and WOOD LANE; it is part of the large, post-World War Two St Bernards Avenue council housing scheme, this element of it being laid out after the time that the 1956 OS map was surveyed. The land it stands on was originally part of Louth's old open South Field.

WOODLANDS

See WELLINGTON ROAD.

WOODVALE RISE

Woodvale Rise runs west from GRIMSBY ROAD and is built on what is said to have been the deepest pit in Louth. Chalk was extracted from this pit to burn for agricultural lime, and the lime works here were run by Jabez Paddison and his widow, Sarah Jane Paddison, from the 1870s through to World War Two, when it was the last lime pit to be worked in Louth. The houses of Woodvale Rise were constructed in the mid- to late 1990s, being sold as new builds in 1997.

WORCESTER CLOSE

Worcester Close runs east from ROBINSON LANE and is part of a late twentieth-century housing estate built to the south of MOUNT PLEASANT. This estate was constructed in the mid-1990s on land that had formerly been used by the Robinson family for its market garden and nursery, and all the roads that run off Robinson Lane are named after varieties of apple.

Bibliographic Note & Further Reading

The accounts of the individual streets offered in this work were primarily formed out of a few core classes of material, which were then supplemented with more specific material where such was available. There is, of course, a vast amount of evidence that might be brought to bear on the history of many of the individual streets in Louth, and in a work such as this I was able to only use a proportion of this material, otherwise the book would have run to several volumes and perhaps never have been finished. I hope that the relatively brief discussions of the streets included here will, therefore, encourage more detailed studies of individual streets, or even individual buildings, which might more fully engage with and utilise the vast array of material that I could sometimes only touch on in this volume.

The first core class of material used in the present work is composed of maps, plans, drawings and paintings of Louth—of particular importance were Armstrong's 1778 plan of the town, the maps relating to the Enclosure Act, Espin's 1808 plan of the town, the 1824 OS (Ordnance Survey) map of Louth, Bayley's 1834 plan of Louth, the 1839 map of the town, and the many OS maps of the town that date between 1889 and 1990. Needless to say, William Brown's preliminary sketches of 1844 and his final Panorama of 1847 (last updated in 1856) also proved invaluable in understanding the state of the streets of Louth in the mid-nineteenth century. The second core class is composed of trade directories, produced by a number of companies, which listed the various businesses, tradespeople and 'gentry' who lived on each street in Louth. Those directories primarily consulted in the following work include the Universal British Directory of 1794; Pigot & Co.'s (later Slater's) directories for 1828–9, 1835, 1841 and 1852; White's directories for 1842, 1856 and 1872; the Post Office directories for 1861 and 1868;

and Kelly's directories for 1885, 1889, 1896, 1905, 1909, 1913, 1919 and 1937, although other volumes were occasionally used too. The third class consists of the various censuses taken every ten years by the British Government from 1841 to 1911. Of these, the 1841 census is the least useful, lacking some key categories in its data and being the hardest to decipher, but they are all enormously valuable to a greater or lesser degree when it comes to understanding the inhabitants of the streets, their occupations and their families. The fourth core class of evidence is physical evidence derived from archaeological excavations and assessments of still-standing buildings, this material being primarily accessed via the Lincolnshire Historic Environment Record, the National Heritage List for England and the individual reports on excavations and buildings produced by various companies, such as Lindsey Archaeological Services. The fifth and final core class of evidence consists of newspaper reports, in particular those drawn from the *Stamford Mercury* and, especially, the *Hull Packet*—as is discussed in the Preface, it would appear that William Brown wrote for both newspapers in the mid-nineteenth century and the detailed record of events and individuals on the various streets of Louth preserved in these reports is used throughout this book.

With regard to secondary sources, a large number of books and articles on the history of Louth were consulted whilst preparing the present text. Of particular importance were the works of David Robinson, especially *The Book of Louth* (Buckingham, 1979), *Adam Eve and Louth Carpets* (Louth, 2010), *The Story of Hubbard's Hills* (Louth, 2007), *The Kidgate Story* (Louth, 1997), and, with Christopher Sturman, *William Brown and the Louth Panorama* (Louth, 2001). Also extremely valuable were Richard Gurnham's *A History of Louth* (Stroud, 2007), Naomi Field's *Louth: the Hidden Town. A Study of its Archaeological Potential* (Lincoln, 1978), J. E. Swaby's *A History of Louth* (London, 1951), and R. S. Bayley's fascinating *Notitiæ Ludæ, or Notices of Louth* (Louth, 1834). Naturally, considerable use was made of the works of R. W. Goulding too, especially his *Annals of Louth, 1086–1600* (Louth, 1918), his *Louth Old Corporation Records* (Louth, 1891), and his many articles published in *Goulding's Almanack*—for example, 'On the court rolls of the manor of Louth' (1901), 'Some obsolete Louth customs' (1922), 'Notes on some Louth houses and their former occupants' (1903), and 'Christian Frederick Esberger, his relatives and his journal' (1902).

Other significant books and articles on Louth consulted include Stuart M. Sizer and Josephine Clark, *People & Boats: a History of the Louth Canal* (Louth, 2005); Bill Painter, *The Story of Louth House of Correction, 1671–1872* (Louth, 2004) and *Upon the Parish Rate: the Story of Louth Workhouse and the Paupers of East Lindsey* (Louth, 2000); David Cuppleditch's *H. L. Howe: a Twentieth-century Louth Photographer* (Louth, 1988), *Joseph Willey: A Victorian Lincolnshire Photographer* (Chedder, 1987), *Louth: the Twentieth Century* (Louth, 1999), *Around Louth* (Stroud, 1995), and *Around Louth: A Second Selection* (Stroud, 2002); Reginald C. Dudding, *The First Churchwardens' Book of Louth, 1500-1524* (Oxford, 1941); A. E. B. Owen, 'Louth before Domesday', *Lincolnshire History and Archaeology*, 32 (1997), 60–4, especially on St Mary's Church; C. S. Carter's articles on 'Old streets, inns and scenes of Louth', in *The Louth Record* (Louth, 1916); Louth Teachers' Centre, *Louth Industrial Trail* (Louth, 1977); K. Redmore, *Louth Town Trail* (Louth, 1979); Stuart Sizer and others, *Louth Local Study Topics 1–4* (Louth, 1978); William Leary and David N. Robinson, *A History of Methodism in Louth* (Louth, 1981); J. W. White, *Part of Old Louth* (Louth, 1960); Geoff Mullett, *Discovering Louth* (Louth, 2010); John Lill, *Louth Playgoers: the First Sixty Years* (Louth, 1992); Meg Wynne, *The Green Lady of Thorpe Hall and Local Ghostology* (Louth, 1974); St Michael & All Angels Church, *A History of St Michael & All Angels, Louth, 1863–1986* (Louth, 1986); and David Kaye, *Monks' Dyke: Golden Jubilee, 1929–1979* (Louth, 1979).

Maps

PLAN of LOUTH

New
Burying
Ground

St Marys
Burying
Ground

THE LUDD

WEST GATE

Gospel Gate

Crow Tree Lane

SCALE

100   200   300 Yards.

THE CLOSE

Carpet Manufactory

by the Canal

James Street

Old House of Correction

Priory

Padehole or ... Str

Bee House

Fish Shambles

EAST GATE

Butcher Market

Market Place

Mill Dam

MONKS DIKE

Mercer Row

Mill Race

Ancel Spring

St Helens Spring

COLLEGE

Quarry and

Sheep Pens

Pig Market

Gallows or others

Saltern Bower

Business Park

GRIMSBY ROAD

TATTERSHALL WAY

Factory

Fanthorpe Lane (Track)

Northfield Farm

A18

B1520

A18

B1520

PH

ARUNDEL DRIVE

BUCKINGHAM RD

FANTHORPE LANE

HILL RISE

ONGLEAT

BADMINTON

DRIVE

GRIMSBY ROAD

GOODVALE RI

ST MARY'S PARK

Deighton Close Farm

MARY'S LANE

CHURCH LANE

PW

The Paddocks

RIVER

LYNDON CRESCENT

MARTIN

KESTREL DRIVE

LYNDON WAY

SWALLOW DRIVE

...INGTON CRESCENT

DAVID AVE

ELM DRIVE

STAINES WAY

The Elms

Oakwood

REDDINGTON ROAD

CHRISTOPHER CLOSE

CHARLES AVENUE

ADA WAY

COCK KEEPERS W

GROSVENOR CRES

GROSVENOR ROAD

MAPLE CLOSE

Louth Canal

ABBEY PARK

PARK ROW

EASTFIELD

...TA ROAD

RIVERHEAD

THAMES STREET

RIVERHEAD ROAD

EASTFIELD ROAD

PARK AVE

NORMANDY G

CHESTNUT DRIVE

F Sta

Pol Sta

COMMERCIAL RD

ABBEY ROAD

Football Ground

Recn Gd

PW

LACEY GARDENS

LACEY GD

TH

TRINITY LANE

...CLOSE

Lacey Gardens Junior School

School

BROADLEY CRESCENT

ST BERNARDS AVE

HARVEYS LANE

BISHOPS CL

ABBOTTS W

FRIER OAK

B 1200
Troutbeck
River Lud
Thorpe Hall
WESTGATE
BREAKNECK
LOVE LANE
IRISH HILL
CROWTREE LANE
Hubbard's Hill
Mill
Playing Fields
Crowtree
Cottage
Club
House
LITTLE CROWTREE LA
Ppg
Sta
VANESSA
Golf Course
Hubbard's Hill
Woldsend
HORNCASTLE ROAD
Water Treatment
Plant
HALFPENNY LANE
Toll Bar

MONKS DYKE ROAD

Pav

PW

Recreation Ground

WALLIS ROAD

QUEENSWAY

THE LINK

BIRCH R

PW

VIRGINIA DRIVE

Wallis
House

Railway Walk

Leisure
Cen

WOOD W

Nursery

MOUNT PLEASANT AVENUE

SPIRE VIEW ROAD

WOOD LANE

PPIN CL

Recn Gd

SYCAMORE DRIVE

School

Y'S LANE

Recn Gd

HAZEL GR

LABURNUM CRESCENT

ALEXANDER DRIVE

MINSTER D

STEWTON G

OAK CLOSE

GRESLEY ROAD

LINDSEY WAY

HAWKER DRIVE

ALDER C

STEWTON LANE

MAYFIELD CRESCENT

PASTURE DRIVE

BARTON GATE

STUTTE CL

BRADLEY CL

ERESBIE ROAD

ALBANY ROAD

ANY C

KENWICK P

B1200

SOUTHLANDS AVENUE

KENWICK C

Agarth

KENWICK GDNS

LEGBF

www.ingramcontent.com/pod-product-compliance
Lightning Source LLC
Chambersburg PA
CBHW060457090426
42735CB00011B/2016